The World in a Grain of Sand

Nivedita Majumdar is Associate Professor of English at John Jay College, City University of New York. She has researched and published on wide-ranging issues in literary and political theories. *The Other Side of Terror*, a volume she edited, offers an analysis of the phenomenon of terrorism on the global stage, delving into its historical and political roots in South Asia as well as literary and historical representations of terrorism.

The World in a Grain of Sand

Postcolonial Literature and Radical Universalism

Nivedita Majumdar

VERSO

London • New York

First published by Verso 2021
© Nivedita Majumdar 2021

All rights reserved

The moral rights of the author have been asserted

1 3 5 7 9 10 8 6 4 2

Verso
UK: 6 Meard Street, London W1F 0EG
US: 20 Jay Street, Suite 1010, Brooklyn, NY 11201
versobooks.com

Verso is the imprint of New Left Books

ISBN-13: 978-1-78873-746-3
ISBN-13: 978-1-78873-747-0 (UK EBK)
ISBN-13: 978-1-78873-748-7 (US EBK)

British Library Cataloguing in Publication Data
A catalogue record for this book is available from the British Library

Library of Congress Cataloging-in-Publication Data
A catalog record for this book is available from the Library of Congress
Library of Congress Control Number: 2020948737

Typeset in Minion by Biblichor Ltd, Edinburgh
Printed and bound by CPI Group (UK) Ltd, Croydon CR0 4YY

For
Vivek and Ananya
My Home in the World

Contents

Acknowledgements

This book was in the making for several long years, but it was a rewarding period. While conceiving of the project, I was fortunate to have tenure affording me both the duration of time and the academic freedom I needed to write the book I wanted. It is a matter of great satisfaction to me that the bulk of the book was written during the years when I was most intensely involved in political work. I was elected for two terms to a principal officer position in my union, the Professional Staff Congress, the faculty and staff union of the City University of New York; it has meant six years of full-time union work. Consequently, large parts of the book were written in between strategy and organizing meetings, in Amtrak stations and airports while traveling to state-wide and national union gatherings, and in a neighborhood café close to my union office. During these years, I benefitted from long hours in the company of wonderful colleagues and comrades like Mike Fabricant, Steve London, Andrea Vásquez, Sharon Persinger, Lorraine Cohen, Bob Cermele, John Pittman, Tony O' Brian, Manny Ness, Dan Pinello, Jerry Markowitz, and many others. I especially honor our union president, Barbara Bowen, an early modern scholar, who sacrificed what undoubtedly would have been a luminous academic career for building one of the most progressive unions in the country. I'm deeply grateful for the support, generosity, and the political education that I have received working with Barbara, and others. The motivating energy underlying this book of literary exploration is fundamentally a political one, so it was a remarkable privilege to be thinking and writing alongside organizing members and negotiating contracts.

I'm grateful to Devin Harner, Paul Narkunas, Alexander Long, Bettina Carbonell, Jean Mills, Liza Yukins, Dale Barleben, Caroline Reitz, Melinda Powers, Richard Haw, Alexander Schultz, and John Staines among others for making my academic home, the English department at John Jay College, a strong contender if there was ever a contest for the most collegial and warm workplace. A special word of thanks to the several chairs at different periods from all of whom I've received unqualified support and encouragement: the late Chris Suggs, Margaret Tabb, Allison Pease and Jay Gates. The companionship and generosity of my buddies, Valerie Allen and Toy Tung, have seen me through the hardships of writing this book and much more.

My dearest friends Aruna Krishnamurthy and Shakti Jaising, both, insightful literary scholars, kindly read and offered advice on several chapter drafts at short notice. I owe a debt of deep gratitude to my friend, Bashir Abu-Manneh for being a rock with encouragement, advice, and camaraderie; Bashir made the book better with his astute feedback on every chapter. Thanks to Avis Lang and Elliot Podwill for the love and support; I owe Avis also for her helpful reading of the manuscript. Ida Cheng, and also, Swati Sharma have been delightful companions offering tea and banter while I kvetched about writing and more.

The Mellon fellowship, grants from the CUNY Research Foundation, and from the Office for the Advancement of Research at John Jay College, provided much appreciated support to the project. A fellowship program at the Center for Place, Culture and Politics, became a source for a stimulating semester of weekly discussions led by David Harvey and Ruthie Gilmore; it helped shape some of the core ideas of the book. Thanks to Shelly Eversley and Matt Brim for their stewardship of the Faculty Fellowship Publication Program at CUNY which has been a source of support and has offered me the privilege of serving as a research mentor to junior faculty. I'm grateful for the invitation to share parts of the project at the Centre for Marxist Studies, Dehradun, the University of Florida, Gainesville, Wits University, Johannesburg, School of Visual Arts, New York, and at the Center for Women's Studies, Zagreb. I'd like to thank Achin Vanaik, Phil Wegner, Vishvas Satgar, Jeremy Cohan, and Karolina Hrga for the opportunities, each of which proved to be wonderful and instructive.

Parts of chapter 1 and chapter 2 were published earlier in *Catalyst: A Journal of Theory and Strategy* and in *The Journal of Postcolonial and*

Commonwealth Studies respectively; thanks to the journals for permission to reprint. At Verso Books, thanks to my editor, Sebastian Budgen for believing in the project, to Duncan Ranslem and the rest of the Verso team for their work on the production process. Sam Smith did an excellent copyediting job.

My mother-in-law, Darshan Perusek has been a source of support and encouragement over the years; her own incisive literary criticism is referenced in the book. I am indebted to my father, and my family in India for the emotional anchoring that sustains my work and life. It saddens me deeply that I am not able to share the book with my mother who passed away in 2009. I was eleven, when over a period of a couple of weeks, she read to me Bibhutibhusan Bandopadhyay's *Pather Panchali,* and we laughed and cried together with the characters. A voracious reader and a gifted writer, my mother instilled in me the love of literature. She would have had a lot to say on the chapter on Rabindranath and Sharatchandra, two of her favorite authors; I'll miss that conversation, but mostly I'll miss her pride and joy in my accomplishment.

The years it took me to write the book were my daughter, Ananya's middle and high school years with all their anxiety and excitement. During this period, she mostly saw me either rushing to union meetings or working on the book, but took it in stride with the effortless resilience that only the young exhibit. The thought of her reading the book someday has often made me smile and work harder. It is hard to be grateful to Vivek because he's so much a part of me. His faith in me and our shared conviction in the underlying premises that shape this project have been my strength. He has read, reread and helped improve every chapter of the book. Our love and comradeship give meaning to this project and to my life.

Introduction: Radicalizing Universalism

In 1987—forty years after India became independent—I began my undergraduate education in the English honors program at Delhi University. Our syllabus started with the Greeks, the classical background to English literature, before beginning in earnest with Chaucer. We were taken through all the central movements and writers: Spenser, Marlowe, Shakespeare, the Metaphysicals, the Romantics, the Silver poets, Milton, the eighteenth century, the Victorians. Our studies ended with the early twentieth century: Eliot, Conrad, Lawrence, and others. Every course was mandatory. There were no electives, no offerings of literatures from elsewhere. Clearly, neither the illustrious anti-colonial movement nor the four decades of robust democratic governance had made an impact on the cultural core of empire: English literary studies. Not until another decade did the university initiate the process of decolonizing the English department's curriculum.

Not coincidentally, it was that very decade, the 1990s, that postcolonial studies took firm hold in academia, challenging the hardened colonial curricula in literature departments and prying them open to include literatures from other regions, especially from the erstwhile colonized world. The discipline's spirited attack on the Western canon, targeting texts and critical reception to uncover the hitherto-ignored presence of colonial ideology, was stunningly iconoclastic. Though feminist and Marxist analyses had highlighted previously unarticulated gender and class dynamics in texts, they still did not fully address how centuries of colonialism had shaped the European psyche and Western cultural production. Postcolonial critics took on the task of exposing the violence and violations of colonial ideology that were lodged in the interstices of the Western canon. The twin phenomena that have by now substantially reshaped the conceptualization of English studies in academia—the reevaluation of the Western literary canon and the opening up of the curriculum to include non-Western literatures—are, I believe, postcolonial studies' most remarkable contributions. By no means has the battle been easy. Entrenched ideological and material interests have protected the mantle of the canon from the other side of the barricades.

Postcolonial critique is now prominent, having acquired a stature far beyond its immediate sphere of influence in English departments. It has been warmly adopted in the social sciences, for example in history, anthropology, and area disciplines such as African studies and Latin American studies. While debates and discussions on the discipline peaked in the early 2000s, there has been an ongoing, steady production of critical discourse on the merits and reach of postcoloniality.[1] In recent years, several journal volumes have been devoted to analyses of the state of the discipline.[2] And if there is now a certain wariness about the necessity of renewed debate on postcolonial studies, this wariness bespeaks the tremendous success of a discipline whose premises have now become almost academic common sense.

----

1 See for instance, Vasant Kaiwar, *The Postcolonial Orient: The Politics of Difference and the Project of Provincialising Europe*, Leiden: Brill, 2014; Graham Huggan, *Oxford Handbook of Postcolonial Studies*, Oxford: Oxford University Press, 2013; Vivek Chibber, *Postcolonial Theory and the Specter of Capital*, London and New York: Verso, 2013; Bill Ashcroft et al., eds., *Literature for Our Times: Postcolonial Studies in the Twenty-First Century*, Amsterdam: Rodopi, 2012; Neil Lazarus, *The Postcolonial Unconscious*, Cambridge: Cambridge University Press, 2011; Julie McGonegal, *Imagining Justice: The Politics of Postcolonial Forgiveness and Reconciliation*, Montreal: McGill–Queen's University Press, 2009; Graham Huggan, *Interdisciplinary Measures: Literature and the Future of Postcolonial Studies*, Liverpool: University of Liverpool Press, 2008; R. Krishnaswamy and J.C. Hawley, eds., *The Postcolonial and the Global*, Minneapolis: University of Minnesota Press, 2007; Sarah Brouillette, *Postcolonial Writers and the Global Literary Marketplace*, Basingstoke: Palgrave Macmillan, 2007.

2 "Marxism and Postcolonial Theory: What's Left of the Debate?," special issue, *Critical Sociology* 43:4–5 (2017); "The State of Postcolonial Studies," special issue, *New Literary History* 43:1 (2012); Patricia Yaeger, "Editor's Column: The End of Postcolonial Theory? A Roundtable with Sunil Agnani, Fernando Coronil, Gaurav Desai, Mamadou Diouf, Simon Gikandi, Susie Tharu, and Jennifer Wenzel," *PMLA* 122:3 (2007), pp. 633–51.

The discipline emerges intact from questions about its "datedness"[3] primarily because interlocutors largely do not contest the premises of its foundational theory, but only whether those premises can be meaningfully applied to a fast-transforming globalized order. The two phenomena typically invoked in challenges to the relevance of the discipline are terrorism and neoliberal globalization. In response to the view that the explanatory framework of postcolonial theory cannot be mobilized to engage with capitalist globalization, postcolonial critics insist on the expansiveness of their categories. Revathi Krishnaswamy and J. C. Hawley assert that "to be global is to be first and foremost to be postcolonial and to be postcolonial is always already to be global."[4] Ania Loomba and her co-editors of the volume *Postcolonial Studies and Beyond* argue that neoliberal globalization in the non-West must be read as a continuation of colonialism and its "imperial structure."[5] In the introduction to *Literature for Our Times*, a volume devoted to the relevance of postcolonial studies in the twenty-first century, Bill Ashcroft celebrates the eclecticism of the discipline, proclaiming that the volume represents "a range of approaches and interests living together in what Amartya Sen might call an argumentative democracy."[6] In the *Oxford Handbook of Postcolonial Studies*, Graham Huggan, similarly making a

---

3 Andrew Pendakis and Imre Szeman, "Introduction," in *Contemporary Marxist Theory: An Anthology*, ed. Andrew Pendakis et al., London: Bloomsbury, 2014, p. 6.

4 R. Krishnaswamy and J. C. Hawley, eds., *The Postcolonial and the Global*, Minneapolis: University of Minnesota Press, 2007, p. 3

5 Ania Loomba et al., eds., *Postcolonial Studies and Beyond*, Durham, NC: Duke University Press, 2005. This is consistent with the view of critics, like Gayatri Spivak, who read globalization as neocolonialism—a phenomenon that develops after colonialism and is "more economic and less territorial." Gayatri Spivak and Robert Young, "Neocolonialism and the Secret Agent of Knowledge," *Oxford Literary Review* 13:1–2 (1991), p. 221. While noting the vast disparity in the economic situation in the industrialized Asian countries like South Korea, Taiwan and Japan, on one hand, and countries like India and Algeria, on the other, Spivak maintains that both regions are operating under neocolonialism. Similarly, Deepika Bahri opines that the turn toward a neoliberal frame in countries like India testifies to the fact that "decolonization generally has failed." Deepika Bahri "Once More with Feeling: What Is Postcolonialism?," *Ariel: A Review of International English Literature* 26 (1995), pp. 51–81, 61. Robert Young contends that even though the "new system that replaced [colonialism] . . . was more subtle," neocolonialism denotes a "continuing economic hegemony [of] . . . the former masters." Robert Young, *Postcolonialism: An Historical Introduction*, Oxford: Blackwell, 2001, pp. 44–5.

6 Ashcroft, *Literature for our Times*, p. xvii.

virtue of the discipline's lack of "methodological coherence or consensual politics," proclaims:

> Postcolonialism, as a loose set of revisionist techniques, is both irrepressibly and incorrigibly combative, quarrelling with the world it wishes to transform but also, and no less obviously, bickering with itself. This is no less, of course, than one might expect of a field whose existence has been persistently fraught since its first institutional appearance in the 1980s, and the increasingly frequent allegation of whose replacement by emergent disciplines such as transnational cultural studies or globalization studies is so far from being the truth that it seems almost pointless to reject. What is closer to the truth, perhaps, is that terms such as "postcolonial," "transnational," and "global" work better together than apart, and help collectively to explain the times we live in.[7]

Far from being eclipsed, the premises of postcolonial theory are now firmly implanted within the firmament of contemporary cultural studies. This is evident not only in related fields such as world literature and decolonial studies, but also in formations such as transnational modernism, which have emerged partly in reaction to postcolonial studies. Thus, while theorists like Aníbal Quijano[8] and Walter Mignolo[9] signal a departure from postcolonial theory in reading capitalism as "economic coloniality" rather than as neocolonialism, they nevertheless base their position on the postcolonial premise that capitalism is fundamentally a Western rather than a global phenomenon. Similarly, the soul-searching in comparative literature led by David Damrosch, Emily Apter and others on the question of what constitutes world literature has been largely spurred by the pervasive influence of postcolonial theory.

The ubiquitous adoption of postcolonial premises within broader cultural theories is not surprising, because these premises represent an academic consensus in response to historical conditions that remain

---

7 Huggan, *Oxford Handbook of Postcolonial Studies*, p. 15.

8 See Aníbal Quijano, "Coloniality of Power and Eurocentrism in Latin America," *International Sociology* 15:2 (2000).

9 See Walter Mignolo, *The Darker Side of Western Modernity: Global Futures, Decolonial Options*, Durham: Duke University Press, 2011.

germane. Postcolonial studies made its definitive entry into academia at a time when the neoliberal agenda of the Reagan-Thatcher era, with its deregulation of markets, free trade, and the decimation of labor unions, had become the reigning doctrine. The discipline emerged under peculiar conditions: on the one hand, labor power had been decidedly trounced, but on the other, social movements had been flourishing for more than a decade. An increasingly diverse student body and popular movements led to fundamental shifts in the content of education, away from canonical texts and toward the democratization of the curriculum. Postcolonial thought emerged in this milieu from the broad umbrella of the New Left, a product of its times that encapsulated the contradictory pulls of liberalism and conservatism. The resilience of its influence during the past quarter century is a testament to the fact that we have not fully transcended the historical conditions that initially gave rise to postcolonial thought.

This study acknowledges the extraordinary achievement of the discipline in contesting and transforming the content of literary studies in academia. Furthermore, and more pertinently, I personally identify with the motivation behind the emergence of the postcolonial discipline: to challenge the ideology of colonial domination in cultural production. At the same time, however, I question the broad consensus in postcolonial theory that what is distinctive and valuable about literary works from the South is that they eschew grand narratives and universal categories in favor of the concrete and the particular—a maneuver lauded by postcolonial theorists on the basis that such universals are often highly parochial projections of European values and experiences onto the rest of the world. Hence, the embrace of the particular, as embodied in postcolonial literary works, becomes part of the more general rejection of Eurocentric universalism.

By contrast, my book argues that postcolonial theory profoundly misunderstands what lies at the core of some of the most influential postcolonial literary works. This body of theory, I contend, insists on reading those works as emblems of a localized and particularistic consciousness, whereas in fact, often the opposite is true. Postcolonial theory's misconceptions derive from an impoverished conceptual and normative repertoire, in which localism and universalism are not merely the only alternatives but are also mutually exclusive. This leaves us with an exotic and essentialized localism, and a Eurocentric universalism, as our sole options. I contend that the rejection of Eurocentric theories can be complemented by embracing another, richer and *non-parochial* form of universalism.

Through explorations of writings from South Asia and the Middle East spanning from the early twentieth century to the contemporary period, I draw a contrast between texts and interpretations that remain mired in categories of essentialized difference, and other texts that embody what I call a *radical universalism*. My analyses show that while they are deeply anchored in lived experience, these latter texts delve into aspects of the local that are not specific to it. Rather, they are expressions of shared concerns and dilemmas, which readers in diverse cultural settings can understand and to which they can readily relate. This is a local that encapsulates the universal.

Critiques

Even as postcolonial studies has become increasingly influential within a relatively short period, there have also been strong dissenting voices. This book builds on a body of critique centrally focused on postcolonial literary studies by Neil Lazarus,[10] Benita Parry,[11] Michael Sprinker,[12] Timothy Brennan,[13] Arif Dirlik,[14] and Neil Larsen[15] among others. In particular, Parry's foregrounding of liberation theory, Brennan's focus on interwar Marxism and Lazarus's reading of postcolonial literature

---

10 See Neil Lazarus, *Nationalism and Cultural Practice in the Postcolonial World*, Cambridge, UK: Cambridge University Press, 1999; *Marxism, Modernity and Postcolonial Studies*, Cambridge, UK: Cambridge University Press, 2002; *Cambridge Companion to Postcolonial Literary Studies*, Cambridge, UK: Cambridge University Press, 2004; *The Postcolonial Unconscious*, Cambridge, UK: Cambridge University Press, 2011.

11 See, for instance, Benita Parry, *Postcolonial Studies: A Materialist Critique*, London: Routledge, 2004.

12 See, for instance, Michael Sprinker, *Edward Said: A Critical Reader*, Oxford: Blackwell, 1992.

13 Timothy Brennan, *At Home in the World: Cosmopolitanism Now*, Cambridge, MA: Harvard University Press, 1997.

14 See, for instance, Arif Dirlik, *The Postcolonial Aura: Third World Criticism in the Age of Global Capitalism*, Boulder, CO, Westview Press, 1997.

15 See, for instance, Neil Larsen, "Toward a Profane Postcolonialism," *Diaspora: A Journal of Transnational Studies* 8:2 (Fall 1999).

against the grain of postcolonial theory have vigorously contested the
orthodoxies of what is otherwise "the only game in town."[16] While the
current study certainly benefits from and builds on the works of these
critics, it also remains in critical dialogue with them. I, for instance, take
exception to Parry's, but more specifically Lazarus's, spirited defense of
Fredric Jameson's "Third-World Literature in the Era of Multinational
Capitalism."[17] Jameson's essay, while acknowledging the danger of
Orientalism in privileging cultural difference, is nevertheless premised
precisely on such privileging, and a defense of Jameson's position marks
the limitations of any postcolonial critique. While noteworthy challenges
to some of the field's weaknesses have emerged over the years, postcolonial critics nonetheless tend to remain constrained by the parameters
of the field. This prevents them from going far enough in their criticisms,
and more important, from offering an adequate alternative.

In a cultural terrain characterized by an aversion to studying
global modernity in relation to the dynamics of capitalism, the recent
volume on world literature by the Warwick Research Collective (WReC),
*Combined and Uneven Development: Towards a New Theory of World-
Literature*, is a welcome venture. Highlighting the failure of postcolonial
scholars from Edward Said to Dipesh Chakrabarty and Ashis Nandy in
the task of anchoring modernity to global capitalism, WReC insists on a
"singular modernity," but one that does not preclude heterogeneity. The
collective rejects the homogenized Imperial West of postcolonial theory,
calling instead for the recognition of a "single but radically uneven
world-system; a singular modernity, combined and uneven; [and] a literature that variously registers this combined unevenness in both its
form and content."[18] In its formulation, the collective firmly ties Leon
Trotsky's theory of "combined and uneven development"[19] to Immanuel
Wallerstein's world-systems theory via Franco Moretti and Fredric
Jameson, positing a capitalist system with a core and periphery "bound

---

16 Lazarus, *The Postcolonial Unconscious*, p. 34.

17 Fredric Jameson, "Third-World Literature in the Era of Multinational Capitalism," *Social Text* 15 (1986), pp. 65–88.

18 Warwick Research Collective, *Combined and Uneven Development: Towards a
New Theory of World-Literature*, Liverpool: Liverpool University Press, 2015, pp. 10–11.

19 Drawing on Marx and Lenin, Trotsky uses the term to describe the functioning
of capitalism in an uneven terrain where capitalist forces of production and class relations coexist with preexisting structures and relations.

together in a relationship of growing inequality." WReC offers four case studies of literatures from across the globe to substantiate its thesis of a "world-system literature" that "registers" the functioning of capital grounded in the "dialectics of core and periphery."[20]

While there is much to commend in WReC's enterprise, it is not clear whether the framework sustains the stated goals. The collective announces its hostility to third-worldism, but then yokes the theory of "combined and uneven development" to world-systems theory, with very little comment or explanation. This is odd, since world-systems theory has been the anchor for third-worldism for much of the recent past. The authors do not consider that there might be a deep incompatibility between the two approaches—of Trotsky on the one hand and Wallerstein on the other—and move rather unselfconsciously between one and the other. It is true that both theories recognize the reality of underdevelopment and assign a role to external forces. But beyond that, they draw on entirely different theories of development and predict quite different paths of ascent for states in the global South. It should be noted that because it reads signs of semi-peripheral status in parts of Europe, including the UK, the collective may well deny any affiliation with a third-worldist perspective. But it remains unclear what precisely is gained by the insistence on a core–periphery model in analyzing the cultural registration of capital in Europe and elsewhere, and why the apparatus of "combined and uneven development" was not sufficient.

That critical problem notwithstanding, *Combined and Uneven Development* deserves acknowledgment for helping build a space outside the siloed East–West paradigm of postcolonial theory. It signals a refreshing break in a critical climate that either steers clear of studying the dynamics between cultural production and the operation of global capital, or misanalyzes the dynamics because of an inability or unwillingness to grasp the functioning of capital as a *single* system. Even though an exploration of the literary registration of capital's global operation is not the primary objective of my book, it is in part what I do, and WReC's insistence on a single capitalist modernity across the globe enhances studies like mine.

Theoretically, my study is more aligned with critiques of postcolonial theory by Aijaz Ahmad, Vivek Chibber and Vasant Kaiwar.[21] In

20 Ibid., p. 51.
21 See Aijaz Ahmad, *In Theory: Classes, Nations, Literatures*, London: Verso, 1992;

consonance with both Chibber and Kaiwar, this book argues that the field's insistence on cultural difference ultimately resurrects the very Orientalism that postcolonialists set out to oppose. Both analysts make the case for a universalist framework that enables a proper appreciation of both the logic of capital and resistance to it. While I am indebted to their insights in these studies, my critique of postcolonial theory is conducted primarily through an engagement with literary studies, a domain they leave largely untouched. And unlike both Kaiwar's and Chibber's works, this study is concerned with the larger postcolonial field, beyond the Subaltern Studies Collective.

Perhaps the closest predecessor in approach and substance is Ahmad's *In Theory*. Though over two decades old, it remains the most comprehensive and insightful critique of the field. While drawing on the same theoretical and ethical commitments, my study is largely distinct in scope and content. Ahmad was responding to a field emerging in the wake of the Thatcher-Reagan assault on the working class, as well as the crisis in newly decolonized nation-states of the South. Since then, the field has evolved in response to geopolitical developments such as international terrorism and the crisis of global capitalism. My book addresses a field shaped by these contemporary phenomena. In addition, whereas Ahmad's focus was largely on the political and intellectual conditions that produced postcolonial theory, I examine its operation in literary discourse.

Radical Universalism

This book maintains that the postcolonial opposition to colonial and other oppressive systems necessitates neither an embrace of historical difference nor a return to the kind of hollow liberalism embraced by many postcolonial theorists.[22] Simon Gikandi grapples with the dilemma

---

Chibber, *Postcolonial Theory and the Specter of Capital*; Kaiwar, *The Postcolonial Orient*.

22 An instance of postcolonial thinkers' affinity to liberalism would be Leela Gandhi's search for alternative Western political traditions of anti-colonialism that have not received due recognition in postcolonial thought—as she describes in her *Affective Communities: Anticolonial Thought, Fin-de-Siècle Radicalism, and the Politics of Friendship*, Durham, NC: Duke University Press, 2006. A worthy project, but all that she manages to retrieve in the repertoire of Western anti-colonial thought is a mere politics

of aligning postcolonial anti-humanism (and anti-universalism) with "powerful ethical concerns, the status of the human, and the status of culture, and the status of moral well-being," but he ultimately remains within the discipline's confines, unable to forge a resolution.[23] Postcolonial theorists fail to appreciate that the commitment to foregrounding subaltern predicaments and agency—what Gikandi terms an "ethical project"[24]—is not only consistent with the acknowledgment of underlying universalisms but is in fact untenable without it.

In his now-iconic essay, Fredric Jameson, while acknowledging the danger of Orientalism in its tendency to privilege cultural difference, nevertheless premised his theory of third world literature on precisely

---

of "friendship," as manifested in the ideas of marginal and marginalized groups such as vegetarians, animal rights activists, and spiritualists. Robert Young's approach to the Israel–Palestine conflict offers another example of the same phenomenon. He believes that it is the spirit of tolerance in Islam—rather than a challenge to Israeli colonialism and its economic and political interests—that holds the key to the conflict's resolution (Robert J. C. Young, "Postcolonial Remains," *New Literary History*, vol. 43, no. 1, 2012, pp. 19–42). Yet another instance can be found in Homi Bhabha's reading of Fanon in his foreword to a new translation of *The Wretched of The Earth*. Bhabha makes a misguided effort to divorce Fanon's ideas from socialist thought, instead asserting that Fanon's politics would align in the present day with demands for debt relief and access to generic drugs for HIV/AIDS, and with the work of NGOs and human rights organizations to realize such goals. Embracing the palliative benefits of liberal institutions as the only possible horizon for politics, Bhabha steers clear of addressing the necessity of systemic deconstruction of capitalism (Homi Bhabha, "Foreword: Framing Fanon" in Frantz Fanon, *The Wretched of the Earth*, New York: Grove Press, 2004, pp. vii–xlii). Also, consider that Stephen Morton upholds Spivak's ambivalence toward organized resistance by characterizing her position as an "ethical commitment to achieving *one-on-one epistemic change* [that] is crucial for altering the structures of inequality" (Steven Morton, *Gayatri Spivak: Ethics, Subalternity and the Critique of Postcolonial Reason*, London: Polity Press, 2007, p. 173). Ironically, a discipline founded to challenge not merely liberal humanism's notion of the autonomous human but also Marxism's residual humanism ends up embracing the hoary liberal idea of effecting structural transformation by changing one person at a time.

23 Simon Gikandi, "Postcolonialism's Ethical (Re)turn: An Interview with Simon Gikandi," by David Jefferess, *Postcolonial Text* 2:1, 2006. Gikandi observes that he can only occupy a "middle space" after rejecting colonialism and nationalism. But why use a nondescript phrase like "middle space" and refuse to consider other critical spaces—of Marxist thought, for instance—that critique both colonialism and nationalism, and grapple with the fundamental moral and political questions that Gikandi raises.

24 Ibid. Note that Gikandi's "ethical project" concerning fundamental questions of oppression and moral well-being is distinct from the "ethical turn" in the discipline away from transformative politics.

such privileging. He examines the drawbacks in building a theory of "radical difference" that accounts for non-Western literature, but cannot envision an alternative:

> It is clear to me that any articulation of *radical difference* . . . is suscep-tible to appropriation by that strategy of otherness which Edward Said, in the context of the Middle East, called "orientalism." It does not matter much that the radical otherness of the culture in question is praised or valorized positively, as in the preceding pages: the essential operation is that of differentiation, and once that has been accomplished, the mechanism Said denounces has been set in place. On the other hand, I don't see how a first-world intellectual can avoid this operation without falling back into some *general liberal and humanistic universalism.*[25]

The present book attempts to demonstrate that it is not only possible but necessary to engage with cultural production from the global South without resorting to either choice considered by Jameson: the Oriental-ist category of "radical difference" or the embrace of "some general liberal and humanistic universalism." Any generalized category of universalism or "common humanity" that is disconnected from hetero-geneities of culture and economy is necessarily vacuous and potentially oppressive. But, contra Jameson and postcolonial analyses, I do not read difference in specificity, or singularity in concreteness.[26] Postcolonial literature, like all literature, must be read with an eye to how it is anchored in cultural specificities and rooted in concrete experiences, both collective and individual.

Through literary texts from the postcolonial world, I try to show that the fine-grained engagement with culture, the mapping of ordinary lives not just as objects but as subjects of history, is often embedded not in the postcolonial notion of "radical difference" but in what I call a radical universalism: a universalism rooted in local realities but also capable of unearthing the needs, conflicts, and desires that stretch across cultures and time. It is a universalism recognized by Marx and embraced by the likes of

---

25 Jameson, "Third-World Literature," p. 77, emphasis mine.

26 See Peter Hallward, *Absolutely Postcolonial*, Manchester: Manchester University Press, 2001, for a critical analysis of the notion of singularity in postcolonial theory.

Frantz Fanon, Amílcar Cabral and C.L.R. James, a universalism steeped in the spirit of anti-colonialism and hostile to any whiff of exoticism.

I would assert that my rejection of the universal/particular binary enables me to unpack and reject a series of other binaries that arise therefrom. In individual chapters devoted to writings from the early twentieth century through the present day—from India, Sri Lanka, Palestine and Egypt—I argue that the typical oppositions set up by post-colonial theory are artificial and unworthy. Among such oppositions are those between the structural and the experiential, between abstract theorization and concrete manifestation, between collective struggles and individual moral agency. I show that these arguments do not merely make theoretical mistakes but also profoundly mischaracterize the works they purport to examine. I further contend that many of the works in question—works presented by postcolonial theory as rejections of all universalizing categories—in fact embody a universalizing ambition.

Architecture

Borrowing from William Blake, I argue that a grain of sand—the local—contains the world—the universal. The book is divided into two parts. Part I, "A Grain of Sand," examines the postcolonial privileging of the local in the idea of historical difference. The main thrust of this first section is to show how the theory fails on its own terms, that is to say, how its attempts to reveal the specificity of postcolonial regions and to excavate the agency of marginal groups end up doing the opposite. Post-colonial theory, I assert, obscures agency, celebrates constraints, and obfuscates the true dynamics at play in the regions on which it focuses. Following part I's exploration of the weaknesses inherent in certain classically postcolonial themes, part II, "The World in the Grain," turns to works that show the promise of a radical universalism. These works are especially noteworthy because, though lauded by postcolonial critics, they are far from fitting the mold favored within the field. In upholding commitments explicitly castigated by postcolonial theory, they lay the foundation for an alternative cultural project: one that avoids both the exoticism embedded in much of postcolonial studies and the parochial, conservative universalism associated with imperial ideologies.

Part I: A Grain of Sand

The opening chapter, on "agency," focuses on how postcolonial theory has based its claim to radicalism on its defense of the quotidian and the marginal, and on instances of agency arising within those domains. It examines those claims as evidenced in three of the field's canonical essays: Gayatri Spivak's "Can the Subaltern Speak?," Homi Bhabha's "The Commitment to Theory," and Ranajit Guha's "Chandra's Death." All three are not simply works of theory but also examples of textual analysis, wherein the reader is shown how to recover instances of agency that the wider scholarly community has either overlooked or denigrated.

In this chapter, I criticize the essays on both grounds, showing that each theorist's reading of the texts is deeply flawed. More significantly, I argue that what Spivak and the others describe as instances of agency are in fact acts of acquiescence. While supposedly showing and defending women's resistance, the chosen examples in fact naturalize domination and evacuate actual instances of resistance in the texts. The contradictory readings raise grave doubts about the conceptual framework generated by the field, since these essays are widely regarded as exemplars of how to undertake postcolonial analysis. Chapter 1 thus serves as an opening theoretical salvo into the field's core, which is then followed by more focused inquiries into literary texts.

Chapter 2, on the "gender question," juxtaposes the works of Rabindranath Tagore and Sharatchandra Chattopadhyay, and examines some of the pitfalls that accompany the embrace of "difference." Tagore is lauded by postcolonial theorists for having explored the interplay of gender and modernity in fin de siècle Bengal. Of particular significance here is his novel *The Home and the World* (1916), which has achieved iconic status within the field for its depiction of the patriarchal character of Bengali *bhadralok* culture. I show that while *The Home and the World* does indict the subordinate position of Bengali women, it remains a deeply patriarchal novel. What is fundamentally at play here is Tagore's naturalization of various gender norms that contribute to the patriarchy he seeks to condemn.

Tagore's conservatism is all the more apparent when we set his work against that of his contemporary Sharatchandra Chattopadhyay. Chattopadhyay was more widely translated in India and had a larger readership. And, unlike Tagore, for whom gender was only one part of a ramified oeuvre, Chattopadhyay was centrally preoccupied with exploring its place in Bengali culture. I set out the contrast between the two by analyzing one of Chattopadhyay's popular novels, *The Final Question* (1931). In it, Chattopadhyay offers a scathing indictment of the inter-related discourses of cultural authenticity and patriarchy. The portrayal of its central protagonist, a brilliant and articulate widow, is strongly critical of *bhadralok* patriarchy while being no less sensitive to the texture of local norms and culture.

Despite his deeper progressivism and his greater resonance with an Indian readership, Chattopadhyay has gone almost unnoticed in post-colonial studies, while Tagore remains a revered figure. I argue that this contrast captures the dilemma in which the field is trapped. Its blanket rejection of universalism inclines its exponents to ignore Chattopadhyay, even though he is far more critical of patriarchy and no less popular with the Indian audience than Tagore. Yet Tagore is celebrated largely because he rhetorically embraces cultural difference, despite his con-servatism on the very issue that postcolonial studies seeks to advance: women's agency. As a result, the field ends up promoting a conservative position on gender.

The third chapter, on "neo-Orientalism," centers on Michael Ondaatje's *Anil's Ghost* (2000), widely hailed as the consummate postcolonial novel, not just in its choice of subject—the Tamil insurgency in Sri Lanka—but also in its approach. Robert Young has praised it for the specificity of its representation of terrorism in the postcolonial world. Although I agree with the categorization of the novel as postcolonial in both focus and approach, I show that this does not bode well for the field.

It is true that Ondaatje makes the Sri Lankan Civil War his focus, but his treatment of the war undermines his objectives. Rather than expli-cate the conflict by taking seriously the context and the forces responsible for its undertaking, the author obscures the conflict by fitting it into a conventional Orientalist frame. The dynamics of the civil war are intro-duced to the reader through the eyes of Anil, the book's protagonist, who approaches the conflict through the lens of a human rights researcher. But as the narrative unfolds, it becomes clear that her perspective—her attachment to a Western conceptual framework that looks for causes, legality, interests, and the like—is simply insufficient to apprehend the nature of the conflict. Gradually Anil's perspective is undermined and overturned by the author's own viewpoint, which depicts the killings as arbitrary and unreadable. Young approvingly describes Ondaatje's depiction of terrorism as beyond the reach of all social and political discourse, to be understood simply as trauma. I, on the other hand, argue that Ondaatje presents a classically Orientalist depiction of the East, and that Young's embrace of it offers up an indictment of the field.

Whereas chapters 2 and 3 explore the poisoned chalice of "difference," chapter 4, "The Neoliberal Logic in Indian Anglophone Literature," moves us closer to the radical alternative by offering a cautionary argument against what I call *neoliberal universalism*. My main contention is that even though postcolonial theory's embrace of the local is deeply flawed, the solution is not an embrace of universalism tout court. I show this by examining a new trend in Anglophone Indian literature: a cosmopolitan patina, wrapped around a highly individualistic and ultimately neoliberal worldview. This approach is embodied in two recent award-winning novels, Jhumpa Lahiri's *The Lowland* (2013) and Neel Mukherjee's *The Lives of Others* (2014).

Both novels reject the exoticism of traditional Anglophone literature and seem to explore dimensions of Indian culture that are typically anathema to this literary tradition: popular struggles and revolutionary politics. For both authors, however, politics remains an external, alien force acting upon their protagonists, impinging on their individuality, rather than being an expression of it. Redemption comes only with a turn away from political struggle; emancipation is expressed as a rejection of the binding force of political commitment. As a result, both books embody the worldview of the upwardly mobile Anglophone middle class, a cosmopolitanism that is comfortably ensconced in the circuits of consumption.

Part II: The World in the Grain

In large part thanks to the efforts of Gayatri Spivak, Mahasweta Devi is among the most widely read writers in the postcolonial field and is celebrated for her depiction of marginal groups in the subcontinent: tribal populations, peasants and especially women. Chapter 5, "Indigeneity as Myth and Message," joins in the celebration of Devi's work but also contends that the postcolonial appropriation of her work is fundamentally mistaken. I situate Devi's contributions within the context of debates on indigeneity in the competing fields of indigenous studies and postcolonial studies, and make the case that, disciplinary tensions notwithstanding, the fields subscribe to an underlying cultural-ism. Focusing on Devi's novella *Pterodactyl, Puran Sahay and Pirtha* (1995), I argue that Devi's compassionate and nuanced portrayal of indigenous culture does not conform to the culturalist template. Never does it separate the experiential universe of the tribal people from the social and political context; always it insists on viewing their condition through the prism of their material condition, rather than the alterna-tive cosmology posited by her commentators. Her portrayal of the rich tribal culture—"a continent that we kept unknown and undiscovered"— is never an end in itself, because Devi does not deal in the politics of recognition. Hers is a demand for equal access to resources and rights for indigenous populations.

My argument in this chapter deepens and advances the analysis of Devi's work that I present in chapter 2, where I show that her depiction of gender relations in her short story "Draupadi" flatly contradicts Spivak's reading of that text. Here I show that Devi's depiction of the title character is not an isolated instance. When we combine it with her portrayal of tribal issues in *Pterodactyl*, we see that postcolonial theory has imposed an interpretive grid on this author that simply erases themes quite central to her work. Excavation of these themes generates a portrait that not only goes against the dominant interpretation but also suggests a radically divergent politics of the local. The chapter ends with a nod to postcolonial ecocriticism, a promising field that has managed to steer clear of culturalist dead ends and is more in sync with Devi's insights.

In chapter 6, "The National and the Universal," I explore the fact that no political form receives as much attention—or as much opprobrium— from postcolonial theory as does the nation, and how this exemplifies the tendency for universalizing discourses to homogenize across local particularities and to suppress any aspirations that cannot be folded into the larger national project. Hence the intellectual project to rescue the local *from* the nation. Through a discussion of the changing fortunes of the critical reception of Jameson's "Third World Literature" essay, argu-ably the most significant intervention in the field on the subject, I comment on the affiliations and the pitfalls of the discipline.

I examine the works of two Middle Eastern novelists, Mourid Bargh-outi and Ahdaf Soueif, to show that the opposition posited by postcolonial theory between the national and the local is overdrawn. Barghouti's memoir *I Saw Ramallah* (1997) documents the return of a Palestinian exile to his homeland, now under occupation. Soueif's novel *In the Eye of the Sun* (1992) is set in Cairo in the 1960s and 1970s, the high point of Egyptian nationalism, and revolves around the life of a young middle-class woman, Asya al-Ulama, the daughter of university professors. Each of the two texts explores its protagonist's longings for self-actualization. For Barghouti, it is the urge to overcome the alienation created by the feeling of exile in his own country, the longing for recognition; for Asya, it is the desire to embrace her position in Egyptian society while simultaneously navigating its patriarchal culture. But in neither case is the protagonist's struggle for individual recognition set against the aspirations for national liberation. Instead of seeing a contradiction between the two, both authors suggest a mutuality. It is true that both texts have deeply problematic aspects—for instance, Barghouti's unsubstantiated critique of collective action, and the class privilege that mires Soueif's perspective. Their drawbacks notwithstanding, we see in these texts two different ways in which the universal resides *within* the particular, not external to it.

This book's final chapter, "The Radical Universalism of A. Sivanandan," showcases a literary exemplar of the project I endorse, a radical universalism, embedded in the local and experiential but connected to the wider human condition. Here I examine Sivanandan's *When Memory Dies* (1997), a narrative set in the same war-torn Sri Lanka as the Ondaatje novel critiqued in chapter 3. *When Memory Dies* tells the story of three generations of a Sri Lankan family, much of it spanning the years of the Tamil insurgency. Sivanandan weaves an intricate tapestry of characters and events, exploring the lifeworlds of his characters, recognizing the abiding influence of the country's colonial history, and connecting the protagonists' inner worlds to this context. The narrative depicts postcolonial subjects actively engaged in the construction of their history; it acknowledges their agency, but always as constrained by their circumstances.

Sivanandan's depiction of the civil war contrasts starkly with Ondaatje's. Whereas Ondaatje's account presents the violence and suffering as something mysterious, uncaused, a product of the Eastern mindset, Sivanandan brings the reader into the war's political history, thereby not merely making the violence more explicable but also allowing the reader to more directly empathize with the plight of his protagonists. Through his depiction, we come to understand the uniqueness of the conflict and its emergence from the particular history of modern Sri Lanka, but we never lose sight of the essential humanity of those caught up in its vortex. Furthermore, *When Memory Dies* also highlights the difference between a genuinely radical universalism, and the alienated, apolitical universalism of Jhumpa Lahiri and Neel Mukherjee discussed in chapter 4. Whereas for Lahiri and Mukherjee politics is something that intervenes in the personal, as an extrinsic force, Sivanandan's characters discover their individualism through political engagement and social ties.

Not unlike Sharatchandra Chattopadhyay's work, Sivanandan's book resides on the margins of postcolonial studies, despite having won prestigious awards and been widely read. Nevertheless, it presents a model of literary production that goes against the grain of the discipline in its insistence on a universalizing project that recognizes the particular and, at the same time, puts forward a radical vision affirming our shared humanity.

PART ONE
A Grain of Sand

1

Political Agency and Postcolonial Studies

Though born in the narrow confines of literature departments in the wake of Asian and African decolonization, the influence of post-colonial theory has increasingly become associated more with direct political commitments. Postcolonial theory today is viewed as an indispensable framework for understanding how power works in modern social formations and, in particular, how the West exercises its dominance over the global South. Even more, it is lauded for its attentiveness to the marginal, the oppressed—those groups that have been relegated to obscurity even by political traditions ostensibly committed to social justice. In academia, the concepts associated with this theoretical stream have increasingly displaced the more traditional vocabulary of the Left, particularly among younger academics and students. Indeed, the two most influential political frameworks of the past century on the Left, Marxism and progressive liberalism, are often described not just as inadequate sources of critique, but as tools of social control.

This chapter proposes to take up an issue that is at the very heart of postcolonial theory—the relationship between social domination and agency, and specifically, how gender is conceptualized as a site of struggle within this framework. It does so via an examination of several of the classic, agenda-setting essays in the field by Gayatri Spivak, Homi Bhabha and Ranajit Guha. Spivak's "Can the Subaltern Speak?"[1] and her

---

1 Gayatri Spivak, "Can the Subaltern Speak?," in *Marxism and the Interpretation of*

commentary on Mahasweta Devi's "Draupadi,"[2] Guha's germinal foray into gender history in "Chandra's Death,"[3] and Bhabha's influential "The Commitment to Theory,"[4] which seeks to reinstate women's agency into a reading of the British miners' strike of 1984 and 1985, thus comprise my focus.

The themes of agency and resistance are, of course, the signposts of the entire postcolonial turn. While the emphasis in the field's early years was on how forms of political agency arose in a colonial and postcolonial context, and became embedded in movements for self-determination, this is no longer the case. Postcolonial theory today, under the influence of Bhabha, Spivak and others, has taken on a far more ambitious agenda, going beyond the specificities of geographic location to generate more encompassing arguments about the nature of agency itself. In this respect, it has, as many commentators have observed, become one of the most influential political theories on the contemporary scene, certainly to the point of rivaling the traditions inherited from the nineteenth and early twentieth centuries. What makes the postcolonial turn especially important is that it foregrounds precisely those forms of agency and political identity that have tended to remain at the periphery of Marxist and liberal considerations—gender, sexuality and race in particular. Whereas these forms of oppression have only recently become analytical foci within the traditional Left, they have been central to postcolonial theory from its inception.

The decision to focus on a small number of central texts is intended to serve a specific purpose. In part, it is motivated by the fact that the works in question have been hugely influential in the field—indeed, so much so that some of them are even identified with it. But, precisely because they exercise such inordinate influence, to criticize them without a careful engagement would be to invite skepticism toward, if not outright dismissal of, my claims. Just as importantly, it is through close examination of these texts that one can also raise the natural

---

Culture, ed. Lawrence Grossberg and Cary Nelson, Urbana-Champaign: University of Illinois Press, 1988, pp. 271–313.

2 Gayatri Spivak, "'Draupadi' by Mahasweta Devi," *Critical Inquiry* 8:2 (1981), pp. 381–402.

3 Ranajit Guha, "Chandra's Death," *Subaltern Studies*, vol. 5, New Delhi: Oxford University Press, 1987, pp. 135–65.

4 Homi Bhabha, "The Commitment to Theory," *New Formations* 5 (1988), pp. 5–23.

question about their reception and canonization in the field. Although other critics have cast doubt on some of the arguments made by Spivak, Guha and Bhabha,[5] the more specific issues that I raise—about the manner in which they conceptualize resistance and subalternity—have rarely been taken up, much less debated. In crucial ways, postcolonial studies has tended to take on board the very aspects of these essays that I find most objectionable. The indictment of the arguments in these texts should also, then, raise some worries about the intellectual culture in the field.

Guha's Small Drama

Ranajit Guha's essay "Chandra's Death" occupies a special place in post-colonial scholarship. Even though it is not as influential as some of the other canonical works in the field, it has been recognized as an agenda-setting piece, not only by postcolonial theory's proponents but also by its detractors. Thus, Sumit Sarkar, an early defector from the Subaltern Studies project, of which Guha was a founding member, regards the essay as offering "glimmerings of an alternative approach" that was, sadly, abandoned by the project.[6] Priyamvada Gopal, also a critic of the subalternists, aligns with Sarkar in her assessment of the essay as a "profoundly humanist" engagement with the histories of the oppressed in its investigation of the layered complexity of human predicaments.[7] What is especially praiseworthy to many readers is its engagement with gender. "Chandra's Death" was published in the pivotal fifth volume of *Subaltern Studies* and was, in some measure, a response to admonishments from feminist scholars that the subalternist project, in its first four volumes, had been largely blind to gender issues. After this essay,

---

5 See Aijaz Ahmad, *In Theory: Classes Nations, Literatures*, London: Verso, 1993; Arif Dirlik, *The Postcolonial Aura: Third World Criticism in the Age of Global Capitalism*, Boulder, CO, Westview Press, 1997; Benita Parry, *Postcolonial Studies: A Materialist Critique*, New York: Routledge, 2004; Neil Lazarus, *The Political Unconscious*, Cambridge, UK: Cambridge University Press, 2011.

6 Sumit Sarkar, "The Decline of the Subaltern," in *Writing Social History*, New Delhi: Oxford University Press, 1997, p. 93.

7 Priyamvada Gopal, "Reading Subaltern History," in *The Cambridge Companion to Postcolonial Literary Studies*, ed. Neil Larsen, Cambridge, UK: Cambridge University Press, 2004, pp. 140–1.

the historian Florencia Mallon lauded Guha for having provided a
"powerful answer" to charges of ignoring women's agency.[8] Gayatri
Spivak praised the essay, too, as having inaugurated the incorporation of
gender into the subalternist project.[9]

The essay is thus unusual in its elicitation of praise from all sides, not
just from advocates for Subaltern Studies or postcolonial theory. Indeed,
there is much in it to admire, not least Guha's prodigious research into
the context for the events he recounts, the clarity with which he presents
his case, and, of course, the commitment to bringing gender to the
center of the subalternist project. Guha's concern in the essay is to
recover an instance of women's gendered agency in which they forge
solidarity in a highly patriarchal setting to preserve their autonomy
against the weight of male authority. I will argue, however, that it fails to
make the case on either of these counts—of showing female agency or
solidarity. My contention is that Guha mistakes self-preservation for
solidarity. Insofar as he tries to make a case for women's agency, he does
so by redefining the concept in such a way as to turn it into its opposite.
In other words, Guha constructs a narrative in which an act of acquiescence is brandished as resistance. This amounts not to a recovery of
women's agency, but to its effacement.

The essay describes the circumstances leading to the death of a young
woman named Chandra in mid-nineteenth-century rural Bengal.
Chandra has had an affair with her brother-in-law Magaram and discovers that she is pregnant. Upon discovering this, Magaram approaches
Chandra's mother, Bhagobati, and informs her that Chandra has two
options available to her: to have an abortion or to be ostracized from the
village as an adulteress—a punishment known as *bhek*, which Guha
aptly describes as a "living death in a ghetto of social rejects."[10] Bhagobati
decides in favor of the abortion and mobilizes her familial network to
procure the necessary drugs. These are then administered to Chandra
by her sister; they have the intended effect, but they also result in Chandra's own demise. Chandra's death is deemed a murder by the colonial
authorities, and Chandra's relatives are tried for the crime.

---

8 Florencia Mallon, "The Promise and Dilemma of Subaltern Studies: Perspectives
from Latin American History," *American Historical Review* 99:5 (1994), p. 1509.

9 Gayatri Spivak, "Scattered Speculations on the Subaltern and the Popular," *Postcolonial Studies* 8:4 (2005), p. 434.

10 Guha, "Chandra's Death," p. 161.

To Guha, this event has an intrinsic significance, which we will consider shortly. But it is also important because of the way it has been absorbed into Indian historiography. Guha observes that the dominant tradition of historical analysis has little interest in small events like Chandra's death, since it is preoccupied with the master narratives of nation building, statehood, capitalism and so on—making historians oblivious to "the small drama and fine detail of social existence."[11] Second, Guha questions the appropriation of the event in legal discourse, which has the effect of reducing the "complex tissue of human predicament"[12] to a mere case. The experience of the event and the humanity of the actors are all erased in the "abstract legality"[13] that turns Chandra's relatives into "murderers."[14] Legal and historiographic discourses remain deaf to the "sobs and whispers"[15] in which the subaltern voices speak.

Against the established weight of such renderings, Guha takes on the task of reconstructing a history of Chandra's death that "by bending closer to the ground . . . [would] pick up the traces of a subaltern's life in its passage through time."[16] So Chandra's death is important not only as an event but also as an analytical exercise, an act of historical recovery that both excavates and honors the agency of actors buried under the weight of academic convention, while also demonstrating the shortcomings of dominant intellectual traditions. Even more, Guha seeks to establish the central role of gender as both a site of oppression and a fount of resistance, which the grand narratives of class and nation inevitably marginalize in their reconstructions of the events.

Guha begins by establishing the context for the decisions Chandra made. Her family belonged to the Bagdi caste, a stratum of landless laborers who resided in a western district of Bengal in the mid-nineteenth century. As rural proletarians, the Bagdis were at the bottom of the agricultural society and reviled as a "filthy deposit" by higher-status castes in the village. In addition to being agricultural laborers, the men were also employed as the village's night watchmen, guarding their employers' property. Yet the men were branded as "incorrigibly prone to criminality,"

11 Ibid., p. 138.
12 Ibid., p. 141.
13 Ibid., p. 141.
14 Ibid., p. 160.
15 Ibid., p. 141.
16 Ibid., p. 138.

and while Bagdi women were routine victims of sexual exploitation by upper-caste men, they were labeled as women of "easy virtue."[17]

In this setting of acute scarcity, the Bagdis relied on a complex system of local caste and subcaste alliances as a survival strategy. Bagdi children would marry within the sections of the subcaste to which they belonged, which amounted to several families in the two or three neighboring villages, so the village cluster was a "kinship region for six Bagdi families."[18] In common with the rest of India and many rural societies, the marriage circles served not only as a site of biological reproduction but also as a crucial source of material support. Finding an appropriate household for their children to marry into was a central part of the survival strategy of these landless laborers. Anything that threatened the viability of that strategy, by extension, also posed a grave threat to the material welfare of the entire subcaste.

When Magaram approached Chandra's mother and confessed his affair with Chandra, the implications were clear. If it were revealed that she had been impregnated by her brother-in-law, it would, of course, disgrace Chandra's mother and immediate family. But it would also land a severe blow to the reputation of the larger group of families within the marriage circle. A woman's honor, her fidelity, was among the most important elements in the reputation of any family and constituted an important marker of a village's ability to establish internal order. The prestige of a caste, Guha points out, was primarily based on its "degree of purity," which translated as a "maiden's virginity, a widow's chastity and a wife's sexual fidelity."[19] A child born out of wedlock in such a setting therefore threatened the delicate system of mutual dependence into which the Bagdis were inserted.

For Magaram, it made little difference whether Chandra opted for bhek or for abortion. Either choice would have insulated him from exposure. But the fact that her mother, Bhagobati, decided in favor of abortion is, for Guha, significant, since it brought with it tasks and risks that bhek would not. The drugs to induce the abortion had to be procured from another village. Her own daughter, her sister, and their husbands and brothers had to be mobilized to arrange the matter. Each

---

17 Ibid., p. 144.
18 Ibid., p. 148.
19 Ibid., p. 152.

of these tasks carried an additional risk of exposure or failure. Chandra's sister Brinda was responsible for administering the drugs, but several men played an important role in arranging payment and then, when it resulted in Chandra's demise, in burying her body nearby. In spite of the greater burdens, what is clear is that Bhagobati managed to secure the cooperation of much of her clan in covering up her daughter's illicit affair.

These are the basic facts about the events and the roles of the various actors involved. Guha does an admirable job of adding context and texture to the fragment that recounts the case, and we are able to locate Bhagobati and her family in their setting and also to understand the awful choice with which she was confronted. Guha brilliantly exposes the brutality of the patriarchal order, the cold logic of which is manifested especially in Magaram, who impregnated Chandra, and in the women's attempts to minimize the inevitable damage to their well-being. As I have noted, Guha carries this out with exemplary clarity and sensitivity. But this is not what has made the essay a classic within postcolonial studies: there, it is seen, we will recall, as a demonstration of subaltern agency, an act of recovery that traditions blinded by master narratives of class and nation systematically marginalize.

For Guha, the acts of resistance are to be found in Bhagobati's decision to abort Chandra's fetus and the women's consequent actions to carry it out. He presents these actions as an assertion of women's autonomy and solidarity. He reads Bhagobati's initiatives to prevent Chandra's excommunication as "a choice made by women entirely on their own in order to stop the engine of male authority from uprooting a woman from her place in the local society."[20] For Guha, the women's actions in the hour of crisis were nothing short of an "act of resistance" against a patriarchal order and in defense of "another woman, to fight for her right to a life of honour within her own society."[21] Further, Guha argues that the response was not merely dictated by the women's desire to protect an immediate family member; to read the "resistance merely in terms of the obligations of kin and kutum is to ignore what is distinctive about it . . . [it is] *an alternative solidarity*—a solidarity of women."[22]

---

20 Ibid., p. 164.
21 Ibid., p. 162.
22 Ibid., pp. 164–5.

So what makes Bhagobati's choice, and those of the other women involved, acts of resistance is that they were motivated by empathy and were intended to undermine patriarchy. The women enacted their agency in ways that are not picked up by dominant historiographic traditions, as a small history, in ways that do not conform to the image of struggle that Marxism, for example, has handed down. Hence, it is only through an approach of "bend[ing] closer to the ground" that we can locate this agency and see the resistance for what it was.[23]

But Guha's argument strains credulity. Take, first, the issue of the women's motivation. Guha observes that much of what transpired was clearly impelled by a pervasive fear among the principals of losing status within the village. This fear bred a kind of solidarity among all the actors, men and women, which was expressed in their cooperation to effectuate Chandra's abortion. Yet, he insists, if we look deeper, we will see that the women were not fundamentally driven by fear: "The solidarity born out of fear contained within it another solidarity activated by a different, indeed contradictory, principle—namely empathy. If it was the power of patriarchy that brought about the first, it was the understanding of the women which inspired the second."[24]

What understanding? From Guha's own account, had Chandra's indiscretion been discovered, the consequences would have been dire for the whole clan, women included. Chandra would have had to accept bhek; in addition, however, for the wider clan, the mere association with her transgression could entail sanctions directed toward them. Guha explains their predicament:

> Any violation of the norms in this respect could pollute all of an offender's kin, especially her consanguines, and undermine the group's ability to sustain and reproduce itself . . . the object of solidarity was also the person who could, by her transgressions, bring shame upon those she would most expect to stand by her when found guilty and share the rigour of all penalties prescribed by the samaj.[25]

---

23 Ibid., p. 138.
24 Ibid., p. 160.
25 Ibid., pp. 152–3.

Given the likelihood of sanctions for Bhagobati and other kin, one can only wonder how Guha can present Bhagobati's actions as solidaristic rather than self-interested. The choice of abortion had one unambiguous merit for the family—unlike bhek, which left a stigma for the entire clan, a successful abortion erased any evidence of Chandra's sin once and for all. Indeed, what risk it entailed was borne overwhelmingly by her. This is not to say that Bhagobati's choice for her daughter could not have been motivated by empathy. Perhaps Chandra expressed a greater fear of social ostracism than of the dangers that came with abortion; perhaps the women were aware of her preferences and acted on these, even though they turned out to also benefit them. It is certainly possible. The point is that Guha does not provide one bit of textual evidence to suggest that this was in fact the case. All we have is Guha, mysteriously turning against his own presentation of the facts, and insisting that what appears to be a choice made out of fear and practicality was in fact an act of resistance.

One can legitimately object here that under the slogan of "bending closer to the ground," Guha is committing the very sin of which he accuses dominant traditions—the erasure of the actual structure of events, while sliding them, instead, into some master narrative. In this case, it is the narrative of "agency" and "resistance" that is the hallmark of postcolonial theory. Whereas for nationalist historians, every historical event is forced into the telos of nation building, and for legal scholars, into the narrative of crime and social order, in this instance a poor woman's death is turned into a heroic saga of collective struggle against patriarchy. This latter interpretation is no less guilty of overreach than are the others.

But that is not the real problem with Guha's interpretation. If that was all there was to the matter, our critique would be no more than an academic quibble about texts. The deeper problem has to do with what his argument implies about resistance as a political act and about agency itself. Bhagobati was given a choice between two awful alternatives, a choice that was the product of the local patriarchal order. Neither she nor Chandra had any means, nor did they show any inclination, to change the choice set or even contest the terms on which the choices were offered. Their agency was limited to opting for one or the other— bhek or abortion. In the end, they went for the latter, and Chandra paid for it with her life. To choose between two options that have been generated by an oppressive social structure is not resistance—it is

acquiescence to that order. It is not, therefore, something to be celebrated, but rather comprises the very circumstance that a critical analysis
ought to insist needs to be changed.

The conservatism of Guha's argument shows itself in even sharper
relief as he expands on what Chandra's relatives achieved and on the
content of their resistance. Chandra's female relatives, he suggests, were
able to resist because they acted within a sphere where they were empowered—that of biological reproduction. Chandra's pregnancy itself
opens up an autonomous space for women, where

> patriarchy retreat[s] in the face of women's determination to assert
> her control over her body . . . in pregnancy . . . [women consciously
> establish ownership of their bodies] . . . This knowledge constitutes a
> challenge which is genuinely dreaded by male authority. For it oper-
> ates in an area of liminality not strictly governed by the will of
> husbands and fathers—an area which appears to the latter as fraught
> with uncertainty and danger, since women speak here in a language
> not fully comprehensible to men and conduct themselves by rituals
> that defy male reasoning.[26]

But it is not clear how the decision was in any way an assertion of
control by Chandra over her body or, in that manner, patriarchy's
"retreat." It was, after all, Bhagobati who made the choice, not Chandra,
which made the act a relinquishment of autonomy by the woman, not
an assertion thereof. Even worse, the decision was made in acquiescence
to the demands laid out by the very "male authority" that Guha sees as
somehow in retreat.

As if realizing the dubiousness of his claim, Guha turns to Simone de
Beauvoir for support, quoting from *The Second Sex*, where she describes
pregnancy as a "drama that is acted out within the woman herself"—
and therefore, we are to infer, an assertion of her individuality.[27] But this
move only deepens Guha's folly, for not only does it misconstrue the
compliance with a command for an assertion of autonomy, but also
quite dramatically distorts Beauvoir's argument regarding pregnancy
and the body. Beauvoir never privileges the body as the site of resistance,

---

26 Ibid., p. 163.
27 Ibid., p. 162.

nor does she consider childbirth as an assertion of autonomy. She insists, to the contrary, that a liberation from patriarchy presupposes a transcendence of the biological and of the domestic sphere, which Guha offers as the natural domains for women's agency. Indeed, when Guha describes women's embrace of natal care as operating in an "area of liminality," speaking in a "language not fully comprehensible to men," and "conduct[ing] themselves by rituals that defy male reasoning," he comes perilously close to excavating not women's resistance, but the hoary idea of the "feminine mystique."

To insist, as I do, on an interpretation that highlights the constraints under which Bhagobati labored, rather than on her supposed resistance, is not to deny her agency. It is to point out that for Bhagobati, and for millions of women in her circumstances, agency is exercised in making the best of a horrible situation, day after day and year after year. It is to call attention to the fact that those circumstances are unjust precisely because no matter which choice is made, the outcome will be unjust. That is why it is the *choice set itself* that needs to be changed, by making it the object of struggle. By celebrating the choice as an act of anti-patriarchal resistance, Guha turns Bhagobati's resignation to her condition into an act of resistance against it—and in so doing, he both devalues and denatures what agency and resistance entail. If merely choosing between the options given to you is to resist them, then why enjoin the oppressed to struggle against the choice set itself?

Spivak's Speech

If Guha finds an act of subaltern resistance in Chandra's death, Gayatri Spivak finds one in a woman's suicide. Since its publication in 1988, "Can the Subaltern Speak?" has taken its place as perhaps the most widely cited essay in postcolonial studies. It is seen as a call for the acknowledgment both of subaltern—especially women's—agency and of its suppression. It has generated a cottage industry of interpretation, no doubt in part owing to the dense prose but also because of the sheer range of issues that Spivak throws into the mix. There are some obvious differences between her essay and Guha's recuperation of Chandra; while Guha draws primarily on archival research, Spivak's intervention is more focused on the landscape of poststructuralist theory. But both seek to recover and acknowledge instances of women's resistance that are either ignored by establishment discourses or suppressed in the exercise of power.

"Can the Subaltern Speak?" is a complex, sprawling essay, the bulk of which is an engagement with contemporary—mainly French— philosophy through the prism of Foucault and Derrida. Spivak seeks to engage the issue of imperialism in its relation to the third world, as well as the problem of revolutionary agency in the contemporary setting. It is therefore interesting that critical commentaries on the essay almost invariably foreground a tiny section at its very end that examines the fate of a young woman, then extricates from the story some conclusions about the nature of subaltern—especially women's—agency. Although the portion of the essay dedicated to women's agency is short, the outsized attention it has garnered is probably deserved, for Spivak draws conclusions from it that carry enormous significance not only for theory but for practice.

Spivak relates the fate of Bhuvaneswari Bhaduri, a relative of Spivak's who hanged herself in 1926 in Calcutta. Bhuvaneswari's story interests Spivak because while her staging of her suicide exemplifies the "interventionist practice" that resistance entails, the absorption of her story into the broader culture reveals the futility of such gestures in the face of the patriarchal order. This patriarchy was instantiated clearly in the debate around widow immolation—known as sati—in British India. Spivak views this controversy as a clear example of the denial of women's agency, in that the two poles of the controversy were both comprised of men—either defending the practice or denouncing it—but neither side ever took into account, or even bothered to discover, women's views on the matter. The absence of women's voices in a debate that was quintessentially about their interests embodies the erasure of subaltern agency.

Bhuvaneswari, an unmarried woman, did not, of course, commit sati. But, for Spivak, her act of suicide was nevertheless significant because it was an instance of resistance against the patriarchal ideology that generated sati—such that through the suicide, Bhuvaneswari "rewrote the social text of sati-suicide in an interventionist way."[28] She did so by carefully transmitting certain signals through the details of how she

_____

28 Spivak, "Can the Subaltern Speak?," p. 103.

staged the event. Bhuvaneswari was careful to hang herself during her menstrual cycle, so that it was clear that she was not pregnant at the time of her death. She did so because, in the patriarchal culture of Bengal, when teenage girls committed suicide, it was typically assumed that they had done so to cover up a sexual tryst that had been or was about to be discovered. Bhuvaneswari knew that like most female suicides, hers too would be viewed as the outcome of an illicit relationship. So, she killed herself when she was menstruating as proof that she was not a victim of failed romantic passion.

We see, then, the significance of the suicide for Spivak. The theological basis of sati is a wife's unwavering devotion to her husband, evidenced in her willingness to end her own life when her husband dies. If Hindu theology, Spivak contends, silenced the woman's voice in this manner, so did imperialist British legal discourse, which, even while banning the practice, remained unconcerned with women's subjectivity: "Between patriarchy and imperialism, subject constitution and object-formation, the figure of the woman disappears . . . into a violent shuttling between . . . tradition and modernization."[29] In Spivak's reading, Bhuvaneswari rewrites this text by inserting female subjectivity into it. By offering physical proof that her death was not a consequence of a failed love for a man, Spivak claims that Bhuvaneswari "generalized the sanctioned motive for female suicide by taking immense trouble to displace (not merely deny) in the physiological inscription of her body, its imprisonment within legitimate passion by a single male."[30]

The actual motivation for Bhuvaneswari's act was revealed years later: her relatives discovered that she had been a member of a militant anticolonial organization and had been given the responsibility of carrying out an assassination. She found herself unable to fulfill her mission, but, mindful of the necessity of keeping trust with the organization, she killed herself. Although Bhuvaneswari kept these details to herself, she clearly wanted it to be known that whatever the motivation for the suicide might have been, it was not the shame of an illicit affair and its consequences. For years, her family remained in the dark about the background to her act, knowing only that it was not because of a pregnancy. It is the mystery that she left behind, the family's cluelessness

29 Ibid., p. 102.
30 Ibid., pp. 103–4.

about her death, that Spivak offers as confirmation of the idea that the
subaltern cannot speak.

In the voluminous commentary generated by Spivak's essay, her
reading of the event has not been without controversy. Critics have
pointed out that Bhuvaneswari can hardly exemplify the subaltern's
inability to speak, given that Spivak herself retrieves her suicide act as a
rewriting of the patriarchal text.[31] Surely the "interventionist act" is a
kind of agency on the young woman's part, which by Spivak's own definition makes it a speech act. Another issue critics have raised is how a
middle-class woman with Bhuvaneswari's comfortable background can
be characterized as "subaltern," so that she falls into the same category
of oppression or marginalization as peasants and workers.[32] Still others
have made the observation that in reconstructing the motivation behind
Bhuvaneswari's actions and making an inference about what her reasons
might have been for ending her life, Spivak is assigning to her the very
unitary subjectivity that she describes as an intellectual fantasy.[33] So we
seem to have here a non-subaltern who does in fact speak, and with a
coherent subjectivity that cannot supposedly exist.

These criticisms have some merit; in response to them, Spivak has
modified or redrawn some aspects of her analysis. In a revised version
of the essay, she holds that in Bhuvaneswari's case, the subaltern did
speak, in a manner, but was silenced by the fact that the broader patriarchal culture had no interest in hearing her.[34] As Spivak recalls, when
Bhuvaneswari's own relatives attempted to dissuade her from gathering
the facts about the suicide, she was "unnerved by this failure of communication." Furthermore, Spivak also allows that there are other forms of
agency that women, and subordinate groups more generally, might have
available to them—a point I will return to shortly. Indeed, she now takes
the view that her declaration in the original essay, that the subaltern
cannot speak, "was an inadvisable remark."[35]

---

31 See, for instance, Abena Busia, "Silencing Sycorx: On African Colonial Discourse
and the Unvoiced Female," *Cultural Critique* 14 (1989–90), pp. 81–104.

32 Rajeshwari Sunder Rajan, "Death and the Subaltern," in *Reflections on the History of
an Idea: Can the Subaltern Speak?*, New York: Columbia University Press, 1983, pp. 117–38.

33 Bart Moore-Gilbert, *Postcolonial Theory: Contexts, Practices, Politics*, London:
Verso, 1997, pp. 104–7.

34 Gayatri Spivak, *A Critique of Postcolonial Reason*, Cambridge, MA: Harvard
University Press, 1999, pp. 306–10.

35 Ibid., p. 308.

So Spivak now agrees that it is possible for the subaltern to engage in resistance. But what has been largely ignored in this debate around her work, and is of deeper significance in any assessment of the politics of postcolonial theory, is what counts as resistance. Spivak's critics have been at pains to note the contradiction in her presentation of Bhuvaneswari's action—that she describes the suicide as an interventionist act, and hence an attempt to disrupt patriarchal discourse, while also denying that it is such an act. But it needs to be emphasized that, in making this criticism, the interlocutors implicitly agree with Spivak on one crucial point: that Bhuvaneswari's action should indeed be understood as an attempt to "rewrite the social text of sati-suicide." Much of the debate thus turns on Spivak's reluctance to acknowledge the full weight of the young woman's disruptive act.

Just as we raised doubts about Guha's presentation of Chandra's death as an act of gender solidarity and resistance, so might we question the very idea that Bhuvaneswari's actions were an attempt to question, much less disrupt, the patriarchal field into which she had been inserted. Let us return for a moment to the specifics of her death. We know that she was entrusted with the job of a political assassination and, for some reason, found herself unable to carry it out—which, in turn, seems to have led her to take her life. She also understood that, given the mores of Bengali culture, her suicide was likely to be apprehended as an admission of moral failure, of being guilty of illicit love. Thus her decision to show emphatically that any such interpretation would be an error, as evidenced by her active menstrual cycle.

What this shows, however, is not that Bhuvaneswari rejected or punctured Bengali patriarchal norms. It does not indicate a denial of the "sanctioned motive for female suicide," as Spivak would have it. What it amounts to is an attempt on the young woman's part to proclaim her innocence of accusations generated by those conventions—and hence, by implication, an acquiescence to those very conventions. Bhuvaneswari was not calling for a rejection of the idea that women should abjure romantic entanglements not approved by their betters. She was merely proclaiming her innocence from the idea that she might have been guilty of such an act. Hence, just as in the case of poor Chandra's untimely demise, Spivak takes an instance of a woman's subordination to her circumstances as an example of her resistance to her subjugation. To be sure, the act did embody agency of a kind—it was a volitional

stance intended to respond to something in her situation. But whatever
else it was, it was also a plea not to be associated with the norms of
impurity and transgression sanctioned by that very same patriarchal
order. Bhuvaneswari went to great lengths to assert her innocence of
accusations of an immoral act, but never questioned the grounds on
which acts such as those were deemed immoral. Her suicide was, therefore, an action carried out very much within the parameters internal to
the order.

Thus, much like Guha, Spivak discovers resistance in this text—
resistance that dominant discourses and conventions supposedly refused
to recognize—not by uncovering it where it had been obscured but by
redefining it—or, more to the point, by turning it into its opposite. What
is especially striking in this instance is that while Spivak valorizes this
act of resignation to the colonial patriarchal regime, she relegates to
obscurity the parts of Bhuvaneswari's life that were unambiguously acts
of resistance—namely, her involvement in the anti-colonial movement.
Spivak brings up this aspect of Bhuvaneswari's practice as part of the
background to her actions, but then banishes it from the discussion, as
if it has no bearing on our verdict regarding subaltern agency.[36]

Can we not, however, insist that this political involvement is not only
relevant but in fact central to the matter? Bhuvaneswari was apparently
an active participant in a movement that articulated the agency and the
"speech" of hundreds of thousands of women in the colonial era. Indeed,
if Spivak had explored a little further, she could have uncovered not just
these actions but a rich archive of thousands of these women, in the
peasant movement and in the Communist movement, which have been
available for years in regional and national archives as well as in oral
testimonies. Some such accounts from just one region of India, published
in a pivotal volume some years after "Can the Subaltern Speak?" was
written, provide some indication of how deeply involved rural women
were in the revolutionary movement.[37] However, the experience of
women in the movement was widely studied and known even by the late
1970s, almost a decade before Spivak set about composing her essay,

---

36 For one of the few instances of this point being raised, see Priyamvada Gopal,
"Reading Subaltern History," p. 150.

37 Stree Shakti Sanghatana et al., *We Were Making History: Life Stories of Women in
the Telangana People's Struggle*, London: Zed, 1989.

which is certainly enough to undermine any doubts about women's capacity for political action.

The effacement of women's agency when it takes organized, collective form is on display again in Spivak's commentary on Mahasweta Devi's "Draupadi." Devi's literary oeuvre offers an invaluable resource for an appreciation of the texture of resistance emerging from the most oppressed sections in postcolonial India; chapter 5 provides a more in-depth discussion of her work. "Draupadi" is set in the context of the Naxalite movement in India, which emerged in 1967 as an armed insurgency by peasants against landed classes in rural Bengal; the movement later spread to urban centers. Eventually, the state unleashed a counteroffensive, employing draconian anti-terrorist laws, and succeeded in suppressing the insurgency's first phase. Against this backdrop, Devi narrates the story of the capture of a young woman, Draupadi, an indigent tribal and a militant in the movement. She is on the run after participating in the assassination of a landlord; her husband, a fellow activist, has been killed by the police. Draupadi is good at hiding in the dense forests, home to her but almost impenetrable to the law enforcement teams. Ultimately, however, she is outwitted by a particularly ruthless and efficient army officer named Senanayak.

Unlike the officials who work for him, Senanayak is something of an intellectual, having steeped himself in revolutionary literature in order to better analyze the Naxalite movement. He views Draupadi's capture as a signal achievement for himself; once she is in custody, he initiates the inevitable process of interrogation. However, as it becomes clear that the young revolutionary is not going to make any revelations, Senanayak's methods become ever more drastic. He eventually orders his minions to "make her" and disappears from the scene. Draupadi is brutally and serially raped all night long. In the morning, she is ordered to clean herself, get dressed, and appear before Senanayak. Draupadi does go out to meet Senanayak, but does so naked, having refused the soap and water that were offered her. She appears before him with her mangled and mutilated body in full view and challenges him: "You can strip me, but how can you clothe me again? . . . What more can you do? Come on, counter me."[38] The story ends with Senanayak unable to move or answer, paralyzed by

38 Spivak, "Draupadi," p. 402.

the terrible specter of this woman standing before him, brutalized but utterly defiant.

"Draupadi" is a key text, illuminating both the brutality of the Indian state's suppression of the Naxalite movement and the heroism and solidarity of the youth who comprised its political cadre. Draupadi joins the movement with her husband; she is clearly trusted and valued by her comrades, as evidenced by her inclusion in a political assassination; and she values the movement itself enough to withstand inhuman torture and rape at the hands of the police. But, if we turn to Spivak's commentary, these political and organizational dimensions of Draupadi's agency are strenuously pushed to the background.

Spivak confines her focus to the final sentences of the story, when Draupadi is presented to Senanayak and refuses to clean and clothe herself for her interview. Draupadi the subaltern revolutionary comes into her own for Spivak only after her gendered brutalization: "It is when she crosses the sexual differential into the field of what could *only happen to a woman* that she emerges as the most powerful 'subject.'"[39] It is in her refusal to follow instructions, in choosing not to act, that she emerges as a conscious agent, so that "she will finally act for herself in *not* 'acting.'"[40] What Spivak means here is that Draupadi only takes control of her volitional self in her decision to refuse to clean up for an audience with Senanayak. It is in this refusal to act that she manages to "finally act for herself." As for her life as a revolutionary prior to her capture, Spivak blithely dismisses it as Draupadi's way of keeping "political faith as an act of faith toward [her husband.]" Her decision to join the movement, we are to assume, is not conscious political agency, but simply expresses her fidelity to her husband. Indeed, her immersion in the revolutionary movement only continues her gendered subordination, which is why, for Spivak, her torture marks a break; it provides her with the opening to emerge out of the shadows of the men in her life. It is only with her response to her torture, then, that the "male leadership stops."[41] By "male leadership," Spivak here refers to Draupadi's dead husband and comrade and, more pertinently, to the leadership of the Naxalite movement.

---

39 Ibid., p. 389, emphasis in original.
40 Ibid., p. 389, emphasis mine.
41 Ibid., p. 388.

Contra Spivak's reading, there is not even the slightest hint in the story that Draupadi joins the movement as her husband's shadow, that her activism is shaped by a distant "male leadership," or even that she sees her final defiant act toward Senanayak as her political awakening. To the contrary, in the events leading up to her capture, Devi offers us a window into her protagonist's thoughts, and we see her—now aware that her capture is imminent—anticipating the inevitable torture, and thinking of . . . what? Escape? Regrets? Bitterness toward the leadership? No, her mind goes to the fate of another comrade, whom she vows to emulate— a young man of twenty-two who bit off his tongue during torture rather than reveal the information demanded of him. "That boy did it," she reminds herself. Then her thoughts return to her martyred husband, also killed in an encounter. "I swear by my life. By my life, Dulna, by my life. Nothing must be told."[42]

Everything we learn about Draupadi's state of mind, every thought that Devi reveals to us in her narrative, is presented to generate an organic link between Draupadi's political conviction, her commitment to her com- rades—male and female—and her contemptuous dismissal of Senanayak's command. The inner sources upon which she draws throughout her ordeal include her gender identity, of course. But they also include a steely courage, a sense of obligation to the sacrifices of others, and an unshak- able commitment not to endanger the lives of other comrades—all of which come from her political conviction as a revolutionary, and all of which Spivak sweeps aside with the back of her hand.

This gesture by Spivak not only devalues and submerges Draupadi's political agency, but reinserts a highly paternalistic, and hence patriar- chal, view regarding her choices. Her subjectivity is affirmed when she steps forth and expresses awareness of her subjugation specifically as a woman—when the brutalization is to her body. Spivak denies her this when Draupadi rejects her brutalization as a class subject and joins in with her comrades to overturn that class hierarchy. So when she fights alongside the male members of her underground squad, she is not yet fully a subject; when she declares to her dead husband, "I swear by my life. By my life, Dulna, by my life," this is merely "an act of faith toward her husband," not an act of political commitment or principle. Why not? Why is she assumed to be a passive follower of commands when she is

42 Ibid., pp. 397, 399.

in the company of men, instead of a political actor fully aware of the imperatives behind her choices? Surely a feminist reading of the text might at least allow for the possibility that she proceeds with an understanding of her interests when she takes up arms against the landlord armies of Eastern India, no less than when she taunts Senanayak while in captivity? [43]

The congruence between Spivak's reading of Draupadi and Bhuvaneswari is striking; in both instances, the protagonists' political commitments are dismissed. But whereas in Bhuvaneswari's case, the facts about her political past were shrouded in obscurity, this is not so with Draupadi. The bulk of the narrative in "Draupadi" is dedicated to highlighting precisely those dimensions of the woman's consciousness that Spivak dismisses as irrelevant. And this is what makes Spivak's interpretation of the narrative especially puzzling. What she holds up as a paradigm of resistance is Draupadi's refusal to obey a single command, not her refusal to abide by an exploitative and patriarchal social order. What Spivak admires is her act as an individual woman, not her willing and conscious participation in a revolutionary movement. As Spivak herself puts it, only when Draupadi experiences violence that "could only happen to a woman" does she come into her own as a historical subject—not when she experiences violence as an indigent peasant or a revolutionary. There is a direct line connecting this argument with Guha's valorization of a woman's biological realm as the natural habitat for her agency—a remarkable return to the very tropes that feminists have tried for decades to overturn.

Bhabha's Negotiation

Homi Bhabha's influential essay "The Commitment to Theory," written just a few years after the British miners' strike of 1984–85, uses that event as an emblem of all the problems that arise from classical socialist views on power and interests, agency and resistance. Much as Spivak and Guha do, Bhabha seeks to rescue women's agency from the narrow

---

43 For a critique along these lines, see Darshan Perusek, "Post-Colonial Realities, Post-Structuralist Diversions: An Unamused Exchange," *Economic and Political Weekly* 29:5 (1994), pp. 243–9.

confines of conventional political theorizing, not to mention the actual practice of class politics. Whereas socialism privileges the politics of class, Bhabha seeks to restore the salience of other interests and identities inevitably ignored under the singular weight of economic issues.

Bhabha does not seem to view the miners' strike, in its essence, as a response to Margaret Thatcher's offensive against working-class families in the mining towns, though of course he does recognize that it was her decision to close down the pits that triggered the conflagration. For Bhabha, the essence of the strike lay in the men's attempt to preserve the traditions and cultures—the way of life—of the mining communities. "The choice," he observes, "was clearly between the dawning world of the new Thatcherite city gent and a long history of the working man, or so it seemed to the traditional Left and the New Right." So it was a clash between two conflicting visions of the social order, both male: the emerging world of the "city gent" and the venerable culture of the "working man." The class culture of the miners was, for Bhabha, constructed around the male identity and hence patriarchal to its roots. He contends that it was around precisely this traditionalism of the laboring classes that the strike was "enjoined": though the strike mobilized entire communities, "the revolutionary impulse . . . belonged squarely to the working class male," with women decidedly relegated to the inevitable "heroic supporting role."[44]

The strike was another instance in which working-class men crafted their strategy to defend not only their economic interests but also their dominant position in the gender order. In other words, it was a demonstration of how one set of interests was promoted at the expense of another. But, as it happened, it became the occasion for a dramatic overturn of the very patriarchal order that the men were trying to sustain. The men relied on the fact that the women would internalize their framing of the issues and fall into line. In fact, the women's approach to the conflict turned out to be "startlingly different and more complex" than that of the men.[45] Once involved in the struggle, "many women began to question their roles within the family and the community—the two central institutions which articulated the meanings and mores of the *tradition* of the laboring classes around which

44 Bhabha, "The Commitment to Theory," p. 12.
45 Ibid., pp. 11–12.

ideological battle was enjoined."[46] The result was a churning of the inner world of the mining communities themselves, as women rejected and then walked away from the world that their men had constructed for them.

Bhabha presents this episode as an illustration of his view that the rise of "class politics" is a discursive creation—a construct created by the placement of a rigid conceptual grid on a world in which interests and identities are, in fact, highly fluid. It finds order only by erasing or suppressing all the myriad complexities that constitute the social world. This complexity goes down to the level of the individual. Hence, for women in the mining towns, the strike opened up both a dilemma and an opportunity. The women were not "class" subjects, as their men defined them. They were also gendered subjects, and both identities coexisted. This created a dilemma: "What does a working woman put first? Which of her identities is the one that determines her political choices?"[47] What many of the women decided, he argues, is that they would embrace their gender identities—which meant a rejection of their imposed class identities and of the social order and priorities that the men were trying to defend.

Bhabha's point is not as simple as saying that the mining women came to discover their gender identities or interests only when they set aside those associated with class. It is the more radical thesis that the very idea of fixed identities or objective interests is mistaken. There simply is no such thing as a class interest, for what we know as "class" is the product of a discursive grid imposed on a fluid and shifting land-scape. Thus, he approvingly quotes Stuart Hall's assertion that even while we might agree that people have interests, "material interests on their own have no necessary class belongingness."[48] Hence, there is no identity or constellation of interests for agents to be wedded to, or to commit to, for they are and remain divided subjects. "There is no simple political or social truth to be discovered," he argues, "for there is no unitary representation of political agency, no fixed hierarchy of political values and effects."[49] What the strike achieved for the women was not a

---

46 Ibid., p. 12.
47 Ibid., p. 14.
48 Ibid., p. 14.
49 Ibid., p. 13.

widening of their social identity, such that it might embrace their status as class actors as well as gendered actors; instead, it supposedly revealed to them the intrinsic artificiality of those categories.

Bhabha therefore describes the effects of the struggle in a very particular manner. When the women joined the struggle against Thatcher's attack—and, in so doing, also brought matters of gender into the movement—they did not merely add a dimension to their political identities. They constructed a new hybrid that is not an additive compound of two elements, but something more—"a rearticulation, or translation of elements that are *neither the One* (unitary working class) *nor the Other* (the politics of gender), *but something else besides*."[50] The question that naturally arises is: What is this new hybrid complex that works upon class and gender identities but leaves both behind? Bhabha never describes it. It remains unnamed and unspecified, but he is quite clear about the notion that, upon emerging from and rejecting their class identities, the women of the mining towns moved on to a new form of social identification that could be described neither as class nor gender.

Bhabha illustrates his argument by drawing on an article written by Beatrix Campbell for the *Guardian* at the one-year anniversary of the strike.[51] Campbell had interviewed a number of women active in the struggle to see how it had affected their lives, both during the conflict and in its aftermath. The interviews are supposed to illustrate how the women were initially divided by their two identities but then, over the course of the strike, transcended both to create a new gestalt.

If we examine the testimonies that Campbell's article relates, however, the picture that emerges is rather different from the one advanced by Bhabha. All of the women interviewed do recall a transformation in their perspectives, if not their lives, as a consequence of their experience in the struggle. Gendered conventions were denaturalized for all of them in varying degrees. Yet not one of the women Campbell interviews viewed their gendered identity to be in conflict with their class identity. These working-class women accepted the logic of the strike, the inherent class contradiction that it embodied, without any hesitation. They all

---

50 Ibid., p. 13.

51 Beatrix Campbell, "Monday Women: Pitting Their Wits? Fate of Women's Support Groups in Aftermath of the Miners' Strike," *Guardian*, August 25, 1986.

seemed to have viewed the attack on the miners as an attack on them no less than on their husbands; they all looked back at the strike with admiration and even nostalgia.

Campbell describes the experience of Margaret Storr, for whom involvement in the strike opened up an entirely new life, even as she continued with her old roles as a housewife and mother of four. After some hesitation, she participated in the strike support efforts, and also joined her husband on the picket line. The decision, she recounts, transformed the relationship: "My husband Paul and I talked a lot during the strike—and since. Our marriage is a lot happier since, because we talk and we say what we feel . . . he listens to me now because he knows I mean it." She continues, "I used to have trouble with my nerves. But I never took a Valium during the strike and I have never taken a tablet since . . . How come I didn't get anxiety during the strike? It gave me strength." Campbell reports that Storr keeps a scrapbook of the strike and finds the need to dive back into it occasionally, for since those heady days "she has sunk back into her shell."

Campbell then turns to Margaret Dransfield, who, unlike Storr, had been politically active all her life. The strike nonetheless transformed her consciousness in complex ways. She realized that she had absorbed most of her political beliefs passively, but after her experience in the struggle, had become more independent in her judgment. "The strike was hard work," Dransfield recounts, "but I thoroughly enjoyed it, and it was a challenge." In its aftermath, Dransfield went through a period of withdrawal, but soon reactivated her political identity: "Politics is very important to me now. I'm in CND [Campaign for Nuclear Disarmament] and I went to the Greenham Common." Lynn Dennett reports that the strike opened up her life in entirely new ways. As an activist, she recalls, "I got a taste for not knowing where I'd be the next day, and I wanted more." After the strike, she divorced her husband. Crucially, she has no regrets; to the contrary, she credits those days with giving her the confidence to strike out on her own. She and three of her friends had been active in fundraising: "Of the three of us who went out fundraising, we've all left our husbands. It was the strike that gave us the confidence to go. I learned how repressed I'd been . . . I'm at peace now." The final woman Campbell interviews is Kim Young, who also divorced after the strike and, like Dennett, credits the strike experience for her transformation. The fault wasn't her husband's, she observes: "Our husbands had their faults, but they were nice men, it wasn't that so much." So, what was it? Campbell asks. It was, Young recounts, that "the strike was a diving board for a lot of women. They were able to say what they actually felt."

In brief, what emerges from these testimonies has almost no connection to Bhabha's summary of them. The women overturned the norms of the patriarchal order, no doubt, but none of them questioned the importance of their class interests, nor of the identities attached to the latter. The strike triggered a restructuring of gender codes, but it simultaneously reaffirmed to them their class identities. In other words, whereas Bhabha's description of the new complex is that with respect to class and gender, it was "neither the one nor the other," the testimony of the women suggests something very different: *it was both the one and the other*. The women grew into and embraced their interests with respect to gender, but did so while continuing to embrace their class solidarity. The latter was not something they grew out of or left behind. To the contrary, it was something they saw as a necessary part of their emancipation and, further, an engagement of which they remained proud. Even the women who left their husbands seemed aware of the necessity of the class response to Thatcher.

The women saw their class interests and identities as real because Margaret Thatcher was kind enough to draw their attention to them. To the men and women in the mining communities, the intent behind the assault was quite clear—to break one of the most powerful unions in the country. The decision to fight back was not motivated by something as nebulous as the defense of a traditional "way of life"—though of course this was part of what the miners were trying to sustain. The struggle was "enjoined" for something far more mundane—to defend their homes and basic livelihoods. All of the women interviewed by Campbell show a clear awareness of this as the animating issue, and none of them place their emancipation from gender constraints in opposition to it. Bhabha's argument relies crucially on a displacement of the logic of the strike, from one grounded in these interests held in common by both genders, to one that pits the women against the men. Even more, he describes it in essentially cultural terms—as a battle to defend the traditions of the working class—rather than the terms in which the women themselves viewed it, which revolved around their very real interests as women and as miners.

Of course, there were many women whose experience of the strike would have been very different from that of the women Campbell interviewed. For many, the strike would surely trigger painful and even negative memories, and it would not be difficult to find women who regretted their participation in it or whose subordination in the home continued or even intensified. Perhaps they would even blame the strike and the traditional mining culture for this outcome. Political conflicts never settle evenly upon individual lives, and the forces that they unleash are often more brutal than the circumstances that give rise to them. The argument here is not that Margaret Storr's testimony captures the essence of women miners' experience in the days of struggle. The point, rather, is that Bhabha thinks that it does—or at least, that his distorted interpretation of it does. His view denies not only the possibility that the class interests of the women were real—every bit as real as their gender interests—but also the possibility that the women might be aware of this and uphold the sanctity of both.

So just as Spivak pushes Draupadi's revolutionary politics to the background when she analyzes Devi's text, so Bhabha effaces the women's working-class agency. In both instances, women are taken seriously as political actors only on the condition that they keep their goals confined to gender issues. Draupadi is deemed a "true subject" only after she undergoes a brutalization specific to women, and the women from the collieries acquire political maturity only when they supposedly grow out of their identification with their class. Even more, when the subjects of these texts express a political consciousness broader than the one assigned to them by these theorists, this consciousness is either dismissed as manipulation (Spivak) or simply ignored (Bhabha). Perhaps this is not quite so confined a space as the one endorsed by Guha, who locates Chandra and her mother's heroism in their embrace of the biological—in this instance, the women are at least allowed some dalliance with politics. But the leash remains tight.

Conclusion

There is something eminently praiseworthy about a theoretical framework setting out to recover the agency of the oppressed, to recognize instances and forms of resistance that so often are buried under the

weight of posterity. To the extent that postcolonial theory has contributed to this enterprise, it is to be lauded and its insights upheld. Guha,
Spivak and others are entirely correct to insist upon the salience of the
local as a site of contestation, and to insist that any political theory
worth its salt has to be able to connect to the quotidian struggles that
extend beyond the economic realm.

They are not, of course, the first to embrace such a challenge. For
decades, socialists and Marxists have understood that political struggles
unfold in specific places and times—in particular workplaces and
specific localities, not on a plane hovering above them. Whatever political analysis flowed from their theory would therefore have to be relevant
at the micro level, not just on some rarified plane reserved for grand
theory. If there is something novel about postcolonial theory, it is not
that its practitioners are the first to insist on the importance of the
local—though they often make out as if they were. Their claim to inno-
vation has to rest on their success in recovering dimensions of agency
that other radical theories are unable or unwilling to recognize.

The essays examined above have achieved notoriety because of their
putative success on this dimension—in highlighting instances of agency
and resistance impugned or ignored by more conventional narratives.
But, as we have seen, this success is based on rather questionable
grounds. Guha and Spivak recover instances of agency only by redefining the concept and, indeed, by transforming it into its opposite—what
they brandish as exemplars of subaltern agency are in fact instances of
acquiescence. Of course, there is something admirable, even heroic, in
the choices made by Chandra and her family, as well as by Bhuvaneswari. What we see are women making the best of the choices that are
handed to them. They are trying to preserve their dignity in circumstances that are intrinsically hostile to them. But they do so while taking
their constraints as a given, not by trying to transform those constraints.
If we are to now accept actions such as these as emblematic of political
action, as episodes of struggle, then there ceases to be any distinction
between a dominant ideology and a critical theory—for it is the signature of a dominant ideology that it enjoins subaltern groups to accept
their location as parametric and to then make the best of what they've
been handed.

Indeed, it is fair to say that what these essays achieve is the denigration of the very concept of agency, something at the very heart of the

postcolonial project. In obscuring the effects of social circumstances, in denying—implicitly or explicitly—the role of structure, the theorists under consideration whisk away what makes political praxis distinctive as a volitional act. For what is political agency if not a form of practice aimed at the structures of power within which it is embedded? Whether it aims to reproduce them, as in ruling-class strategies, or seeks to transform and undermine them, as is the case with subaltern classes, political agency is defined by its relation to these fields of power. But with Spivak and, in particular, Guha, it seems that it is the simple exercise of will that enables the actions of their protagonists to serve as political agency—and even those actions are an acquiescence to their subjugation.

If we turn to the question of gender in particular, the conservatism of all three theorists is unmistakable. There is a baseline commitment to uphold the distinctiveness of patriarchal domination, to insist that it cannot be collapsed into class—which is entirely laudable and has to be the lynchpin of any sustainable feminist politics. But all three theorists go much further than that. In Spivak's and Bhabha's cases, the political agency of the women in their texts is not so much recognized as it is whittled down, so that it is recognized on the condition that it is confined to issues of gender. Bhuvaneswari and Draupadi are both dedicated militants in revolutionary movements, yet in neither case does Spivak acknowledge, much less analyze, the importance of their choices in this domain. Bhabha takes a story of women's amalgamation of their gender identity to class solidarity and turns it into a struggle of one against the other. Guha, for his part, demarcates and then sanctifies the biological as not merely an acceptable domain of struggle for women, but the natural one. The accompaniment to this curious promotion of gender as the preferred site of resistance for women—however narrowly defined—is the consistent denigration not just of class politics, but of organized politics in most any form. It is not that struggles of the latter kind are denigrated tout court, but that they are presented as irrelevant or unnatural for women.

What makes this contrasting characterization of the women characters' politics interesting is that the denigration of their agency in organized politics is not a case of unbalanced treatment. It is not that Spivak and Bhabha, for example, just give more importance to one aspect of their women's political involvement than to another. Rather, they suppress altogether aspects of the texts that would invite another interpretation. The elements of the narratives that highlight the women's commitment to organized politics are simply ignored. We only learn about them by reading the texts ourselves. In other words, aspects of political agency that are very much part of the textual record are suppressed by the narrative favored by the theorists—the very sin of which they accuse the holders of grand narratives. In this case, it is a quite particular and narrow conception of gender politics' displacement and marginalization of the various dimensions of the women's broader political agency.

My reading confirms the observation made by other critics: that postcolonial theory has not so much enriched the critique of a globalizing capitalism as it has weakened the resources to resist it. No struggle can be waged without a clear conception of what counts as resistance—how to distinguish between strategies that question the dominant order and those that accept its terms—and how to organize to make that resistance more effective. Women's collective agency around their gender and class interests have to be indispensable parts of deepening that resistance. It is remarkable that in these essays, which are foundational to the development of postcolonial theory, such concerns are either denigrated or dismissed altogether. What is even more striking is that, in all the commentary they have generated, these maneuvers have either gone unnoticed or have been set aside as being of minor consequence. Both of these facts are redolent not just of the direction that the theory has taken, but also of the larger intellectual culture of the field. In the next chapter, I remain with the question of gender as it plays out in the critical reception of the works of two stalwarts of Indian literature, to further elucidate the pitfalls of postcolonial theory.

2

Rabindranath, Sharatchandra and the Gender Question

Sharatchandra Chattopadhyay's *The Right of Way* (*Pather Dabi*, 1926) and its charismatic revolutionary protagonist Savyasachi, the scholar-warrior par excellence, made an indelible impression on a nation struggling for independence. The British Indian government was quick to ban the novel for encouraging sedition. In response, Chattopadhyay asked Rabindranath Tagore, his contemporary, to join the widespread protests against the ban—a request denied by Tagore on the odd and novel grounds that the British actually deserved praise for the ban because it showed their appreciation of the power of Chattopadhyay's work. Tagore's position was symptomatic of his ambivalence toward mass politics in general and militant activism in particular. Today, while Tagore is a revered figure in South Asian postcolonial studies, there is barely any engagement with Chattopadhyay's works.

This exclusion is especially curious in light of the fact that Chatto-padhyay has been by far the most popular novelist in India and was a major figure in the intellectual scene of the early twentieth century. He is credited with having ushered in the golden age of the Bengali novel, and the acclaimed Hindi writer Jainendra Kumar has observed, "Where is that Indian language in which he did not become the most popular when he reached it?"[1] In his authoritative *History of Indian Literature*,

---

1 Manik Mukhopadhyay and Satyabrata Roy, eds., *The Golden Book of Saratchandra*, Bengal: All Bengal Sarat Centenary Committee, 1977, p. 51.

Sisir Kumar Das, referring to the "phenomenal popularity" of Chattopadhyay, notes that Indian publishers "never tired of reprinting his
works . . . [He was] the most translated, most adapted, most plagiarized
author till today, sixty years after his death . . . [and] an important force
in Indian cinema."[2] Chattopadhyay's literary stature makes the postcolonial silence on his works surprising, especially given the considerable
engagement with Tagore and other regional writers of that period.

What accounts for postcolonial studies' differential treatment of the
two literary giants? In this chapter, I address that question by exploring
both specificities and differences in the authors' worldviews, and how
they align or clash with postcolonial thought. If Tagore's views on historical difference, on nationalism, on culture and cultural identity are
largely in sync with postcolonialism, Chattopadhyay's positions have a
different hue. Within a conceptual domain marked by its claims to
radicalism, the privileging of Tagore is instructive, not merely because
of Tagore's retreat from politics, but also given that the author was the
subject of stringent critique, even in his own time, for his bourgeois
sensibilities. Unlike Chattopadhyay, however, Tagore has been an
acclaimed figure in the West from well before the advent of the New Left
or postcolonial studies. The fact that postcolonial critics rarely question
the stature of Tagore as an icon of the East and in fact build on his
celebrity status, at the same time as they ignore his contemporaries like
Chattopadhyay, illuminates the discipline's preoccupations and biases in
telling ways.

For both Tagore and Chattopadhyay, who wrote in the context of the
anti-colonial movement of a nascent nation, issues of coloniality, race,
historical difference and national identity were of primary concern, and
both writers were keenly aware of how these issues converge on the
question of women's status. This chapter examines the two authors'
views by focusing on one novel by each of them: Tagore's *The Home and
the World* (*Ghare Baire*, 1916) and Chattopadhyay's *The Final Question*
(*Shesh Prashna*, 1931). Both novels were authored by writers at a mature
stage of their literary career, and in the substantial oeuvres of both
Tagore and Chattopadhyay, these novels stand out, and each is the
product of a mature writer. Tagore wrote his novel partly as a response

---

2 Sisir Kumar Das, *A History of Indian Literature: 1911–1956*, New Delhi: Sahitya
Akademi, 1995, p. 43.

to criticisms aimed at his rejection of the 1905 *swadeshi* movement, which called for a boycott of British goods and services; the novel was meant to answer his critics by laying out the reasons for his political position. Chattopadhyay's novel, the last he completed, was in many ways a summation of his lifelong literary exploration of issues relating to culture and gender. Both novels are striking for their engagement with political and philosophical issues and for the evident challenge of using literary form as a vehicle of intellectual exposition.

Rabindranath

Tagore's biographical background, familiar in South Asian historical and literary circles, acquires relevance when contrasted with that of Chatto- padhyay. The Tagores (or Thakurs) were zamindars—landowners—with considerable estates and a recorded family history going back more than three centuries. This aristocratic family had a rich history of social and cultural contributions to art, music and literature, as well as to social and religious reform. Tagore was raised in a household immersed in the Bengali cultural renaissance. As a result, growing up, he was surrounded by musicians, playwrights and artists, and had the privilege of witness- ing the many cultural performances and literary debates his family hosted. For the most part, he studied at home, but he later went to England to pursue, though not complete, a law degree. In an illustrious career spanning more than six decades, Tagore became the first non- European to win the Nobel Prize and eventually became India's prophetic cultural ambassador to audiences across the world. Widely credited with revolutionizing modern Bengali poetry, Tagore also broke new ground with his short stories, novels and essays; in addition, he created a new genre of music, significantly influenced modern Indian painting, and founded a university with an innovative mission.

Tagore is widely considered a visionary endowed with a liberal and internationalist sensibility. While that stance is taken to be consistent across his works, *The Home and the World* is regarded as having special significance, not only because of its critical engagement with the nation- alist movement, but, even more, because of its intervention on the gender question. It is here, on the woman's question, that Tagore's democratic sensibility is seen to be most fully developed—far ahead of the prevailing nationalist position. The novel is taken as a rejection of cultural nationalism in favor of a more cosmopolitan outlook, evidenced most of all in its enlightened approach to gender. I argue that Tagore's critics are correct in seeing his views on gender as indicative of his approach toward nationalism. But I view the connection through a quite different lens from that of the conventional interpretation. Far from indicating a distaste for traditional patriarchal norms, the novel displays a degree of comfort with them, even a partial endorsement. There is a remarkable continuity between the nationalist stance on the woman's question and Tagore's own understanding of it. Not surprisingly, this conservatism bleeds into other dimensions of his political views, confirming the idea that *The Home and the World* provides a window into Tagore's relationship to the various strands in the independence movement.

Tagore's putative critique of nationalism and his affirmation of universalism in *The Home and the World* have received round applause. Ranajit Guha respects Tagore's capacity to perceive the drawbacks of the nationalist movement;[3] Tanika Sarkar holds that the novel's "critique of extreme nationalism . . . [carries] enormous new significance";[4] Ashis Nandy celebrates his rejection of the "post-medieval western concept of nationalism";[5] and for Sumit Sarkar, the "profound dimension" of the novel is its rejection of "fetishisation of the Nation."[6] It is noteworthy that critical appreciation of Tagore's stance on nationalism in the novel is always accompanied by either a silence on the writer's position on gender or by an unqualified approval of his position on the issue. Sarkar's essay, for instance, begins with the aim of addressing the issue of women in the novel but, curiously, concludes with the claim that the novel remains valuable for its portrayal of the struggle between alternative conceptions of masculinity. My analysis goes against the grain of

3 Ranajit Guha, *Dominance without Hegemony: History and Power in Colonial India*, Cambridge, MA: Harvard University Press, p. 199.

4 Tanika Sarkar, "Country, Woman and God in *The Home and the World,*" *Rabindranath Tagore's* The Home and the World: *A Critical Companion*, ed. P. K. Datta, London: Anthem, 2005, pp. 27–44, 27.

5 Ashis Nandy, "Illegitimacy of Nationalism," in *Return From Exile*, Delhi: Oxford University Press, 1998, pp. 108–10.

6 Sumit Sarkar, "Nationalism and Stri-Swadhinata," in *Beyond Nationalist Frames: Relocating Postmodernism, Hindutva, History*, New Delhi: Permanent Black, 2004, p. 125.

established criticism of *The Home and the World* in contending that
Tagore's stance on nationalism is in tune with the dominant nationalist
movement. Furthermore, mapping the neglected terrain of gender is
central to a grasp of Tagore's position on the nation and nationalism.

Nationalist Universalism

In *The Home and the World*, the author attempts a fictional representation of his views on nationalism and its pitfalls through the vehicle of
its central protagonist, the aristocratic landlord Nikhilesh, mostly
referred to as Nikhil in the novel. The narrative is set in Bengal in the
early twentieth century, and Bimala has been married to Nikhil for nine
years; she follows the tradition of seclusion, whereby women remain
largely restricted to the inner quarters of the household. Nikhil,
Western educated and liberal, however, has different plans for his wife.
He provides her with a modern education by employing an English
governess, and he insists she come out of seclusion. Overcoming her
initial reluctance, Bimala breaks the family tradition and meets with
Nikhil's longtime friend Sandip, a revolutionary freedom fighter.
Soon, she finds herself intensely attracted to the charismatic and virile
Sandip, with his revolutionary speeches, his passionate outlook, and his
fervent adulation of her. In refusing to curb the freedom of his wife,
even after he realizes the depth of her infatuation with his friend,
Nikhil passes the ultimate test posed by his cherished belief in individual freedom. Eventually, on her own, Bimala discovers the falsity of
Sandip's charisma and learns to appreciate her husband's superior
moral character. Nikhil's implied death at the end of the narrative,
however, signals the destruction of the "home" brought about by Bimala's emancipation. Bimala's attraction to Sandip plays out in the broader
context of the emerging differences between him and Nikhil. Nikhil
stands firmly opposed to what he views as Sandip's idealized brand of
nationalism. Sandip's deification of the nation leads him to justify a
politics of coercion in the interest of the nationalistic cause. He feels
justified in forcing poor people to adopt strategies of national resistance, even if it hurts their immediate material interests. Nikhil, by
contrast, holds that it is precisely because Sandip's idea of the nation is
a mere abstraction that he can justify coercing the actual people who

constitute the nation. In the face of growing opposition from Sandip and his followers, Nikhil remains loyal to his liberal ideal of freedom of choice for the individual, even as the ideal conflicts with a collective nationalistic resistance.

Nikhil's position on nationalism encapsulates the author's own views, developed over many years. In a series of lectures delivered in Japan and the United States, Tagore tried to convince the world that "nationalism is a great menace"[7]—a critique derived from his faith in a spiritual ideal of the "universal man," cast in the image of the creator. According to this view, the abstract logic of nationalism goes against the spirit of universality, against all that is spontaneous, moral and decent in human beings. The cold rationality of nationalism thus hollows out all that is worth preserving in humanity.

Tagore's critique of nationalism rests on an ingrained universalism; in a lecture on nationalism, he contended that "there is only one history— the history of man." He insists, however, that this common human history can be apprehended only through the prism of *distinct civilizations*. While Tagore is contemptuous of the "self-idolatry of nation-worship," he also rejects the "colourless vagueness of cosmopolitanism."[8] The "history of man" that he celebrates emerges from the distinctive but complementary histories of the East and the West. Thus, while he chastises Britain for believing that East and West shall never meet, his position is different from that of imperial Britain's only in that he believes that the two *distinct* civilizations need to interact and learn from one another.

Tagore's civilizational perspective, while upholding the idea of common humanity, also maintains that Eastern and Western civilizations are destined to perform separate and specific roles in the unfolding of human history.[9] Consistent with this view, Tagore is

---

7 Rabindranath Tagore, *Nationalism*, London: Macmillan, 1917; repr., Delhi: Rupa & Co., 1992, p. 87.

8 Ibid., p. 48.

9 Tagore's civilizational perspective needs to be understood as distinct from the contemporary civilizationalism avowed by Samuel Huntington. Huntington's reading of the post–Cold War world is one divided by irreconcilable cultural differences between the "West and the rest." It is an arguably racist formulation motivated by the goal of the retention of Western supremacy. Tagore, on the other hand, offers a humanitarian model of civilizationalism, with its insistence on fraternity and dialogue. I am grateful to my anonymous reviewer for alerting me to this distinction between Tagore and Huntington's civilizationalism.

prepared to accept the presence of the British in India as "providential," for "someone must show the East to the West, and convince the West that the East has her contribution to make to the history of civilization." Acknowledging some valuable dimensions of Western civilization in his lectures, he names key elements for the East to learn from the West: the value of the public good above those of the family and the clan, the importance of the rule of law and, significantly, the pursuit of liberty. The central thrust of Tagore's lectures, however, stresses the distinct identity of the East, shaped by the "wisdom" it has "stored for centuries"—its treasure house of spiritual wealth, which the West ignores at its own peril. He holds up Japan as an exemplary case of an Eastern civilization that has embraced the material advancements of the West while remaining firmly rooted in its own traditions. And, to the people of his own country, his advice is that it would be "no good to compete with Western civilization in its own field"; India "cannot borrow other people's history" but rather must follow its own destiny.[10]

Tagore rejects what he considers the mechanized discourse of nationalism, which robs people of their humanity. Instead, he posits a spiritual universalism underscored by the "ideals of humanity."[11] Owing to the devastation wrought by nationalist ideology, the West has all but lost sight of these humanistic ideals, he asserts. But, when the West loses its ill-gotten dominance, as it must, "the eternal light will again shine in the East—the East which has been the birthplace of the morning sun of man's history."[12] In other words, even as Tagore rejects the discourse of nationalism for India, his commentary is framed by India's superior moral position. Moreover, he asserts that India should follow a distinct path of social and cultural regeneration, and guide its "history to its own perfect end."[13] In his unshakable faith in the uniqueness of spiritual India, the nation looms large in Tagore's vision of universalism.

Consistent with the rhetoric of "Eastern destiny," Tagore claims that India's task is the recognition and reform of the social and spiritual life

---

10 Ibid., p. 85.
11 Ibid., p. 83.
12 Ibid., p. 45.
13 Ibid., p. 99.

of its people, not the pursuit of the political. In colonial India, Tagore's rejection of the political translates into skepticism about a prominent strain of anti-colonial struggle:

> The extremists, who advocated independence of action ... their ideals were based on Western history ... Political freedom does not give us freedom when our mind is not free ... We must never forget in the present day that those people who have got their political freedom are not necessarily free; they are merely powerful. The passions which are unbridled in them are creating huge organizations of slavery in the disguise of freedom ... Those of us in India who have come under the delusion that mere political freedom will make us free have accepted their lessons from the West as the gospel truth and lost their faith in humanity.[14]

The ideological struggle between Nikhil and Sandip thus echoes Tagore's distinction between the spheres of the spiritual and the political.[15] Sandip represents the extremist political leader who harbors the sole aim of independence from the British but is out of sync with local issues, whereas the liberal and aristocratic Nikhil, spokesperson for the author, is rooted in his community and takes personal responsibility for its predicament. The ideological difference between the two principal characters is less about the divide between nationalism and universalism, and more about different versions of nationalism. Indeed, Tagore's "universalism" as avowed by Nikhil has a strongly nationalist core.

---

14 Ibid., pp. 88–94.

15 E.P. Thompson, praising the separation of the political/economic from the social/spiritual, observes that "Tagore, more than any other thinker of his time, had a clear conception of civil society, as something distinct from and of stronger and more personal texture than political or economic structures" (E. P. Thompson, Introduction, Rabindranath Tagore, *Nationalism*, p. 14). However, the appreciation of civil society, it needs to be said (and I believe Thompson would agree), remains hopelessly inadequate if it is not enriched by a conception of the *relationship* between civil society and political and economic structures. Tagore refuses to address how his desired social and cultural reformation in civil society could be brought about in the face of political slavery and economic drainage. Unburdened by the problematic of unequal power relations, he maintains that the moral superiority of the East will ultimately prevail.

Nation and Gender

The critique of the extremist phase of nationalism notwithstanding,
Tagore's views are in fact quite in tune with the dominant nationalist
discourse. It is not surprising that, despite their public differences on
many issues, Tagore maintained a lifelong companionship with the
central figure of the nationalist movement, Mahatma Gandhi.[16] Gandhi
shared Tagore's suspicion of "exclusive nationalism" and his faith in
"universal brotherhood." In Gandhi, as in Tagore, universalism coexists
with an abiding cultural essentialism. Tagore's rhetoric of "Eastern
destiny" finds a practical voice in myriad aspects of Gandhian politics.
Hence it is not surprising that these two stalwarts of modern India
share the same intellectual perspective on the issue of gender.

The East/West dichotomy in Tagore's political thought translates into
the masculine/feminine binary in his conception of women and their
social role: "The ideal of stability is deeply cherished in woman's
nature . . . All her forces instinctively work to bring things to some
shape of fullness,—for that is the law of life . . . [While] the masculine
creations of intellectual civilization are towers of Babel, they dare to defy
their foundations and therefore topple down over and over again."[17] The
"feminine principle," in this view, is accorded a higher and a more
necessary function in the civilizational task than the masculine one.
There is, of course, a price tag attached to the glorification of the "feminine," and the price is embedded in the author's description of the

---

16 Interestingly, in a devastating review of *The Home and the World*, Georg Lukács
finds not a single redeemable feature in this "completely worthless" novel. He asserts
that it is through the character of Sandip, who is a "contemptible caricature of Gandhi,"
that Tagore launches his attack on the anti-colonial movement and thus proves to be
Britain's "intellectual agent in the struggle against the Indian freedom movement."
Unfortunately, Lukács's critique remains irremediably flawed by his inadequate knowledge of Indian politics. Tagore, for all his reservations about the Indian national
movement, was no sympathizer of the empire. Also, he was a lifelong companion of
Gandhi, and the politics of the novel, in its repudiation of violence and its espousal
of universal humanism, comes very close to Gandhian politics. What Lukács misses is
that Tagore's internationalist politics with all its attendant problems is very much
compatible with mainstream Indian nationalist ideology. Georg Lukács, "Tagore's
Gandhi Novel Review of Rabindranath Tagore: *The Home and the World*," pp. 8–11.

17 Rabindranath Tagore, *Personality: Lectures Delivered in America*, London:
Macmillan, 1917, p. 171.

"passive qualities of chastity, modesty, devotion and the power of self-sacrifice" with which a woman is endowed "in a greater measure than man is."[18] Tagore fails to recognize that these passive qualities are actively and institutionally demanded of women in a patriarchal society.

One institution that demands all the aforesaid "qualities" in women is widowhood, one of the most egregious manifestations of Indian patriarchy. Gandhi justified the same institution: the "ideal of widow-hood" for Gandhi "is one of the glories of the Hindu religion."[19] His support of patriarchal institutions flows from an essentialist premise regarding gender identical to that of Tagore: "Nature has created sexes as complements of each other. Their functions are defined as their forms."[20] And, like Tagore, Gandhi passionately believed in and worked for the social upliftment of women—a project perfectly consistent with patriarchy.[21]

The similarity between Tagore's and Gandhi's worldviews points to the fact that Tagore's universalism and his gender politics are both consistent with the mainstream nationalist culture. Partha Chatterjee's observations on the interlocking discourses of nation and gender at the turn of the century facilitate an understanding of Tagore's politics.[22] Chatterjee sets out to explore why the condition of women, an issue so central in mid-nineteenth-century Bengal, seemed to have disappeared from public debate by the dawn of the new century. He shows that in fact, it is not the case that women's status ceases to be an issue during the more advanced stage of nationalist politics; instead, it acquires a different character by being appropriated within the larger discourse of nationalism, such that it is no longer an issue in its own right.

---

18 Ibid., p. 173.

19 Pushpa Joshi., comp., *Gandhi on Women: Compilation of Mahatma Gandhi's Writings and Speeches on Women*, Ahmedabad: Navajivan Publishing House, 1988, p. 45.

20 Ibid., p. 313.

21 For Marxist-feminist critiques of Gandhi's position on gender, see Sujata Patel, "Construction and Reconstruction of Women in Gandhi," *Economic and Political Weekly*, February 20, 1988, pp. 377–87; and Madhu Kishwar, "Gandhi on Women," 2 parts, *Economic and Political Weekly*, October 5, 1985, pp. 1691–702 and October 12, 1985, pp. 1753–8.

22 Partha Chatterjee, "The Nationalist Resolution of the Woman's question," in *Recasting Women: Essays in Colonial History*, ed. Kumkum Sangari and Sudesh Vaid, New Delhi: Kali for Women, 1989.

Chatterjee analyzes the contrary pulls of tradition and modernity in the Indian nationalist struggle and their impact on gender politics.[23] His analysis is consistent with a large body of feminist criticism about the ambivalent role of the project of nation formation on women's issues.[24] Deniz Kandiyoti, for instance, points out that feminists share the common belief that the "integration of women into modern 'nationhood' . . . somehow follows a *different* trajectory from that of men."[25] The source of this difference, Kandiyoti observes, can be traced to the "Janus-faced" quality of nationalist discourse, which "presents itself both as a modern project and melts and transforms traditional attachments in favor of new identities and as a reaffirmation of authentic cultural values culled from the depths of a presumed communal past."[26] Chatterjee describes precisely this nationalist project in colonial India—a project that simultaneously aspired both to modernity and to a definable cultural identity. In this endeavor, women become the site for the negotiation of contradictory aspirations. On the one hand, the nationalist elite seeks to "emancipate" women, consistent with the larger project of modernity. And yet the new patriarchy of the emergent nation-state, in its search for cultural identity, also makes women the bearer of tradition. Thus the "emancipated" woman of the new nation has the "'spiritual' signs of her

23 For some other critical accounts on the gender question in nineteenth-century India, see Ghulam Murshid, *Reluctant Debutante: Responses of Bengali Women to Modernization, 1849–1905*, Rajshahi: Rajshahi University Press, 1983; Sumit Sarkar, "The Woman's Question in Nineteenth Century Bengal," in *Women and Culture*, ed. Kumkum Sangari and Sudesh Vaid, Bombay: SNDT Women's University, 1986.

24 The contradiction between women's emancipation and nationalist ideology has been a subject of sustained theoretical discussions. It has been shown that nationalist elites at once appropriate and suppress issues of women's rights and demands. See, for instance, Maxine Molyneux, "Family Reforms in Socialist States: The Hidden Agenda," *Feminist Review* 21 (Winter 1985); Catharine MacKinnon, "Feminism, Marxism, Method and the State: An Agenda for Theory," *Signs* 7:3 (1989), pp. 515–44; Varda Burstyn, "Masculine Dominance and the State," in *Socialist Register 1983*, ed. Ralph Miliband and John Saville, London: Merlin Press, pp. 45–89; Maria Mies, *Patriarchy and Accumulation on a World Scale*, London: Zed, 1986; Nira Yuval-Davis and Floya Anthiased, *Woman-Nation-State*, London: Macmillan, 1989; Anne McClintock, "Family Feuds: Gender, Nationalism and the Family," *Feminist Review* (Summer 1993), pp. 61–80.

25 Deniz Kandiyoti, "Identity and Its Discontents: Woman and the Nation," *Millennium: Journal of International Studies* 20:3 (1991), pp. 429–43, 430.

26 Ibid., p. 431.

femininity . . . clearly marked—in her dress, her eating habits, her social demeanor, her religiosity."[27]

Both Gandhi's and Tagore's gender politics conform to the model described by Chatterjee. As discussed below, Tagore's text is centrally invested in testing Bimala's capacity to chart the waters of modernity while remaining anchored in her traditional world, and the narrative logic of the novel harshly judges her for failing this test. *The Home and the World* is, in this sense, a classic instance of the ideology of the new nationalist patriarchy, which sought to resolve the woman's question with a carefully crafted dose of modernity. The fact that Tagore, a man of his times, would subscribe to the dominant consensus on the issue of modernizing women is not surprising. What is remarkable is that most contemporary critics of *The Home and the World*, such as Sarkar, Guha, Nandy and Atkinson, either circumvent the gender issue or applaud the narrative stance on gender in the text. Either they remain silent on Bimala's predicament or, like Nikhil and his author, they judge Bimala for her failure to become the model of the "new woman" as prescribed by nationalist patriarchy. In so doing, the critics of the novel thus *reflect* rather than *critique* the phenomenon described by Chatterjee.

The Home in *The Home and the World*

In early twentieth-century India, women became the site for negotiating the dynamics of opposing forces such as tradition and modernity, and Westernization and self-reliance. Recognizing the extensive and intricate ideological nature of the task, one social commentator of the time declared that women must be "refined, reorganized, recast, regenerated."[28] It is this attempt by the native elite to produce the brand-new nationalized woman that lies at the heart of Tagore's novel. Nikhil, the liberal landlord, disagrees with the tradition of women's seclusion. If women lack perspective and depth, he believes, it is not they themselves who are responsible. Women's minds, he declares, are "like the feet of Chinese women . . . the pressure of society [has] cramped them into

---

27 Chatterjee, "The Woman's Question," p. 130.

28 See Koylaschunder Bose, "On the Education of Hindu Females," in *Nineteenth Century Studies*, ed. Alok Ray, Calcutta: Bibliographical Research Centre, 1975, p. 214.

pettiness and crookedness . . . They are like pawns of the fate which
gambles with them. What responsibility have they of their own?"[29]
Putting his beliefs into practice, he challenges his age-old household
tradition of secluding women and facilitates his wife's entry into the
social sphere.

Nikhil's stance on the question of women derives from his belief that
the greatest good lies in the realization of the individual moral self. His
principal difference with his friend Sandip is based on their divergent-
perceptions of the value of patriotism for the individual and the
community. Sandip deifies the nation and contends that placing a high
value on patriotism is the only way to reclaim the country. For him, a
politics of force and fear is justifiable for the greater goal of Indian
independence. For Nikhil, however, no political goal can justify the
coercion of the individual. As a corollary to his faith in the free development of the individual, Nikhil also upholds what he believes to be a
liberal modernist position on women. From the authorial perspective,
the text is thus meant to be an expostulation of both liberal humanism
and female emancipation.

Echoing the author's liberal sentiments, Nikhil declares, "I longed to
find Bimala blossoming fully in all her truth and power. But the thing I
forgot to calculate was, that one must give up all claims on conventional
rights, if one would find a person freely revealed in truth."[30] The prior-
itization of women's self-actualization and freedom over conventional
female roles is of course a profoundly liberal value. The question, then,
is whether Nikhil indeed gives up his "claims on conventional rights," or
instead persists in asserting those rights, albeit in modified fashion.

While Nikhil wishes to believe he has set his wife free, in actuality, she
is never truly free to determine the nature and direction of her ambitions. And, while he alleges he would like to see Bimala blossom in *her*
"truth and power," he also maintains definitive views on the "real nature"
and "true role" of women. Bimala in her "freedom" is thus strongly
pressured to conform to a particular ideal of femininity—an ideal foregrounded through Nikhil's expectations and disappointments, as well as
through a narrative logic of nostalgia for a previous era when an even

---

29 Rabindranath Tagore, *The Home and the World*, trans. Surendranath Tagore,
New York: Macmillan, 1919; repr., London: Penguin, 1985, p. 22.

30 Ibid., p. 41.

more stringent patriarchal ideal of femininity reigned supreme. Nikhil's own ideas on the woman's question reflect what Chatterjee has shown to be the prescribed role for the nationalized woman.

Nikhil's expectations from his wife should be located in the context of the debates on the woman's question that raged in Bengal during the latter half of the nineteenth century. This, in fact, is the setting for the emergence of the "new woman," who must walk the tightrope of tradition and modernity, and thereby symbolize the identity of the new nation. The nationalist elite constructed this woman within the parameters of its own privileged class. As opposed to the situation of the working-class country woman, the explicit distinguishing mark of the modern, nationalized woman is that she receives an education. This constitutes the greatest concession to modernity made by the nationalist elite. Nevertheless, tradition makes a backdoor entry through the nature and content of her education.

Strictly guided by the belief in the gender-specific roles of women, female education exhibits an excessive focus on purity, moderation and religiosity. In an insightful analysis, Sumanta Banerjee shows that the construction of the nationalized woman involved not only a qualified embrace of modernity but also a rejection of a certain stream of tradition. Education aimed at expunging from the lives of privileged women the "forthright, aggressive and ribald tone of women's popular culture" and the "coarse 'untutored' expletives and expressions that they shared with women of the streets."[31] The new patriarchy perceived a threat in cross-class women's solidarity and the implied acknowledgment of independent sexuality. As a result, the regenerated woman of the emergent nation—educated, conversant with literature and the arts—existed within the context of "companionate marriage," wherein she could impress her husband with her accomplishments. But, as Banerjee reminds us, the new woman must never forget her "total dependence on the male head of the family and strictly adhere to traditional responsibilities of a respectable home."[32]

It is useful to read Nikhil's desire to "educate" Bimala with reference to the carefully constructed framework of female education in the early

31 Sumantha Banerjee, "Marginalization of Women's Popular Culture in Nineteenth Century Bengal," in Sangari and Vaid, *Recasting Women*, p. 163.
    32 Ibid., p. 165.

part of the century. Bimala, however, stumbles as she braves the tight-rope between "enlightenment" and its pitfalls. In keeping with the expectations of her liberal husband, she receives a Western education and steps out of the inner quarters into the larger social sphere. But instead of being grateful to her husband and repaying him with renewed loyalty, she falls in love with his friend—a development that presents the author and his hero with a dilemma that challenges their liberal think-ing. For Nikhil, to obstruct Bimala from following the dictates of her heart and suppress her freedom would be to admit the limited scope of his liberalism. But to allow Bimala to proceed on her chosen path would mean the destruction of his home and the loss of his beloved wife. This interesting dilemma and its resolution are at the core of the novel.

What Nikhil chooses is the emotionally painful but morally satisfying option of refusing to be an impediment to his wife's self-discovery, even when it takes the form of her infatuation with another man. In facilitat-ing his wife's education and entry into the outer world, Nikhil is partly motivated by the desire to test his wife's love for him beyond the confines of the home. Insisting that Bimala step out of the inner quarters, he says to her: "If we meet, and recognize each other, in the real world, then only will our love be true."[33] He, of course, learns the hard way that he was right to test his wife's love and devotion. And, when he fails to earn her love beyond the restricted confines of the home, he convinces himself that he must abandon his conventional rights over her:

> "My wife"—Does that amount to an argument, much less the truth? Can one imprison a whole personality within that name? . . . Bimala is what she is. It is preposterous to expect that she should assume the role of an angel for my pleasure. The Creator is under no obligation to supply me with angels, just because I have an avidity for imaginary perfection.[34]

Now, if these were the last words of the novel—that is, if the painful resolution of Nikhil's dilemma was the closing sentiment of the text— *The Home and the World* would be a different book. But Tagore has it otherwise. While Nikhil is allowed the nobility of his difficult choice,

---

33 Tagore, *The Home and the World*, p. 23.
34 Ibid., pp. 64–5.

Bimala is not. Paradoxically, even as a man's liberalism in allowing his wife her own means to self-realization is applauded, the wife's desire to realize herself is not.

One means by which the condemnation of Bimala is achieved in the novel is its cyclical narrative structure. The book begins with Bimala's reminiscence about her mother, presenting the reader with an evocative and somewhat grandiose image of the traditional Indian woman, imbued with the twin ideals of service and sacrifice. Bimala believes that her mother's example had given her the "golden provision to carry on" in a similar spirit.[35] Thus it was her own devotion and service that she most cherished in her relationship with Nikhil. But that, Bimala then recalls, was before she was "educated and introduced to the modern age in its own language."[36] It is because of her education, she now believes, that she wavered from the rightful path of her true vocation as a woman and a wife. The story is then related, in retrospect, by a repentant Bimala, bemoaning the tragic turn of events. In the concluding scene of this cyclical narrative, Bimala is convinced that it was her irredeemable lapse in the fulfillment of the ideal of womanhood that brought about the destruction of her husband and home.

The cardinal sin committed by Bimala, according to Tagore, is her discovery of her own sexuality. The disciplining of female sexuality is of course one of the central tenets of any form of patriarchy. Even in the midst of her infatuation with her husband's friend, Bimala is hardly free of the spell of patriarchal ideology. Her ruminations while trying to reconcile her own deeply held beliefs with her newfound sexual awakening echo the author's views: "Possibly this is woman's nature. When her passion is roused she loses her sensibility for all that is outside it. When, like the river, we women keep to our banks, we give nourishment with all that we have: when we overflow them we destroy with all that we are."[37] Reminding herself of the wisdom of patriarchy, Bimala feels guilty for having wavered from the "right path." More significantly, Nikhil, the supposed upholder of enlightened liberal values, takes refuge in the same ideology that compartmentalizes the roles of the sexes:

---

35 Ibid., p. 17.
36 Ibid., p. 51.
37 Ibid., p. 110.

We, men, are knights whose quest is that freedom to which our ideals call us. She who makes for us the banner under which we fare forth is the true Woman for us. We must tear away the disguise of her who weaves our net of enchantment at home, and know her for what she is. We must beware of clothing her in the witchery of our longings and imaginings, and thus allow her to distract us from our true quest.[38]

As soon as the project of freeing his wife takes an unforeseen turn, Nikhil becomes obsessed with his own freedom. He wishes to be free from his attachment to his wife. To be sure, Nikhil and his author's argument will be that Bimala's lack of sexual discipline meant she was not following the designated path of a woman's "true freedom."

Sandip, the outsider, the destroyer of home, draws on a different ideology to explain his relationship with Bimala. Sandip, the antithesis to everything Nikhil stands for, wants the "western military style to prevail" in politics.[39] In the sphere of personal relationships, he again derives his values from the West, where passion is something to be celebrated. So, when Sandip finds Bimala riddled with doubts in her attraction for him, he tries to make her "come to the conviction that to acknowledge and respect passion as the supreme reality, is to be modern—not to be ashamed of it, not to glorify restraint."[40] Thus, he uncritically glorifies Western modernity and repudiates his native culture in the spheres of both the "home" and the "world," the latter of which is evident in his approach to the nationalist movement.

The purportedly devastating potential of "illicit" female sexuality is equated with the novel's second target: radical nationalism. Bimala herself makes the connection between sexual passion and radical nationalist politics:

I saw my country, a woman like myself, standing expectant. She has been drawn forth from her home corner by the sudden call of some unknown. She has had no time to pause or ponder . . . as she rushes into the darkness ahead. I know very well how her very soul responds to the distant flute strains . . . There is no call to her of their children

38 Ibid., pp. 93–4.
39 Ibid., p. 113.
40 Ibid., p. 81.

in their hunger, no home to be lighted of an evening, no household work to be done . . . She has left home, forgotten domestic duties; she has nothing but an unfathomable yearning which hurries her on—by what road, to what goal, she recks not. I also am possessed of just such a yearning . . . Both the end and the means have become equally shadowy to me.[41]

However, Bimala is not the only person to compare her sexual awakening with the nationalist movement. When confronted with the possibility that he will have to choose between the political cause and Bimala, Sandip coalesces the two and declares, "I will make Bimala one with my country."[42] Furthermore, as critics have noted, the ideological conflict between Nikhil and Sandip represents their struggle for Bimala, who is symbolic of the nation. Indeed, the comparison of a woman, ruled by her sexual passion, with a nation, aroused by violent radicalism, is intended to be one of the central motifs of the text. As mentioned earlier, Tagore had developed a clear distaste for the extremist brand of nationalist politics that involved violence and coercion. Commenting on the equation of female sexuality with what the author perceives to be violent nationalism, Sangeeta Ray correctly observes that through the "imagining of nationalism as a devouring female . . . Tagore's critique is rendered shrilly censorious."[43]

Multiple examples among Tagore's fiction propose woman as cultural conscience. Anandamayi in *Gora* (1910) and Ela in *Four Chapters* (*Char Adhyay*, 1934) perform similar functions. Anandamayi, arguably more than any other of Tagore's female characters, embodies cultural authenticity. Bimala and Ela, on the other hand, lose touch with their "true feminine" selves, thereby triggering loss and destruction. As a result, these women either emerge as the repository of cultural values (Anandamayi) or, to the extent that they waver from the "rightful path" (Ela, Bimala), disrupt the moral universe of the narrative. Applauding the gender binary in Tagore's vision, Ashis Nandy observes that while Anandamayi "represents in her womanliness the spirit of India," Ela's and

---

41 Ibid., p. 84.

42 Ibid., p. 84.

43 Sangeeta Ray, "Woman as Nation and a Nation of Women: Tagore's *The Home and the World* and Hossain's *Sultana's Dream*," in *En-gendering India*, Durham, NC, and London: Duke University Press, p. 100.

Bimala's "personal tragedies come from the pursuit of values embedded in the . . . principle of egalitarian patriarchy rather than from any genuine reaffirmation of feminine values."[44]

Critical Reception

Much of the critical adulation of *The Home and the World* is based on an unequivocal embrace of Nikhil's/Tagore's worldview and an elision of the significance of Bimala's character.[45] To a considerable extent, the novel has been read as a struggle between the two male characters, with Bimala assigned a symbolic status. David Atkins, for instance, believes that Bimala represents the "beauty, vitality and glory of Bengal," and Nikhil and Sandip's battle for her symbolizes "a battle for the future of Bengal, as they represent two opposing visions." Whereas Sandip asserts the irrelevance of moral standards, Nikhil is the "enlightened human-ist who asserts . . . truth . . . [and] freedom."[46] In his otherwise more nuanced reading of the novel, Ashis Nandy, too, asserts that "Bimala, symbolizing Bengal . . . is shown confronting two forms of patriotism. Nikhil . . . is [initially] outshone by Sandip's flamboyance till a tragic . . . sequence . . . reveals his true heroism to Bimala."[47] The celebration of the novel's putative enlightened humanism is not restricted to post-colonial scholars. Philosopher Martha Nussbaum, for instance, char-acterizes Nikhil (and Tagore) as upholding the "substantive universal values of justice and right."[48] Echoing postcolonial critics, Nussbaum places the onus of the novel's tragic ending and of Bimala's failed eman-cipation squarely on Bimala herself: "The entire tragic story is told by the widowed Bimala, who understands, if too late, that Nikhil's morality was vastly superior to Sandip's."[49] From this vantage point, the novel

44 Ashis Nandy, "Illegitimacy of Nationalism" in *Return From Exile*, Delhi: Oxford University Press, 1998, pp. 41, 42.

45 For yet another appreciative reading of Tagore's political stance, see Anita Desai's introduction to the 1985 Penguin edition of *The Home and the World*, pp. xxi–xxviii.

46 David Atkinson, "Tagore's *The Home and the World*: A Call for a New World Order," *International Fiction Review* 20:2 (1993), pp. 95–8, 96.

47 Nandy, "Illegitimacy of Nationalism," pp. 12–15.

48 Martha Nussbaum, "Patriotism and Cosmopolitanism," in *For Love of Country: Debating the Limits of Patriotism*, ed. Joshua Cohen, Boston: Beacon, 1996, p. 5.

49 Ibid., pp. 15–16.

becomes a classic morality tale, and Bimala the tragic but reformed beneficiary of its message.

Sumit Sarkar's historical approach to the novel provides yet another illuminating instance of the same phenomenon. Sarkar begins with the observation that his current reading is meant to offer a corrective to his earlier commentary on the novel, which failed to provide an analysis of the gender dynamics in the text. Unfortunately, Sarkar then proceeds to provide an analysis that once again not only marginalizes the issue of Bimala's emancipation but also justifies Tagore's position that Bimala is not "worthy of true independence."[50] To read Tagore's work in terms of Nikhil's "enlightened humanism" and Bimala's merely symbolic worth is to remain trapped within the implicit authorial intention for the novel. Such readings fail to interrogate either Tagore's position on nationalism or his gender politics.

Bimala's potential self-realization remains hostage, first to her husband's agenda and then to her lover's attempts to appropriate her selfhood. This is consistent with Chatterjee's claim that a new form of patriarchy frames the national bourgeoisie's project of women's emancipation. Bimala's exploration of her own sexuality is frustrated by Sandip's maneuvering to impose on her his discourse of passion and its desirability. While Sandip's supposedly Western ideology is clearly repudiated in the text, Nikhil's desire to facilitate his wife's entry into the wider world is upheld. Yet there are moments in the novel that expose the hollowness of Nikhil's "enlightened" attitude toward his wife. For instance, at Sandip's urging, Bimala donates a large sum of money to Sandip's nationalist organization without consulting Nikhil. The incident is narrativized as Bimala's "theft" from her own home, a serious act of transgression. Despite all the "freedom" bestowed on her by her husband, Bimala is not free to make a monetary donation without her husband's prior knowledge and acquiescence. On the other hand, we learn early in the novel that Nikhil himself, despite Bimala's displeasure, has long been making donations to Sandip. But that, the reader is expected to understand, is his male prerogative.

Notwithstanding the author's explicit ideology, the basic vacuity of "providing freedom" to women reveals itself in the text. Bimala suffers deeply in her attraction to Sandip, as she is torn by the agony of having

---

50 Tagore, *The Home and the World*, p. 148.

to reconcile her spontaneous attraction to another man with her unflinching loyalty to her husband. Patriarchal ideology renders her incapable of comprehending, let alone justifying, her own psychological and physical needs. And Nikhil, with all his liberal magnanimity, is unable to comprehend Bimala's struggle. It is his own attempt to detach himself from Bimala that occupies him, and in a seeming act of great self-abnegation, he tells her she is under no obligation to him and should consider herself free. Her response captures the worthlessness of this gesture, which negates the contextual complexity of her situation: "And then the other day in the garden, how easy my husband found it to tell me that he set me free! But can freedom—empty freedom be given and taken so easily as that? It is like setting a fish free in the sky."[51]

Sarkar asserts that the novel, in fact, "places a strong question mark against what, after Partha Chatterjee, has been commonly described as the 'nationalist resolution of the woman's question.'"[52] Sarkar offers an analysis of Tagore's engagement with the issue of women's freedom in the novel to argue, contra Chatterjee, that the woman's question was never fully appropriated by the nationalist discourse, but remained relevant in its own right. Even though Sarkar believes that the novel represents Tagore's faith in "genuine women's freedom,"[53] his reading only ends up highlighting the limitations of the benevolent male reformism that results in Bimala's failed emancipation. Echoing other postcolonial critics, Sarkar blames Bimala for lacking the "self-development" that would make her "worthy of true independence," and the "dominant note" of the novel for him is "Nikhil's agonized determination to respect the autonomy of Bimala."[54] Ironically, even as Sarkar wants to highlight the novel as an instance of Tagore's recognition of the autonomy of women, he defines its "dominant note" as the good intentions of its male protagonist. Sarkar is quite right, however, in suggesting that *The Home and the World* is not so much about Bimala's emancipation as it is about her husband's belief in women's liberation. Consequently, in displacing the issue of women's emancipation from its proper register—women's struggle for autonomy—and shifting it to one of patriarchal reform,

51 Ibid., p. 137.
52 Sarkar, "The Woman's Question," p. 132.
53 Ibid., p. 147.
54 Ibid., p. 148.

Tagore's novel becomes an illuminating instance of what Chatterjee has described as the "nationalist resolution of the woman's question."

Some postcolonial critics have resisted reading the novel in the light of Chatterjee's framework of an inner/outer divide within the nationalist discourse. Supriya Chaudhuri, for instance, expresses uncertainty that Chatterjee's "distinction holds" between a pre-nationalist and nationalist phase; instead, she prefers to see the novel as Tagore's critique of a passage into modernity.[55] For Chaudhuri, the novel "is not a conservative work, but . . . a deeply unhappy one. Bimala's sentimental education leads her from a traditional ideal of womanhood to a state of radical incompleteness . . . leaving her in the confusion and uncertainty that Tagore saw as a characteristic of modernity."[56] Surely, however, to the extent the "deep unhappiness" of the novel is generated by a modernity that marks the loss of "a traditional ideal of womanhood," the work does embrace a deeply conservative stance on gender. Rekha Basu similarly questions the idea that the novel represents women's subordination by what Chatterjee describes as the "new patriarchy" of the nationalist phase.[57] Basu contends that the novel "interrogates the contrasting yet common patriarchies represented by the discourses of Sandip and Nikhilesh."[58] In support of the claim that the novel questions Nikhil, Basu points to his obliviousness to the depth of the gendered suffering of his sister-in-law, Bara Rani, even as the two share a close friendship. The problem with this reading is that the nationalist "new patriarchy" and its liberalism are capable of accounting for the suffering of widows. Indeed, the paternalism of the patriarchy is not threatened by the reform of the institution of widowhood, as it is by the implicit demand for female autonomy represented by Bimala's transgressions. So while Basu is right about the condemnation of the egregious aspects of the patriarchal institution of widowhood in the novel, it does not amount to a critique of the "new patriarchy." The operation of the "new patriarchy" when analyzed with

---

55 Supriya Chaudhuri, "Dangerous Liaisons: Desire and Limit in *The Home and the World*," in *Thinking on Thresholds: The Poetics of Transitive Spaces*, London: Anthem, 2013, pp. 87–100.

56 Ibid., p. 93.

57 Rekha Basu, "The Nationalist Project and the Woman's question: A Reading of *The Home and the World* and Nationalism," in *Applied Ethics and Human Rights: Conceptual Analysis and Contextual Applications*, ed. Shashi Motilal, London: Anthem, 2010, pp. 237–45.

58 Ibid., p. 243.

reference to Bimala's choices, does bear out Chatterjee's view that "by associating the task of 'female emancipation' with the historical goal of sovereign nationhood, [the new patriarchy] bound [women] to a new, yet entirely legitimate subordination."[59]

The turn of events that leads to the novel's tragic outcome leaves the reader with many unanswered questions. Beneath Sandip's charismatic personality is a crooked, self-serving hypocrite, and Bimala, finally able to see the man for what he is, finds herself repelled. But how, a reader might wonder, would the conflict be resolved if Sandip were not a villainous character? Similarly, Nikhil had to be a heroic, self-effacing, morally righteous man for Bimala to see the stark contrast between the object of her infatuation and her husband. What if Nikhil were not the hero that the author makes him out to be? And finally, what if Bimala could have viewed the choice between her husband and her lover as secondary to the possibilities for self-actualization? Such questions are ultimately irrelevant, primarily because they are extraneous to the intent of the text. The novel, not meant to probe the psychological twists and turns of its characters, is intended even less to inspire the liberation of women.

Ultimately, *The Home and the World* is a fable that preaches the importance of disciplining women. As in all fables, the characters represent ideas. In the conflict between the world and the home, Sandip, the outsider, personifies the threat to the disciplined and harmonious domestic sphere. As Indrani Mitra rightly notes, Nikhil, beneath his Western education and liberal views, is an "agent for the preservation of an older familial system and its associated values."[60] Indeed, Nikhil represents the desirable nationalist fusion of liberal ideology with traditional identity. But it is women, as Chatterjee reminds us, who must personify the combined strength of native identity and modernity. Bimala's tragedy in failing to serve as this nationalist icon of womanhood serves as a warning of the precarious but necessary balance to be maintained between the forces of the home and those of the world.

---

59 Chatterjee, "The Woman's Question," p. 130.

60 Indrani Mitra, "I Will Make Bimala One with My Country: Gender and Nationalism in Tagore's *The Home and the World*," *Modern Fiction Studies* 41:2 (1995), pp. 243–64, 248.

The World in *The Home and the World*

The story is told through the first-person narratives of the three princi-pal characters: Nikhil, Bimala and Sandip. The strategy of using multiple first-person narratives can either suggest the pluralistic nature of truth, *or* it can offer a version of truth that is seemingly well examined. *The Home and the World* attempts to do the latter. Telling the story from three different perspectives might imply the existence of several possible and equally valid interpretations of events. In actuality, however, both Bimala's and Sandip's narratives, while evoking sympathy, serve primar-ily to reveal the flaws in their reasoning and judgment. Rather, it is Nikhil's voice that elicits empathy and endorsement.

In fact, I would argue that the chosen narrative strategy offers a reflection of the nationalist project. Nikhil, in this sense, embodies an emergent elite and patriarchal nationalism claiming to represent the interests and aspirations of disparate social groups. Historically, nation-alist ideology had to perform a double maneuver: it had to be sufficiently porous to allow various social groups and their interests to be incorpo-rated into its fold, and at the same time, it had to suppress certain aspects of those other interests in order to make the process of incorpo-ration consistent with the project of bourgeois nation building. Sandip's brand of radical, populist nationalism and Bimala's female sexuality represent disparate aspirations within the nation. Elitist nationalism had to simultaneously *incorporate* such aspirations and yet *marginalize* them. In Nikhil's world, the interests represented by Bimala and Sandip are, in a sense, already incorporated—he is, after all, the loving husband of one and a dear friend of the other. The novel becomes the story of the marginalization of these aspirations in the interest of the elite, patri-archal nationalism symbolized by Nikhil.

The simultaneous mobilization and disciplining of women in the nationalist cause is consistent with the native elite's treatment of other subaltern groups. The novel has been applauded for reflecting a progress-ive critique of the *swadeshi* movement, which was organized around the economic boycott of British goods and services, and of the resultant deleterious impact on the underprivileged classes. Nikhil reflects his author's view that the nation's poor should not have to make sacrifices for the nationalist cause. The boycott of cheap yet superior imported merchandise in favor of locally produced, expensive, inferior items spelled financial disaster for small merchants who could not find a market for their goods. The militant leadership of the movement, according to Tagore, was out of touch with the everyday needs and interests of the masses. It remained oblivious to the fact that it is the poorer sections of the population that suffered most from a movement forcing them to boycott all trade in foreign goods.

In his critical account of the elitist character of the anti-colonial movement, Ranajit Guha praises Tagore's opposition to swadeshi in the novel as representing a self-conscious moment in the nationalist struggle—a moment when the realization took hold that if "patriotism were allowed to base itself on fear and coercion rather than persuasion, that would be altogether self-defeating for the nationalist cause."[61] Ashis Nandy also applauds the novel for its suggestion that "a nationalism which steam-rollers society into making a uniform stand against colonialism, ignoring the unequal sacrifices imposed thereby on the poorer and the weaker, will tear apart the social fabric of the country."[62] Similarly, Tanika Sarkar opines that for Tagore, "the nation cannot impose the burning of cheap foreign cloth that the peasant buys and sells just because it is foreign. Foreign rule should go because it offends universal ideas of morality."[63]

If Guha and Nandy uphold the idea of a broad-based, inclusive nationalism, I submit that Tagore's critique of swadeshi offers no such alternative. What he presents is only an appeal for tactical changes, not a rejection of the elitist orientation of the national movement. The fact that the underprivileged pay a steep price for joining the struggle against colonialism need not, in and of itself, be viewed as problematic; rather, it is in the interests of the working classes to fight colonialism and envision a just social order. The involvement of the underprivileged classes becomes questionable only when the native leadership harnesses the movement in the service of its own interests of financial and political power. Now, that might well have been the trajectory of the Indian independence movement, but Tagore does not differentiate between bourgeois and popular forms of anti-colonialism. As a result, there is a

---

61 Guha, *Dominance without Hegemony*, p. 110.
62 Nandy, "Illegitimacy of Nationalism," p. 19.
63 Tanika Sarkar in Datta, *Rabindranath Tagore's* The Home and the World, p. 43.

critical contradiction in his position, in that his critique of the movement for its treatment of the poor never led him to question the feudal
system of landownership that creates and perpetuates a class of indigent
peasantry. Tagore's critique of *swadeshi* is thus made very much from
within the class position of the nationalist elite.

Nikhil, the benevolent feudal landlord, like his author, is pained by
the existence of poverty on his estate and is always ready to lend a
helping hand to the needy. His relationship with Panchu, the poor
merchant who is caught between the demands made of him both by the
swadeshi movement and the *zamindar* (landlord) class, captures much
of Tagore's own searching ties with the poor peasantry of his estate.
Pradip Kumar Dutta discusses Tagore's abiding relationship with his
poor tenants and his need to make sense of what Tagore called the
"reality of life." Dutta observes: "Rabindranth's preoccupation with rural
upliftment formed the hub of a larger concern with solving national
problems. In a letter to his friend Kalimohon Ghosh, Rabindranath
observed that the area concentrated in itself all the problems of the
nation, for it was poorly developed and peopled by poor, illiterate,
indebted Hindus, Muslims and low-caste Namasudras."[64]

The value of Tagore's sympathy for the underprivileged notwithstanding, he never turned his back on the feudal system as he did on
the *swadeshi* movement. A feudal landlord himself, Tagore did not
consider it desirable to overhaul the feudal system; he simply wanted
to make the system more humane. And herein lies the commonality
between the author's positions on class and on gender. Tagore's belief
that the condition of the impoverished requires alleviation parallels
his conviction that Indian women should be ushered into the modern
age through education and social exposure. What *The Home and the
World* does not address are the *structural causes* for gender and class
disparity: patriarchy and feudalism. Tagore's hero, Nikhil, represents
the nationalist elite that sincerely believes in "reaching out to the
masses" while actively working to keep traditional hierarchical structures in place.

---

64 Datta, *Rabindranath Tagore's* The Home and the World, p. 6.

Sharatchandra

Tagore, speaking of Sharatchandra Chattopadhyay,[65] offered what is
the deepest possible appreciation of one writer by another: "He
belongs entirely to his country and age. That is no light matter."[66]
Chattopadhyay's works capture an era when social reform and
rejuvenation—particularly in relation to the modernization of the status
of women—were integral elements of the dominant discourse, and his
writings offer intimate portrayals of the interstices of a traditional world
influenced only tangentially by the reigning discourses. His portrayals,
while sharply critical of oppressive traditional structures, are always
rendered with the compassion of an empathetic insider. It is this profound connection with his subjects—usually women straining against
patriarchal structures in rural settings—that reveal the hollowness of
the nationalist elite's discursive constructions of the modern woman.
Chattopadhyay's works critique both the traditional order and the
emergent nationalist response, as well as explore alternative possibilities,
all the while remaining firmly anchored within the local and the
affective.

In contrast to Tagore and his aristocratic background, Chattopadhyay
was born in rural Bengal and raised in dire poverty. Nevertheless, he did
inherit a love of literature and travel from a father who was more a
dreamer than a man of the world. In addition, his stoic mother, who
raised seven children under impoverished conditions, imbued him with
a respect and empathy for women that became the hallmark of his
writings. Unable to complete a university degree because he couldn't pay
his exam fees, Chattopadhyay spent a few years doing odd jobs in
Calcutta, trying to support his family. Later he moved to Burma, where
he worked as a clerk at a government office for more than a decade. It
was in Burma that Chattopadhyay started writing seriously, and eventually the success of his publications permitted him to devote himself
entirely to literature.

---

65 The name "Chatterjee" is an Anglicization of the Bengali name "Chattopadhyay."
While I have retained the original name for my discussion of the author, editors and
critics often refer to him as Sharatchandra Chatterjee.

66 Quoted in Amitava Das, "Introduction," Sharatchandra Chatterjee, *The Final
Question*, ed. Arup Rudra and Sukanta Chaudhuri, Delhi: Permanent Black, 2001, p. viii

Apart from his literary career, Chattopadhyay was politically active. He participated in the noncooperation movement in 1921 and was elected president of the Howrah District Congress Committee for fifteen years. Even though Chattopadhyay was a committed member of the Indian National Congress, in 1934 he openly criticized Gandhi's displeasure at the ascendance of socialists in the government. Gandhi had resigned from Congress, stating that he could not remain a member of a party dominated by socialists. In response, Chattopadhyay, who was otherwise respectful of Gandhi's leadership, opined that Gandhi's antipathy to socialists stemmed from his close ties to capitalists and that his resignation from the party would be in both his own and the party's best interests. Till his final days, Chattopadhyay remained closely tied to the anti-colonial movement.

In novels such as *Palli Samaj*, *Bardidi*, *Dena Paona*, and *Grihadaha*, he chronicled the stifled suffering of the individual spirit, especially of women, in a society governed by orthodoxies of religion and tradition. Repeatedly, his fiction centralizes the outcastes of the patriarchal order—so-called fallen women, widows, women yearning for escape from marital bonds—thereby offering, as Amitava Das notes, a "virtual inner history of women's liberation."[67] Because Chattopadhyay's strong condemnation of societal mores stems from an even stronger sense of connection to and belonging within that same society, his characters' desire for liberation always seeks a social fulfillment. Supriya Chaudhuri rightly observes that if "the feminism of his earlier works is inseparably linked to the moral function of sentiment," in his more political and more intellectualized later novels, such as *Pather Dabi* and *The Final Question*, Chattopadhyay adopted a different approach, perhaps because he realized that the "idealization of women's suffering and sacrifice" gets absorbed in the patriarchal order with little disturbance.[68]

Sharatchandra's Final Question

In a context where the woman's question was largely coopted within the nationalist project, *The Final Question* signals a striking departure from the phenomenon. The novel questions every possible aspect of the

67 Amitava Das, p. x.
68 Supriya Chaudhuri, "Afterword," in *The Final Question*, pp. 287–8.

fashioning of female identity in the interest of an "authentic" nationalist project. The characterization of Kamal, the central protagonist, is at once the strength and the weakness of the text. Unlike Bimala, Kamal undergoes no transformation in the course of the narrative; from the start, her character is fully formed, displaying an impressive, even daunting, unity of belief and action. And that is precisely the weakness of the novel: the reader has minimal access to this admirable character's inner life. Indeed, Chattopadhyay fails to make the kind of affective connection between character and reader that is the strength of realist fiction.

And yet Kamal's characterization was certainly a conscious choice, made by an author who understood well the role of affect and empathy in the forging of characters, especially female characters. One might identify the artistry of *The Final Question* in the author's attempt to transcend the limitations of his earlier work. Here, Chattopadhyay grappled with the possibilities for weaving the political and the literary, leading to a novel that was the product of his mature political and cultural views. That Kamal becomes the vehicle for those views may be a drawback, but it also forces us to pay attention to the implications of such a choice. In a Brechtian move, Chattopadhyay preferred to prioritize the development of a political position over that of the interiority of his character, thereby attempting to avoid the pitfalls of a realist narrative whose message is easily assimilable by the political structure.

If in its characterization of Kamal the novel marks a departure from the established realist mode, it also signals a significantly different political position on the dominant nationalist ideology. At a juncture when the fashioning of female identity was a key component of the nationalist project, Kamal challenges the fundamentals of that project. In *The Home and the World*, sexual morality is the cornerstone of the nationalist project for forging female selfhood. In *The Final Question*, by contrast, Kamal offers a thoroughgoing critique of that morality.

Born in Assam, Kamal is the daughter of a "mixed marriage" between a white Christian man and a poor Indian woman. Following the death of the father, Kamal's mother worked as a maidservant in an affluent home. Young, beautiful and intelligent, Kamal is structurally handicapped by poverty as well as a questionable heritage. Despite her accomplishments, the disparity in class status alone would typically guarantee that she remain distant from the more privileged members of the community. But the novel set in the North Indian city of Agra allows for certain departures from social conventions consistent with an expatriate location. As part of a group uprooted from their home setting and keen to forge communitarian bonds, Kamal has free access to the homes of more economically privileged individuals. Nevertheless, the community does look askance at Kamal's life choices and their ostensible implications for sexual morality.

Right at the outset of the narrative, Kamal's views on Agra's famed monument, the Taj Mahal, set her apart and set the stage for deeper differences between her and the community. Ashu Babu and other characters subscribe to the conventional view that the Taj signifies an emperor's undying love for his beloved wife. Kamal argues against the idea of single-minded devotion and points out that the same emperor had many other wives. She acknowledges that the "contemplative and poetical" emperor did build a beautiful monument but stresses that it was only incidentally dedicated to one of his wives. Thus, Kamal supports the celebration of the Taj, but only for the aesthetic pleasure it offers, not as a paean to eternal love.

Opposition to various discursive constructions of sexuality looms large in Kamal's personal life. Widowed at an early age, she lives with Shibnath in a "marriage" that was a perfunctory rite performed for social acceptability. Though her marriage has no legal standing, Kamal is unperturbed by its dubiousness. When alerted to the fact that Shibnath might desert her without suffering any consequences, she accepts that the "truth" of her relationship is transient but that a proper marriage would not change that: "Could it be that . . . the truth would sink out of sight and I would tie him down by a ritual I don't myself believe in?"[69] In juxtaposing her "truth" against mere "ritual," Kamal posits experiential truth over the nationalist construction of authenticity.

Ashu Babu is an elderly widower, much liked and respected by Kamal for his patience and emotional generosity. But Kamal has very little regard for his glorification of the memory of his deceased wife as the most prized possession of his inner life, or his decision to remain celibate for his remaining years. His choices, she holds, signify a mythification of restraint untethered to experiential life. Kamal's judgment contrasts with Bimala's attachment to patriarchal rituals whose value is

---

69 Sharatchandra Chattopadhyay, *The Final Question*, p. 42.

asserted not merely by her but also by the narrative structure of Tagore's novel.

After Shibnath leaves Kamal for another woman, Ashu Babu asks her whether she is pained by the separation. Yes indeed, she responds, but that pain is not the entirety of her experience:

> It's not that I haven't suffered misery, but I haven't accepted that as the ultimate truth of my life. Shibnath gave me whatever he had to give, I took whatever was mine to receive. Those little moments of joy are treasured like jewels in my heart. I have neither turned them to ashes in my soul's fire nor stood with hands outstretched for alms before a dried-up fountain.[70]

Subsequently, when an attraction develops between her and Ajit, Kamal expresses the desire for an uncommitted relationship with him, rather than marriage. Much distressed, Ajit tries to convince her otherwise:

> "[Marriage] is the rightful claim born of your love. But you didn't claim your right: what you asked for is as short-lived as a bubble, and just as unreal."
>
> Kamal said, "Its lifespan may be short, but why should it be unreal? I'm not one of those who want to cling to a long life as the only reality."
>
> "But this joy has no permanence, Kamal."
>
> "It may not. But I don't agree with those who, because real flowers wither, adorn their vases with everlasting flowers made of pith. I told you once that no joy is lasting: it has its allotted span of transient days. That's the highest treasure of human life. If you tie it down, you kill it. That's why marriage has permanence but no joy . . ."
>
> . . . His [Ajit's] mind was filled with revulsion at such monstrous contempt for this ancient and holy ceremony of the human race.[71]

Kamal's mistrust of the institution of marriage derives from what she considers its artificiality but also from its deleterious impact on women. The single-minded privileging of the institution in a woman's life necessarily carries a heavy cost, as Kamal tries to explain to Ashu Babu: "You

---

70 Ibid., p. 225.
71 Ibid., p. 196.

too must realize that marriage is one event in life out of many—no more. The day people took it as the ultimate end for a woman—that's the day the biggest tragedy of women's life began."[72] In a similar vein, she characterizes the institution of motherhood as a patriarchal instrument that, while disguised as a "woman's ultimate fulfillment, defrauded the entire race of women."[73]

In spite of their differences, Kamal shares a close bond with Nilima, a widow well respected in the community. Nilima is admired because even though she is not only widowed but also childless, she has devoted herself to running the household of her brother and taking care of his motherless son. Her commitment is viewed as selfless service, born of love for the extended family, and Nilima herself fully embraces that persona. Nilima's character dovetails with Gandhi's elevation of the institution of widowhood and also resonates with Tagore's portrayal of the latter. Tagore, while sensitive to the suffering of widows, is never fully critical of the institution; ultimately, he remains bound by its rationale and age-old solidity. In fact, the open ending of *The Home and the World*, which strongly suggests Bimala's future widowhood as punishment for her transgression, subtly advocates the institution as a means of patriarchal control.

Chattopadhyay's novel takes a different tack. Here again it falls on Kamal to expose the true nature of widowhood as an institution, which she does by simply foregrounding who suffers and who benefits. Even though she feels affection for Nilima, Kamal openly criticizes her for her life choices:

Harendra said . . . pointing to Nilima . . . "She is my ideal . . . You [Kamal] have no respect for Indian antiquity; the ideals of India don't attract you. But tell me where else do you find such glory, such ideals ascribed to womanhood? Boudi ["sister-in-law," referring to Nilima] is the mistress of this house; to sejda's [Kamal's brother's] motherless son, she's like a mother. The entire responsibility of this household rests on her shoulders. But she has neither any personal interests nor any entanglement. Now tell me, in which country do widows give so much of themselves?"

---

72 Ibid., p. 263.
73 Ibid., p. 242.

Kamal's face lit up with a little smile. She said, "Where's the good in it, Haren Babu? Perhaps there's no such instance in the world of being the selfless mistress of someone else's house and a selfless mother to someone else's son. Its uniqueness might make it strange or rare, but how can it make it good?"

... Nilima opened her eyes wide with astonishment and looked fixedly at Kamal. Kamal aimed her next words at her. "However people might glorify it with splendid words and clever epithets, nobody can respect this play-acting of a housewife's part ... This is how men intoxicate us with activity. When we drink in the heady wine of their applause, our eyes glaze over and we treat it like the fulfillment of our womanhood. I remember Harish Babu of our tea garden. When his sixteen year old sister was widowed, he brought her to his house, showed her his horde of children, cried and said, 'Dear sister, from now on they are your children; why should you worry sister? Bring them up, become their mother and the mistress of this house, make your life meaningful. This is my blessing upon you.' Harish Babu was held to be a good man, the entire garden rang with his praise. Everybody said, 'Lakshmi's a lucky girl.' Indeed she was. Only women know that there's no greater misery, no greater fraud. But by the time this becomes clear, it's too late to correct it."[74]

Kamal's castigation of a cherished patriarchal institution embodies a nuanced critique of ideology. Widows, especially if childless, were deprived of property rights. Remarriage was extremely rare. Sexual abstinence was the norm, as was severe austerity in lifestyle, including food and clothing. At the same time, widows were held in high regard for their domestic "service." Widowhood was an exploitative institution, based on both deprivation and extraction. The invocation of the "feminine" ideals of selflessness, service and moderation legitimized it ideologically. Precisely because it enshrined those supposedly feminine qualities, Gandhi glorified it. But in her own portrayal of widowhood, Kamal not only highlights the success of the ideology but also points to the intrinsic limitations of all ideology. Women, she declares, consume the "heady wine" that is offered in the form of praise for the way widows are made to live, while at the same time, their suffering cannot be

74 Ibid., pp. 101–2.

negated by such ideological whitewashing. Ultimately, women realize the "great fraud" perpetrated on them.

Kamal's views on issues ranging from nationalism and cultural revivalism to patriarchal practices are at odds with the beliefs of the other characters, just as they are with the world outside the novel. The only way the other characters can come to terms with her is by attributing her distinct worldview to biological and contextual differences. Ajit, for instance, is attracted to Kamal but unable to engage with her intellectually, and thus, almost predictably, he takes solace in reminding her that she doesn't actually "belong to our kind. Your blood, your beliefs, all your education are foreign. You can never overcome their violent impact on you."[75]

Ajit's brand of comforting relativism ensures that cultural perspectives and positions remain self-referential and free of scrutiny. Viewed thus, Kamal's character—shaped by her birth and upbringing—may be dismissed as simply the product of an alien value system and therefore of little relevance. Yet she also defies easy dismissal, primarily because of her bonds of love and friendship with the other characters. Her seemingly hedonistic outlook notwithstanding, Kamal maintains an austere lifestyle and displays considerable reserves of both empathy and generosity. And, precisely because Kamal is anchored in her community, the narrative attention can persuasively pivot to the defiant positions she articulates on cultural and political questions. Whereas *The Home and the World*, for all its flirtations with modernity, remains ensconced in traditional structures of patriarchy and feudalism, Chattopadhyay's novel adamantly rejects the inegalitarian comforts of the old world, even as its characters struggle to define the contours of a new order.

Conclusion

Postcolonial critics who celebrate Tagore's critique of nationalism fail to identify the conservative core of his philosophy, especially as it relates to gender. Given the broader orientation of the field, specifically its tendency toward culturalist constructions, this stance is perhaps predictable. Their almost-unqualified admiration of *The Home and the*

---

75 Ibid., p. 198.

World, and of Tagore in general, is consistent with Rosinka Chaudhuri's observations about the curious celebration, especially by Bengali post-colonial critics, of the author, "that icon of the middle classes," who in his own time was often reviled for his elitist background.[76] Chaudhuri discusses two instances of misreadings of Tagore by subaltern scholars. First, Ranajit Guha upholds what he considers to be Tagore's critique of historiography for its attachment to dry facts, and his favoring of a creative engagement with the past in literary discourse. Chaudhuri persuasively shows that in the specific context of defending himself against the charge of being an ahistorical writer, Tagore had observed that literature and historiography serve different purposes. The distinction Tagore made between literary and historiographic writing was never meant to signal the superiority of one over the other, as claimed by Guha. In a similar vein, Dipesh Chakrabarty celebrates Tagore for supposedly incorporating the prosaic elements of modernity in ways that ultimately demonstrate the superiority of a poetic imagination and its ability to transfigure the actuality of urban life. Again, Chaudhuri is right in arguing that Chakrabarty attempts to read literary modernism in Tagore by relying "too heavily on a false construct: that of an oppositional relationship between the prosaic and the poetic." In so doing, Chakrabarty misunderstands the nature of literary modernism and its complex relationship to the urban landscape. What stands out in the two instances identified by Chaudhuri is the privileging of binaries—literature versus history, prosaic versus poetic—that speak less to Tagore's work and more to the culturalist agenda of the subalternists themselves.

Postcolonial and subalternist scholars' endorsement of Tagore similarly dovetails with their privileging of cultural difference. The critical upholding of Nikhil's liberal masculinity, together with the denunciation of Bimala's choices, fully conform to the nationalist logic of what Chatterjee identifies as a dichotomization of the inner and outer spheres. By endorsing the essentialist dichotomy underlying the inner/outer divide, they affirm the conservatism of the nationalist embrace of tradition—in which *difference* defines the cultural identity of the nation in

---

76 See Rosinka Chaudhuri, "Flute, Gerontion, and Subalternist Misreadings of Tagore," *Social Text* 22:1 (Spring 2004), pp. 103–20.

the domestic sphere. Bimala, in this reading, remains guilty of the inability to play the part demanded of her by the new nationalist patriarchy. The conservatism on gender that characterizes *The Home and the World* is echoed in Tagore's universalism, similarly premised on a culturalist divide between East and West.

All of this contrasts strongly with Chattopadhyay's politics, which, while culturally anchored, rejects an identity based on tradition and embraces egalitarianism both in gender relations and in relationships between nations. But unlike Tagore, Chattopadhyay, much like numerous gifted authors from the global South, is a scarcely recognized figure in the West. It might be expected that the postcolonial discipline, with its stated objective of challenging Western political and literary hegemonies, would attempt to elevate a writer like Chattopadhyay. Instead, the discipline turned to Tagore, an established figure in the Western canon.

To contrast the authors is not to castigate Tagore. He both reflected and questioned the contradictions of his tumultuous era, and did so masterfully not only in his fiction but in his essays, music and paintings. His writings—especially short stories such as "Streer Patra" ("Letter from a Wife") and "Haimanti"—exhibit genuine empathy toward women and rage at the price that patriarchy pitilessly extracted from them. However, Tagore's empathy for women, unlike Chattopadhyay's, remained bound within the confines of a liberal humanist patriarchy. Consequently, the contrast between Tagore and Chattopadhyay is significant not so much for an appreciation of the difference between the writers themselves as for mapping their *differential reception* by postcolonial critics. Ironically, followers of postcolonial thought—a thought premised on questioning essentialist constructions—have upheld the gender conservatism and culturalism of a writer acclaimed in the West, while remaining largely silent on another more regionally popular writer whose works are characterized by a radical egalitarianism on questions of gender and culture.

3

Neo-Orientalism in Postcolonial Literature

The previous chapters argue that postcolonial theory presents a deep contradiction, evidenced in some of its canonical texts. While they place the recovery of agency at the center of their project, their analyses instead end up suppressing subaltern agency—in particular, that of women. This chapter continues that line of analysis but connects it to another issue central to contemporary literary theory. Here, I examine how postcolonial theorists' confusion about agency also implicates them in debates around Orientalism. The vehicle for this discussion is Michael Ondaatje's acclaimed novel *Anil's Ghost* (2000).[1] Widely regarded as a quintessentially postcolonial novel and praised for its depiction of the Sri Lankan Civil War, *Anil's Ghost* in fact typifies many of the weaknesses of contemporary cultural theory.

While the novel focuses on the widespread violence unleashed by the 1980s conflict between an ethnic majority state and a militant Tamil resistance, it also glances back to another mass insurrection, led by students in the 1970s, which was violently repressed by the state. The narrative eschews any *overt* political stance; rather, it examines the experience of violence from the perspectives of an expatriate investigator and local actors. The central note of the narrative is to establish that a conflict-ridden postcolonial setting calls for a non-Western epistemology.

---

1 Michael Ondaatje, *Anil's Ghost*, Toronto: McClelland & Stewart, 2000.

Anil's Ghost has been roundly applauded for encapsulating a post-colonial critique of Western discourses and for its focus on the phenomenological dimension of postcolonial conflict. Critics contend, for instance, that Ondaatje's treatment of the Sri Lankan situation foregrounds the critique of dominant historiography "as an exclusively western epistemological form."[2] Western historiography, the argument goes, privileges the grand narrative of the nation and of subjects governed exclusively by reason,[3] while these critics see Ondaatje as steering clear of such dominant Western notions, which gloss over the complexities of the postcolonial experience.[4] The turn away from conventional Western narratives is evidenced in the author's eschewal of any partisanship, and in the stress he places instead on the overarching human tragedy.[5] His depiction of the extreme suffering of people caught in the country's civil war is commended for its "attentiveness and concern for the particular."[6] The broad critical consensus is that in its treatment of the war, the narrative constructs a quintessentially "post-colonial ethic."[7]

Robert Young's appraisal of the novel is especially noteworthy in this regard and deserves attention because of his pivotal role in historicizing and defining the field. His commentary on Ondaatje's novel is an instance of the discipline's ambivalence toward materialist historiography and an embrace of Orientalist tropes. In his essay "Terror Effects," Young echoes other critics in praising the novel for demonstrating the futility of Western frameworks for understanding the Sri Lankan

---

2 Antoinette Burton, "Archive of Bones: *Anil's Ghost* and the Ends of History," *Journal of Commonwealth Literature* 38:1 (2003), p. 40.

3 See Mrinalini Chakravorty, "The Dead That Haunt 'Anil's Ghost': Subaltern Difference and Postcolonial Melancholia," *PMLA* 128:3 (2013), p. 555.

4 See Victoria Burrows, "The Heterotopic Spaces of Postcolonial Trauma in Michael Ondaatje's 'Anil's Ghost,' *Studies in the Novel* 40:1–2 (2008), pp. 161–77.

5 See Geetha Ganapathy-Dore, "Fathoming Private Woes in a Public Story—A Study of Michael Ondaatje's *Anil's Ghost*," *Jouvert: A Journal of Postcolonial Studies* 6:3 (2002).

6 Manav Ratti, "Michael Ondaatje's *Anil's Ghost* and the Aestheticization of Human Rights," *Ariel: A Review of International English Literature* 35:1–2 (2004), pp. 121–41.

7 See, for instance, Ryan Mowat, "An Aesthetics of War: The Postcolonial Ethics of *Anil's Ghost*," *Journal of Postcolonial Writing* 49:1 (2013), 28–39; and Victoria Cook, "Exploring Transnational Identities in Ondaatje's *Anil's Ghost*," *Comparative Literature and Culture* 6:3 (2004), pp. 6–15.

conflict.[8] Those trained in the West approach the civil war through the lens of interests, rights, legal frameworks and linear historical causation; Ondaatje shows, we are told, how the war transcended these categories and entered the realm of pure trauma—something perceived, but no longer attached to causes, social forces or political interests. To understand this thus requires a leap into another conceptual universe, one that eschews the nostrums of Western theory.

Young contends that whereas in the first world, terrorism is connected to the abstract "fear of immigrants and the imagined threat that they embody," in the postcolonial world its operation is far more real and visceral. For him, the virtue of Ondaatje's novel is its deep appreciation of this difference:

> It is in Michael Ondaatje's *Anil's Ghost* that we vicariously experience the full extent of a terrorism that has descended into a civil war in which the different sides . . . have become indistinguishable: train killings, massacres, beheadings, crucifixions, night visitations, kidnapping, murders in broad daylight . . . Here terror has moved from the dialectics of traditional terrorism into a porous landscape in which terror has leaked into unreadable forms of arbitrary violence beyond the realm of all political and social institutions of power: in short into trauma.[9]

The novel's portrayal of the scale of violence may well be historically accurate. But what makes Young's reading noteworthy is that he not only accepts but also endorses Ondaatje's description of the two sides as "indistinguishable." In so doing, Young refuses to engage with the complexity of a specific juncture in a country in the global South. Indeed, he describes the very idea of such an engagement as futile. The implication is that the Sri Lankan conflict does not lend itself to the kind of analysis applied to the sectarian strife in Ireland or Basque separatism in Spain. In this gesture, Young follows Ondaatje into the Orientalist universe, wherein conflicts in the South are deemed beyond the reach of political discourse, accessible only as "trauma." Other critics have

---

8 Robert Young, "Terror Effects," in *Terror and the Postcolonial*, ed. Elleke Boehmer and Stephen Morton, West Sussex: Wiley-Blackwell, 2015, pp. 307–28.

9 Ibid., pp. 323, 156–7.

similarly drawn on literary trauma theory to highlight Ondaatje's treatment of trauma "that so often blights the existence of many postcolonial subjects."[10]

The idea that there is something ineffable about Eastern political culture, that it cannot be apprehended through Western categories, is a familiar trope in postcolonial theory. In praising *Anil's Ghost* along these lines, critics like Young assimilate the novel into the postcolonial canon while eschewing concerns of social origins and political forces. These commentators are right to recruit Ondaatje into the project of postcolonial theory. But they are mistaken to suggest that this approach enables a deeper comprehension of the human costs of Sri Lanka's turmoil. The novel, in fact, fails precisely on the grounds on which critics announce its success—the recognition of its characters' agency as well as the recovery of forms of political understanding that have been buried under the weight of Western modernity and that reveal the true nature of the conflict. More to the point, not only does Ondaatje fail to offer a new, indigenous framework that might replace the Western one; what he actually offers are several quite conventional Orientalist constructions of the "inscrutable East."

Indeed, the two failures are connected. Ondaatje's inability to appreciate his characters' motivations—the reasoning behind their choices—as well as his slide into Orientalism, are two sides of the same coin. Social agency is a form of action that does not blindly reproduce social roles. Rather, it is action undertaken with a consciousness of the *context* in which people are located, and it is intimately connected to *reflection* on one's social situation. As a result, it is impossible to understand someone's action, their agency, without due consideration to their context. That is exactly what the examination of causation, history, interests and constraints seeks to achieve—and what Ondaatje evacuates from his narrative. The result is not only that he makes his characters' motivations and solidarities quite mysterious, but also that he ends up flattening the political landscape in which they function. Sri Lanka no longer

---

10 Burrows, "Heterotopic Spaces," p. 162. While Burrows draws on trauma theory in the works of Lawrence Langer, Shoshana Felman, Dori Laub, Saul Friedman and Dominick LaCapra, as well as Kali Tal and Cathy Caruth, in her analysis of the novel, she claims that the theorizing of trauma has remained "bound up in the privileges of whiteness" and silent on the experience of the kind of postcolonial trauma that Ondaatje represents.

emerges as a nation with specific social classes, political conflicts or
historical dilemmas that his characters are trying to navigate. Instead, it
is hypostatized as an abstract "other" of the West. Thus, the same meta-
physical maneuver that strips his actors of the context for their actions
also creates a quintessentially Orientalist Sri Lanka. The suppression
of agency and the slide into Orientalism go together. The final chapter of this book offers another instance of a literary text also set in
modern Sri Lanka, A. Sivanandan's *When Memory Dies* (1997),[11] but
one that presents a sharp contrast in its treatment of postcolonial history
and agency. In order to understand the divergent fortunes of these two
works, some basic facts about the historical context are in order.

The Context

Sri Lanka was torn by civil war for over two decades. The underlying
issues had to do with both ethnicity and economics. The Sinhalese, the
main ethnic group of this small island nation, comprise three-quarters
of Sri Lanka's inhabitants. The remainder of the population includes
Sri Lankan Tamils (about 12 percent), concentrated in the north and
east of the island; Muslims (about 8 percent); Upcountry Tamils (about
5 percent), primarily tea plantation workers from the hill country in the
south central part of the island; and a smattering of Christian Burghers.
The conflict is between the two largest groups, the Sinhalese and the Sri
Lankan Tamils, and is connected in important ways to the country's
earlier, class-based Marxist insurrections that took place in 1971 and
between 1988 and 1989. Both were the work of the People's Liberation
Front, and both involved only the Sinhalese segment of the population.
Staged primarily by rural Sinhalese youth, the insurrections were
grounded in a strong sense of socioeconomic deprivation, manifested
in extremely uneven industrial development and in rural poverty. The
first insurrection ended with a government operation that killed more
than 15,000 citizens; in the second, more organized insurrection of
1988 and 1989, a similar military crackdown cost over 50,000 lives.
Other than its heavy-handed military response, the government did
little by way of substantive reforms to address the issues raised by the

---

11 A. Sivanandan, *When Memory Dies*, London: Arcadia, 1997.

insurrections—except for one course of action that ended up fueling the interethnic conflict.

Rather than create more employment and educational opportunities for all, the government instituted programs that would benefit the majority Sinhalese population at the expense of the Tamils. The criteria for university admissions, for instance, were changed so as to reduce the number of Tamils and increase the number of Sinhalese. The disaffection caused by the new education policy became a major cause of Tamil militancy. But the seeds of the Sinhala-Tamil conflict were sown much earlier, and by the time of independence in 1948 the separate nationalisms were deeply entrenched. The Sinhalese used their numerical dominance to cast aside the goals of secularism and a pluralistic polity, in favor of a race-based nationalism.

Yet, in spite of their numerical preponderance, the Sinhalese political elite forged an identity as an embattled people protecting a religion (Theravada Buddhism) and a language (Sinhala) followed by a minuscule fraction of the world's population. From that perspective, the Tamils represented an intrinsic cultural threat because despite being a minority within Sri Lanka, their language (Tamil) and religion (Hinduism) were, and are, *regionally* far more powerful. Therein lay the logic for the flourishing of Sinhalese nationalism. As a result, in 1955 the country abandoned the two-language policy and adopted an official Sinhala-only language policy, and in 1972 Buddhism was enshrined in the constitution as the religion to be officially fostered and protected. Such institutional marginalization of the Tamil population, combined with the shrinkage in educational and employment opportunities fostered by the post-1989 reforms, caused the emergence of militant Tamil nationalism. The present state of hostilities has been fostered by repeated and often systematic attacks on Tamils during the riots of 1958, 1977, 1981 and 1983—attacks in which the complicity of the government has been only too evident.

The central Tamil nationalist demand is for a separate homeland, *Eelam*, carved out of the north and northeast, where the Tamils constitute a clear majority. The movement began to develop in the early 1980s, when several organizations claimed to represent Tamil demands. Eventually, the Liberation Tigers of Tamil Eelam (LTTE) emerged as the sole voice of the population, mainly by having decimated all other organizations. The LTTE, with its leftist ideology and organized

structure, became the central player along with the government in a
civil war that claimed some 70,000 lives and caused the displacement of
nearly 2 million people. Suicide attack was the main weapon used by
the LTTE against political, economic and military targets. Especially
during the group's early decades, such attacks had a high rate of success:
among the many people whose lives they have taken were two prominent political leaders, former Indian prime minister Rajiv Gandhi, in
1991, and Sri Lankan president Ranasinghe Premadasa, in 1993. After
several rounds of negotiations and ceasefire agreements between the
government and the LTTE, the LTTE was finally defeated in 2009 and
dropped its central demand for a separate Tamil state in favor of a
federal solution.

Ghostly Histories

Set against this backdrop, *Anil's Ghost* follows the story of Anil Tissera,
a US-based forensic pathologist employed by the UN. Teaming up with
a state-employed archaeologist, Sarath, she returns to her homeland of
Sri Lanka on an assignment to investigate possible human rights violations by the government. They discover a skeleton at a site to which
only government workers had access, thus pointing to abuse and a
cover-up. It then becomes Anil's mission to establish the identity and the
history of the skeleton, which would serve as evidence of systemic
human rights violations.

Anil, a woman with a man's name, displays a kind of certitude and
passion in her work that is supposedly masculinist. Even as Sarath
works with her, he rejects her sense of purpose and tries to both alert her
to the political minefield they are navigating and also deflate her ethical
drive to find evidence for criminal wrongdoing. For Sarath, the situation
in Sri Lanka is too complex for ethical grandstanding by anyone, but he
especially objects to Anil's "positivist" stance, given her outsider status
in the country. Sarath succeeds little in deterring Anil from her mission.
It thus falls on Palipana, Sarath's former teacher, an exile in every sense
of the term, to challenge Anil's worldview.

Palipana offers a contrast to Anil's faith in scientific methodology and
the social value of evidence. He is an epigraphist who, after earning the
highest professional accolades, turned away from academia because

there was no place in that arena for his kind of knowledge. Through what we are given to understand as a non-Western epistemology, Palipana challenges the Western forms of knowledge that Anil upholds. His initial publications, we learn, questioned European notions of the East that treated "Asian history as a faint horizon where Europe joined the East." In contrast, he construed Europe itself as simply a "land mass on the end of the peninsula of Asia."[12] But he was not content with nationalist histories that merely questioned the *content* of Western history; he proceeded to reject the very *form* of established historiography. From being a meticulous researcher for whom every piece of archaeological data had to be reconfirmed, every carving drawn and redrawn, he moved on to produce the kind of work that made the discipline shun him for not maintaining minimal professional standards. It began with his publication of a series of interpretations of rock graffiti that illuminated political undercurrents in sixth-century Sri Lanka. His work initially stunned the academic establishment both at home and abroad for its brilliance. Later, however, a group of historians discovered a complete lack of evidence for his study. The runes he had cited could not be located; the textual evidence on which he had supposedly built was simply nonexistent. His work led to professional denunciation, reminding us that "forgery by a master always meant much more than mischief, it meant scorn."[13] Yet, from another point of view, he had simply outgrown the necessity of disciplinary methodology and was able to intuit what to him was the truth:

> It seemed to others he had choreographed the arc of his career in order to attempt this one trick on the world. Though perhaps it was more than a trick, less of a falsehood in his own mind; perhaps for him it was not a false step but the step to another reality, the last stage of a long truthful dance . . . He approached runes not with a historical text but with the pragmatic awareness of locally inherited skills. His eyes recognized how a fault line in a rock wall might have insisted on the composure of a painted shoulder . . . And he began to see as truths things that could only be guessed at. In no way did this feel to him like forgery or falsification . . . The point was not that he would ever be

---

12 Ondaatje, *Anil's Ghost*, p. 79.
13 Ibid., p. 82.

proved wrong in his theories, but that he could not prove he was right.[14]

Palipana, as one commentator remarks, is a "fictional subaltern studies hero."[15] He has transcended the limits of conventional historiography and embraced an epistemology rooted in local knowledge that makes its own claim to truth. His connection with a decidedly Eastern worldview is highlighted in other, even less subtle ways. While Palipana might have been banished from academia, he also chooses to exile himself from the civilized world altogether, in line with older sects of Eastern mystics. Nurturing his orphaned niece, he pursues a deeply austere life in the "grove of ascetics." All this stands in stark contrast to Anil's unrooted existence, free of sustained attachments.

Through the contrasting portrayals of Anil and Palipana, the novel highlights what, for its author, are two fundamentally distinct perspectives, two divergent modes of engagement with the world. The immediate occasion that foregrounds their respective approaches is the question of reconstructing the skull of the skeleton that Anil and Sarath discovered at a restricted site. Because their finding potentially implicates the state, Anil and Sarath have few institutional resources at their disposal to conduct the investigation. Given the circumstances, Sarath takes Anil to see his old mentor, Palipana, seeking his aid in their quest to reconstruct the skeleton's identity. After all, Palipana was a master of reconstructing lost and forgotten artifacts of civilization. This meeting is the occasion for both Anil and Palipana to learn of each other's expertise and to discover much mutual respect (although there is a clear authorial bias toward one of them).

Sarath informs Palipana how Anil, using "contemporary methods," can determine a skeleton's exact age. As Palipana is curious to understand better, Anil explains:

"You put the cross-section of bone under a microscope. It's got to be one-tenth of a millimeter—so you can see the blood-carrying canals. As people get older, the canals, channels really, are broken up, fragmented, more numerous. If we can get hold of such a machine, we can guess any age that way."

---

14 Ibid., pp. 81–3.
15 Burton, p. 44

"Guess," he [Palipana] muttered.

"Five percent margin of error. I'd guess that the person whose skull you inspected was twenty eight years old."

"How certain . . ."

"More certain than what you could know feeling the skull and the brow ridges and measuring the jaw."

"How wonderful." He turned his head to her. "What a wonder you are."[16]

Since Anil does not, in this situation, have access to her "contemporary methods," it is now Palipana's turn to reveal his expertise in the quest for the skull's identity. He does that by telling them of the ancient practice of "Netra Mangala," a highly ritualized practice of painting the eyes of a holy statue. Drawing on his scholarship, Palipana observes: "Coomaraswamy points out that before eyes are painted there is just a lump of metal or stone." But after this act, "*it is thenceforward a God*."[17] He then mentions a fine practitioner of this art who could help with the reconstruction of the skull. Anil is quite taken by the description of the ancient practice as well as by the fact that kings patronized and rewarded the artisans. Anil, we are meant to understand, values knowledge and certainty regardless of their origin. Palipana may appreciate the worth of certain forms of knowledge, but he rejects Anil's comforting faith in the quest for truth. Thus, even as Anil expresses appreciation of the kings' valuation of the artisans, Palipana reminds her that

"kings also caused trouble in those days . . . Even then there was nothing to believe in with certainty. They still didn't know what truth was. We never had the truth. Not even with your work on bones."

"We use the bone to search for it. 'The truth shall set you free.' I believe that."

"Most of the time in our world, truth is just opinion."[18]

The above exchange encapsulates the opposition in which the novel is centrally invested. Anil represents a commitment to objective knowledge

---

16 *Anil's Ghost*, pp. 95–6.
17 Ibid., p. 97.
18 Ibid., p. 102.

based on Western epistemologies, with its unquestioned reliance on science and technology. Palipana, on the other hand, while not necessarily averse to the benefits of technology, summarily rejects the possibility of objective knowledge. Having chosen to rely more on traditional forms of knowledge, he prefers to embrace the contingency of truth claims. Through its characters, the narrative thus constructs a classic Orientalist East/West binary.

Since the narrative's central investment is in the Orientalist dualism of East and West, it proceeds to dismiss and deny the oppositions and the conflicts *within* the East. Even as the civil war in Sri Lanka constitutes the setting of the novel, it remains uninterested in the history of the conflict, the material contexts of its origin, and the political dynamics at play. But the politics of the novel are not merely a disengagement with the political, as some critics have contended. The disengagement extends only to the actual history of oppression that has sustained the war, while the narrative is positioned to *implicitly legitimize the state*. By depicting an oppressive state in a favorable light and denying agency to local actors, the narrative rejects the possibility of a historicized reading of a postcolonial setting that recognizes systems of oppression as well as the struggles of ordinary people. Yet both the novel and its critics have largely steered away from a situated political reading and instead reinforced a statist perspective.

The epistemic dualism in the characterization of Anil and Palipana underwrites their approach to the war. While the novel certainly remains sympathetic to Anil, if not her philosophical and life positions, it unambiguously privileges Palipana's choices and beliefs over Anil's. I would contend that the positions represented by *both* Palipana and Anil are questionable, and that the novel rejects the possibility of alternative. We must now ask how the two positions translate politically. Anil's perspective on the conflict in Sri Lanka is rooted in human rights discourse. By turning bodies into "representatives of race and age and place,"[19] she seeks to discover patterns that can identify both victimizers and victims. It is because of this faith in the value of her work that she makes it her mission to discover the identity of "Sailor," the name that she and Sarath give to the skeleton they find in the site accessible only to state workers. Since it is a truism in her field that "you could not find a suspect until

19 Ibid., p. 55.

you found the victim,"[20] she believes that the discovery of Sailor's identity would help establish a pattern of human rights abuses by the state.
At times, the brutality and the sheer scale of violence would make her
question the worth of her work. Her findings "would be reported, filed
in Geneva, but no one could ever give meaning to it."[21] She would also
wonder if establishing the single case of Sailor would change anything,
as he was "a victim among thousands." It is at this point that she reminds
herself of the words of her American teacher: "One village can speak for
many villages. One victim can speak for many victims."[22]

It is not merely her own doubts about the efficacy of her work that
plague Anil, for her colleague Sarath also repeatedly deflates the intrinsic value that she attaches to her work. His is a double-pronged critique
of Anil. For Sarath, the Sri Lankan political landscape is simply too
complex for Anil's juridical methods to work. It is "not like Central
America," he tells her. "The government was not the only one doing the
killing. You had, and still have, three camps of enemies . . ." In this
scenario, he warns Anil, "there is no hope of affixing blame."[23] Sarath
questions not just Anil's methodology but also her "outsider" status in
the country: "I'd believe your arguments more if you lived here," he said,
"'you can't just slip in make a discovery and leave.'"[24] It is Palipana,
however, who represents the greatest challenge to Anil's position. Anil's
basic fact-finding mission in quest of truth is a misguided one for Palipana because for him such truths do not exist.

Palipana has little to *overtly* offer concerning the political landscape
of Sri Lanka. He does not take any position on the conflict. Indeed, a
clear political stand would undermine the portrait of a man who, we are
given to understand, has transcended politics. His only connection to
the civil war is his niece, the daughter of his murdered sister and
brother-in-law—a child whom he rescued from an orphanage and raises
as his own. Since Palipana represents the kind of wisdom privileged by
the novel, his political stance is instructive. While he does save his
severely traumatized niece and nurse her back to emotional health, he is
completely unable or unwilling to nurture her social consciousness. She

---

20 Ibid., p. 176.
21 Ibid., p. 55.
22 Ibid., p. 176.
23 Ibid., p. 17.
24 Ibid., p. 44.

lives a secluded life with him. Moreover, after his death, we are told, she just "went into the forest."[25] Seemingly, therefore, the only form of worthwhile engagement is a profound human connection, but one that is divorced from society. It is unclear what kind of social vision, if any, Palipana's mode of engagement upholds.

The novel seeks to offer a study in contrasts between Anil, on the one hand, and Sarath and Palipana, on the other. Nevertheless, the immediate differences notwithstanding, there is an *underlying similarity* among the three positions. The fundamental commonality is that all three maintain a stance of political disengagement. In Anil's case, despite her commitment to the discovery of truth, she displays no interest in or involvement with contextual specificity. She travels from one strife-ridden part of the world to another, conducting her work of victim identification with little investment in the lives and struggles of the people who are the subject of her work. At times, Anil voices a bland, generalized repudiation of state terror: "When I was in Central America there was a villager who said to us: When soldiers burned our village they said this is the law, so I thought the law meant the right of the army to kill us."[26] There are no contextual details regarding the particular conflict, the response or resistance of the people, the kind of state. The reader does not even learn which country in Central America Anil is referring to. In her construction of a world where powerless people are routinely brutalized, historical specificities are rendered inconsequential. Instead, in her empathy with victims, she focuses on affect: "She saw that those who were slammed and stained by violence lost the power of language and logic. It was the way to abandon emotion, a last protection for the self."[27]

Sarath criticizes Anil for being unanchored, for having a metropolitan sensibility oblivious to local actualities. Sarath's own reading of the conflict in Sri Lanka is closer in spirit to Palipana's: he remains politically disengaged from a war he deems irrational. The reality of which he is acutely aware, however, is how the war makes everyone vulnerable. He repeatedly warns Anil that she is treading a minefield that cannot possibly lead to any answers, because there are none to be had. Ultimately,

---

25 Ibid., p. 107.
26 Ibid., p. 44.
27 Ibid., pp. 55–6.

even as he is critical of Anil, his position is not very different from hers. He may be more knowledgeable about the factual aspects of the political landscape, but, like her, he does not concern himself with questions of justice or power or resistance. Instead, for him, "the reason for war was war."[28] He identifies the three forces in the civil war as Tamil separatism, the "insurrection of the insurgents"[29] and state counterterrorism. While the Tamils and the state are well-known actors, Sarath's take on the insurrection remains elusive. Much like Anil's "Central America," the insurrection is not explained. Sarath adopts a neutral stance in which all guilt is shared: "'Now we all have blood on our clothes."[30]

Palipana, as discussed earlier, is portrayed as having transcended politics and turned to a mystic life in the "grove of ascetics." But in an arena that is politically fraught, an apolitical stance usually hides a very problematic politics. In Palipana's case, we know, for instance, that he was a nationalist and the "main force of a pragmatic Sinhala movement."[31] Even though the novel does not care to connect these two facts, a significant connection resides there. In the Sri Lankan political landscape, with its history of institutionalized discrimination against its minority Tamil population, a Sinhalese nationalism is, in its most charitable form, an exclusionary ideology. In actuality, given that the Sinhalese comprise the overwhelming majority, that they wield state power, and that they have an established history of persecuting the Tamil minority, this ideology incorporates aspects of fascism. Sinhalese nationalism is no different from ideologies of Hindu nationalism in India or anti-Islamic nationalism in the UK.

Other facts about Palipana's life uncritically position him on the conflict's Sinhalese side. His brother was a monk, and it is known that monks played a key part in the escalation of fight against the Tamils. Yet again, this is not something the text engages with. It does tell us, however, that the brother had been murdered in the civil war, and although doubts are raised as to the identity of his murderers, it is clearly signaled that Tamil fighters were responsible. Nor is this the only murder that Palipana had to deal with. His sister and her husband, too, were

---

28 Ibid., p. 43.
29 Ibid., p. 42.
30 Ibid., p. 48.
31 Ibid., p. 79.

murdered—in the presence of their twelve-year-old daughter. Once
again, though implicit, it is clear who would have been responsible. True
enough, the killing of Sinhalese civilians by Tamil fighters is certainly
historically plausible. But within a politically fraught scenario, when
only one side's victimization is represented sympathetically, the politics
of the text must relinquish claims of neutrality.

The contradictions in these supposed objective portrayals of violence
are exemplified in yet another character: Sarath's brother, Gamini, an
emergency room doctor who works with victims of the civil war. He is
consumed by his vocation to the extent that he is unable to have any
meaningful personal relationships. His is a voice that the novel privileges:

> Fifty yards away in Emergency he had heard grown men scream for
> their mothers as they were dying. "Wait for me!" "I know you are
> here!" This was when he stopped believing in man's rule on earth. He
> turned away from every person who stood up for war or the principle
> of protecting one's land, or pride of ownership, or even personal
> rights. All of those motives ended up somehow in the arms of careless
> power. One was no worse and no better than the enemy. He believed
> only in the "mothers sleeping against their children, the great sexual-
> ity of spirit in them, the sexuality of care."[32]

If Gamini echoes the novel's generalized condemnation of violence, he
also reflects its ingrained contradiction by laying claim to an apolitical
stance and reflecting a complicity in the dominant power structures.
Thus, when Gamini learns of the nature of Anil's mission in the country,
he is severely critical:

> "It's the wrong time for unburials. They don't want results. They're
> fighting a war on two sides now, the government. They don't need
> more criticism."
>   "I understand that," Sarath said.
>   "But does she?" Gamini paused . . . "these guys who are setting off
> the bombs and who the Western press calls freedom fighters . . . And
> you want to investigate the *government*?"[33]

---

32 Ibid., p. 119.
33 Ibid., pp. 132–3.

In response to Gamini, Sarath does point out that innocent Tamils are being killed as well. Given Gamini's forceful denunciation of Anil's investigation of the state, this is a perfunctory nod to the other side, and it is met with a noncommittal response from Gamini: "We're all fucked, aren't we . . . Just no more high horses please. This is a war on foot."[34]

Critics of the novel commend the stand-alone graphic vignettes of extraordinary violence as depictions of trauma. What goes unremarked in the novel's critical reception is that in these depictions, the perpetrators are invariably either the Tamil separatists or the anti-government protestors (i.e., the Marxist "insurrectionists"). Counterinsurgency operations by the state are barely represented and, when mentioned, are swiftly followed by broad generalizations in which everyone is deemed an equal culprit. Thus, right after mentioning the two unauthorized detention centers in Colombo where individuals are tortured for the purpose of acquiring information, Sarath moves on to a generalization that is supposed to be profound but is actually vacuous in its inability to relate to the political scenario: "I wanted to find one law to cover all of living. I found fear."[35]

At one point, Gamini is abducted by LTTE activists and taken to their camp because they need doctors to care for their wounded comrades. The placement of a central character in the midst of a political group already cast as "terrorist," a group allegedly unfit for further analysis or understanding, could have been used as an occasion for challenging the discourse of statist terrorism. Instead, yet again the ruminations of a sympathetic character are tired, unanchored condemnations, perfectly in tune with the state's framing of terrorism: "He [Gamini] had to keep reminding himself who these people were. Bombs on crowded streets, in bus stations, paddy fields, schools had been set by people like this."[36] The period during which Gamini lives and works with the LTTE offers an opportunity for the narrative to explore the perspective of the Tamil separatists, to examine their motivation and rationale through his eyes. But Ondaatje makes no move in this direction.

Taking in the broad sweep of *Anil's Ghost*, we see that it could have been possible, even within Ondaatje's setup, to make the very

---

34 Ibid., p. 133.
35 Ibid., p. 135.
36 Ibid., p. 220.

distinctions that Young deplores. Recall that Young approvingly describes Ondaatje as taking the view that the different sides in the war are "indistinguishable." But it does not take much to glean that the three players—the Marxist insurrectionists fighting for economic justice, the Tamil freedom fighters primarily struggling for political justice, and the state brutally demolishing both kinds of resistance—are quite distinct. That all sides have adopted strategies of violence against civilians does not change their distinctive political characters. And so, a reading that refuses to engage with the politics in a politically fraught arena carries its own political consequences.

The novel's admirers in postcolonial studies praise the fact that it "makes no binarized assumptions about Tamil or Sinhala sides of the civil war."[37] This, however, is far from the case. The contradiction in Palipana and Gamini's stance—the proclamation of a neutral perspective while hewing to the dominant state discourse—actually captures the novel's own perspective. Ondaatje shows his hand when he avers that, for both the insurrectionists and the Tamil fighters, "the reason for war is war." In other words, the violence is an end in itself. But the description does not enable the text to escape or transcend the political, as Young and other admirers would have it. In fact, it only reinforces the dominant political position of the state, while erasing issues of oppression and injustice. The text whisks away the relevant context for the Tamils' and Marxists' resort to violence, and hence empties the movements of their political antecedents and aims. The addition of a perfunctory nod to state repression is not sufficient to alter the imbalance of the narrative

The implicit alignment with the statist position is thrown into especially high relief in one telling instance. In the course of the novel, Sarath is tortured and killed by law enforcement authorities because of his role in aiding Anil to expose extrajudicial killings by the state. However, in Young's interpretation, it is not the state but rather Anil who bears the responsibility for Sarath's death. Young castigates Anil for ignoring the superior nature of "local responses," and instead continuing with her investigative project based on Western notions of human rights, thereby becoming "responsible for effecting the death of her co-worker Sarath."[38]

---

37 Burrows, "Heterotopic Spaces," p. 167.
38 Young, "Terror Effects," p. 325.

That a postcolonial scholar would absolve the state—Sarath's actual torturer and killer—of responsibility is remarkable. From this perspective, a human rights worker is a greater culprit than a repressive state.

A twin move is at work in both the novel and the postcolonial commentary engendered by it: a rhetoric of transcending the political along with a tacit complicity with the dominant statist position. This perspective is consistent with the belief that resistance against structures of power, as exemplified by human rights discourse, is ultimately futile, if not counterproductive. Ultimately, the position amounts to an undermining of oppositional acts—of *agency*. The novel's decrial of Anil's human rights project is not the only instance in which it undermines agency, a move ironically typified by Orientalist historiography. There is a novelistic insistence on inaction, which Young approvingly interprets as "controlling yourself, detaching yourself, rebuilding yourself . . . and moving out of the normative realm of the social to establish a different relation with the temporality of the world beyond the human."[39] What Young applauds as the novelistic "voyage into the . . . space of . . . the post-human" may or may not work as individual therapy,[40] but it translates politically as a denial of the efficacy of all forms of collective agency.

The singular focus on death enacts a similar erasure of agency. Anil's parents are dead; Palipana's brother and sister-in-law are killed; he himself dies; Ananda's wife is abducted and, in all probability, killed; Gamini deals with death on a continual basis; Sarath is killed. The dominant trope for the civil war is death and decay. Repeatedly the images harnessed are of "disappearances of schoolboys, the death of lawyers by torture, the abduction of bodies from the Hokandara mass grave. Murders in the Muthurajawela marsh."[41] Death functions in the text as a silencing mechanism. It prevents an engagement with questions of power and justice, rendering the postcolonial subject voiceless.

After Gayatri Spivak, the death of the subaltern subject occupies a prominent place in postcolonial theory. While the privileging of the subaltern's death may be justified as a plea to draw attention to their plight, it can readily amount to a collusion with dominant historiography

---

39 Ibid., pp. 324–5.
40 Ibid., p. 326.
41 Ondaatje, *Anil's Ghost*, p. 157.

in denying agency and subjectivity to the subaltern. Another telling instance of this phenomenon in *Anil's Ghost* occurs in a narration of the assassination of President Katugala by a suicide bomber that fictionally recreates the actual 1993 assassination of President Ranasinghe Premadasa by an LTTE bomber. In the recreation, the narrative again exposes its political alignment with the state and its vilification of the resistance. Every detail of the final moments of the president's life leading up to the assassination are carefully constructed. Only the suicide bomber remains unidentified. Nothing illuminates who this person might have been, what *his* final moments were like, what cause compelled *him* to destroy himself along with the perceived enemy. No, in a pointed way, Ondaatje refuses even to name the perpetrator: he is referred to merely as R- and, following his death, by a few fragments of flesh. Not only is the subaltern unable to speak. The subaltern, we are encouraged to believe, does not even deserve to speak.

Conclusion

In a review in *The Nation*, exceptional for its critique of the novel, Tom LeClaire observes: "Sarath and Gamini criticize Western journalists for swooping into Sri Lanka, tossing off some reductive political analysis and leaving. I don't see the difference between that and Ondaatje revisiting his native land, observing victims, avoiding political analysis and then retreating to Canada."[42] I do think LeClaire makes a valid point. It needs to be noted, however, that postcolonial theorists would cite such a critique as exemplary of an irresolvable bind. The idea is that the postcolonial writer/critic is ethically bound to represent that world but, given their own location, will never quite succeed. Thus, for instance, while holding that the subaltern cannot speak, Spivak also emphasizes that the postcolonial historian must remain engaged in the recovery process. In *Anil's Ghost*, this dilemma is represented by Sarath's commitment to the truth but also by his knowledge that there may be no such thing:

> Sarath had seen truth broken into suitable pieces and used by the foreign press alongside irrelevant photographs. A flippant gesture

42 Tom LeClaire, "The Sri Lankan Patients," *The Nation*, June 2000, thenation.com.

towards Asia that might lead, as a result of this information, to new vengeance and slaughter. There were dangers in handing the truth to an unsafe city around you. As an archaeologist Sarath believed in truth as a principle. That is, he would have given his life for the truth if the truth were of any use.[43]

Sarath is certainly correct in identifying the perils of the commodification of news often perpetrated by Western media. Disengaged journalism, in which postcolonial reality becomes a consumable item, exacts a cost. Nevertheless, it is unclear why any and every search for answers would therefore be an exercise in futility. That notion, suggested in Sarath's ruminations, evinces a strong postcolonial assumption. Starting from a critique of reason as employed in the interests of colonial enterprise, it is deduced that reason itself is a problematic concept. Or, in this case, beginning by noting the distortion of postcolonial reality in shallow, context-free journalism, Sarath concludes that the search for truth itself may not be of "any use." The possibility of a rooted, historicized alternative for the exploration of postcolonial reality is rejected.

Anil's Ghost seeks to expose the perils of applying Western discourse— such as that of human rights—to postcolonial contexts like the civil war in Sri Lanka. The novel ends up, however, offering a portrayal of that time and place without embedding it in politics or history; rather, it simply highlights the deadly effects of war and legitimizes an oppressive state. The only redemption, the novel suggests, lies in an individualistic transcendence of social context altogether. Ironically, in so doing, the text and its subsequent celebratory commentaries deny agency to the postcolonial world, thereby reinstating the Orientalist historiography that they decry.

If Ondaatje's novel reflects the postcolonial bind, it raises the question of whether there are other literary depictions that escape this predicament. Part II of this book argues that it is possible to be faithful to the stated aims of postcolonial theory—recovering the agency of the colonized world—while also avoiding the pitfalls exemplified in writers like Ondaatje. The final chapter offers a more specific contrast to Ondaatje through the discussion of another text also set in war-torn Sri Lanka that illuminates the path not taken by *Anil's Ghost*: to show postcolonial

---

43 Ondaatje, *Anil's Ghost*, pp. 156–7.

actors not merely as objects, but as active subjects of their own history. But before turning to Part II, the next and final Chapter of Part 1 presents an analysis of a postcolonial perspective that while avoiding the trap of neo-orientalism, is still constrained by a conservatism that fails to meaningfully engage with the lives and struggles of ordinary people in the South.

4

The Neoliberal Logic in Indian Anglophone Literature

The postcolonial era in the global South has produced its share of exoticizing and Orientalist literature, of which Ondaatje's *Anil's Ghost* is just one example. By no means, however, has Orientalism been the only stream of literary production. Most of the post-Rushdie generation of Indian Anglophone writers—freed of the colonial compulsion to hone into cultural particularities that constitute the logic of the exotic—have chosen instead to explore universalist themes. Over the past decades, there has emerged a full and variegated body of work that presents the country's social conditions as part of a shared global process and refuses to view the local as unique or incommensurable with the dynamics of the West.[1]

This new direction in Indian Anglophone literature has emerged as the nation experiences the advent of neoliberalism and the decline of progressive nationalism. It is a period during which an upwardly mobile middle class has turned away from even the rhetoric of egalitarianism and embraced the global neoliberal order, with its promise of continuing economic advancement for their own class.[2] And even when

---

1 Some instances are Indira Sinha's *Animal's People*, Vikas Swarup's *Q & A*, Kiran Desai's *The Inheritance of Loss*, Amitav Ghosh's *The Hungry Tide* and Aravind Adiga's *The White Tiger*.

2 For an insightful commentary on the contemporary neoliberal order, see Arundhati Roy, *Capitalism: A Ghost Story*, Chicago: Haymarket, 2014.

bourgeois individualism has failed to deliver, it has continued to thrive on the ideology that there is no alternative to its market doctrine. Not surprisingly, organized resistance challenging this myth of inevitability and questioning the legitimacy of the neoliberal worldview has evoked only indifference, if not hostility, from the ambitious upper-middle-class strata that largely benefit from the system.

It is in this milieu that writers have chosen to focus on the social and political travails of the popular classes, portraying what critics call the "dark India."[3] As Lisa Lau and Ana Cristina Mendes have noted, instead of exoticizing aspects of poverty, these authors have given "voice and hearing to those who have not been able to partake in India's boom and prosperity."[4] The rooted and empathetic representations achieved by writers as varied as Amitav Ghosh and Aravind Adiga are underpinned by a universalist perspective. The literary universalism emerging from these writings, rather than being an offshoot of Western parochial universalism, is anchored in the exploration of postcolonial realities.

To partake in a universalizing outlook can, however, generate its own brand of conservatism. While it is certainly true that the refurbished essentialism of much postcolonial theory fails to comprehend the conflicts sweeping across the global South, there are other routes to the very same conundrum. The present chapter addresses two novels, Jhumpa Lahiri's *The Lowland* (2013) and Neel Mukherjee's *The Lives of Others* (2014), that embody this tendency: a universalization that, in fact, neither comprehends nor sympathizes with the social and political contradictions in contemporary South Asia.

---

3 See, for instance, Robbie B.H. Goh, "Narrating 'Dark' India in *Londonstani* and *The White Tiger*," *Journal of Commonwealth Literature* 46:2 (2011), pp. 327–44. Other instances of recent critical attention to social justice novels in the larger postcolonial context include Toral Jatin Gajarawala, *Untouchable Fictions: Literary Realism and the Crisis of Caste*, New York: Fordham University Press, 2012; Ulka Anjaria, *Realism in the Twentieth-Century Indian Novel: Colonial Difference and Literary Form*, Cambridge, UK: Cambridge University Press, 2012; Neil Lazarus, *The Postcolonial Unconscious*, Cambridge, UK: Cambridge University Press, 2011; Dougal McNeill, *Forecasts of the Past: Globalisation, History, Realism, Utopia*, Oxford: Peter Lang, 2012; Joseph R. Slaughter, *Human Rights, Inc.: The World Novel, Narrative Form, and International Law*, New York: Fordham University Press, 2007; Eleni Coundouriotis, *The People's Right to the Novel: War Fiction in the Postcolony*, New York: Fordham University Press, 2014.

4 Lisa Lau and Ana Cristina Mendes, "Authorities of Representation: Speaking to and Speaking for; A Response to Barbara Korte," *Connotations* 22:1 (2012/13), pp. 137–43, 142.

Both novels place at the center of their narrative what is commonly referred to as the Naxalite movement, which began in 1967 with a peasant uprising in Naxalbari, a village in northern Bengal near the Nepal border. Initially led by armed members of the Communist Party of India (Marxist), the movement later broke away to form the Communist Party of India (Marxist-Leninist) and has largely followed Mao's doctrine of "people's war." Begun in the countryside, it spread to the cities during the 1970s, attracting significant numbers of educated, unemployed youth energized by the peasants' struggle for rights and recognition. A brutal counteroffensive, empowered by draconian anti-terrorist laws, brought the first phase of the movement to an end. In both novels, the central figures are Naxalite militants. Their immersion in the movement, together with the fallout of their decisions on the lives of those around them, largely propels the narrative in both.

By placing an emancipatory movement at the core of their novels, Lahiri and Mukherjee also place the politics of resistance front and center. And yet, even though both novels are structured by the political actions of key characters, neither author is able to muster an empathetic understanding of their characters' actions. Moreover, the very idea of a life of struggle is made to appear at best quaint, at worst objectionable. In both novels, politics remains something imposed on the characters, an external, impinging force—but never a source of self-actualization. Instead it serves as a source of dislocation, self-doubt, broken relationships and disrupted lives. Each novel exposes its author's inability to perceive the political as an intrinsic aspect of the individual being.

Hence, while each of the authors locates a politics of resistance at their novel's center and views that politics through a universalizing prism, neither can fathom its attraction. Such an approach to emancipatory politics reinforces the neoliberal view that all resistance is doomed because there are no possible alternatives to the current order. And although both authors seem to want to escape an ethos where resistance is viewed as futile, neither is able to do so. As a result, neither is able to engage, much less express, the internal lives of their own central characters. Because of this, they remain limited, not just as postcolonial novels but simply *as novels*.

Commentary on the novels, while alert to other shortcomings, has glossed over this central failing. Lahiri's critics have pointed to a disjuncture between *The Lowland*'s characters and setting, resulting in a lack of narrative coherence;[5] a prose that can appear "naggingly synthetic"[6] or sprinkled with "banal profundities" that do little to deepen the plot or elucidate character.[7] While Mukherjee's critics have largely hailed his novel as "haunting"[8] and "masterful,"[9] it, too, has been subjected to critique for insufficient empathy for its characters. The common thread underlying these critiques is that they barely address how the treatment of the political connects with the failings of the two novels. For both authors, and for their critics, the politics of resistance—though central to the plot—remains an extraneous issue unrelated to the narrative dynamics. Together, the novels and their critical reception reflect a neoliberal consensus that has relegated transformative politics to the periphery of imaginative and critical consciousness.

Lahiri: Humanizing Neoliberalism

Prior to *The Lowland*, Jhumpa Lahiri's fiction engaged almost exclusively with immigrant angst in its many hues. But Lahiri does not like to be categorized as an immigrant writer, and *The Lowland* is her strongest argument against being thus pigeonholed. In the novel, partly set in Calcutta in the 1960s and 1970s, during the throes of the Maoist Naxalite movement, Lahiri steps out of her familiar sphere of immigrant fiction and frames the novel with a political movement of which she has no experiential knowledge.[10] Like Lahiri's earlier work, *The Lowland* made a splash; it was a finalist for both the prestigious Man Booker

---

5 Siddhartha Deb, "Sins of the Brothers: Jhumpa Lahiri's *The Lowland*," *New York Times*, September 27, 2013, nytimes.com.

6 Ron Charles, "Review: *The Lowland* by Jhumpa Lahiri," *Washington Post*, September 25, 2013, washingtonpost.com.

7 Randi Boyagoda, "Review: Jhumpa Lahiri's *The Lowland*," *Financial Times*, September 6, 2013.

8 Harsh Sawhney, "*The Lives of Others* by Neel Mukherjee," *New York Times*, December 26, 2014, nytimes.com.

9 Patrick Flanery, "*The Lives of Others* by Neel Mukherjee, Review: 'Masterful,'" *Telegraph*, October 14, 2014.

10 Maureen Corrigan, "Out of Lahiri's Muddy 'Lowland,' an Ambitious Story Soars," *NPR*, October 7, 2013, npr.org. Unfortunately, some critics insist on reading the novel within the paradigm of the immigrant narrative. See, for instance, Seyedeh Zahra Ghoreishi, "Postcolonial Hybrids," *Advances in Language and Literary Studies* 7:2 (2016), pp. 41–7.

Prize and the National Book Award for Fiction. And yet, as noted earlier, almost every major review of the novel has remarked on the stagnant quality of the narrative, the flat, detached characters, and the tepid pace. None, however, identifies the cause for this failure by an otherwise extraordinarily skilled writer. The single reason sometimes cited is Lahiri's inability to translate her mastery of the short story form into that of the novel. But her first novel, *The Namesake* (2003), does not suffer from this supposed shortcoming, so that explanation remains unconvincing.

Lahiri's failure in *The Lowland* is not one of style but of sensibility. She has little writerly investment in the ethos and spirit of the political culture she chooses to depict, exhibiting neither imaginative curiosity toward that era and its politics nor genuine sympathy for the cause that motivates some of her characters. Remarkably skilled at mapping the tapestries of emotions, Lahiri flounders here in the construction of compelling characters. Naxalism is the catalyst for the plot, and her characters' actions are often shaped by the movement, but because Lahiri herself cannot muster much sympathy for her characters, the affective is hollowed out of political meaning and the central characters denuded of a compelling structure of motivation. That failure is not general, however; aspects of the novel that are more distantly connected to the political movement do not fare as poorly. In fact, characters who remain untouched by Naxalism are delineated with the precision and care that have long been characteristic of Lahiri's fiction.

The novel starts out in the Tollygunge area of Calcutta in the 1950s, centering on a middle-class family with two little boys. The bright and sensitive brothers, Subhash and Udayan, share an unusually close bond. But the bond breaks in the late 1960s as Udayan becomes involved with the Naxalite uprising and Subhash finds himself unable to fully relate to the movement. Choosing his own path, Subhash leaves to pursue doctoral studies at a university in Rhode Island. He returns home after receiving news that Udayan has died, killed by the police for his involvement in the movement. While in Calcutta, Subhash meets Udayan's pregnant widow, Gauri, whom he then marries and takes back to Rhode Island. Their relationship never works, and Gauri is unable to connect even with her daughter, Bela. Subhash, however, proves a tender father to the girl. When Bela is twelve, Gauri moves to California to pursue an academic career, abandoning both daughter and husband. After decades of separation and angst for all characters, a certain secret from the past is revealed relating to Gauri's role in the Naxalite movement. In the end, there is a redemption of sorts for all characters.

At the heart of the novel are two killings: the assassination of a policeman by Udayan and his comrades, and Udayan's own subsequent execution by the police. In response to the brutal repression of peasant uprisings, the Naxalite movement in urban areas had adopted what was called the "annihilation program," targeting people in uniform such as police officers and paramilitary personnel. Udayan's involvement in the assassination, we are given to understand, was connected with this Naxalite strategy. He participated in planning the act and in procuring crucial information, he was present when the police constable was stabbed to death, and he painted a slogan with the blood of the dead man. We learn of Udayan's attempt at escape from the authorities, his haunting guilt for his action, his capture, and his family's bearing witness to his execution without trial by the police. The manner of Udayan's execution is consistent with the history of a brutal anti-insurgent operation that included on-the-spot shooting of recognizable Naxalite cadres.

While the reader is offered thorough representations of Udayan's militant act and subsequent execution, the novel is empathetically invested in only one of those events. There is a clear narrative distinction in the way the two deaths are treated. On the one hand, Udayan's execution by the police is presented as objectionable, even regrettable. But Lahiri does not dwell on the incident; she offers little to elicit the reader's sympathy for Udayan, nor does she encourage our moral outrage. And while we know that Udayan participated in the assassination of a policeman, the text does not enable us to relate to the motivations behind that act. Indeed, there is no depiction of the world or inner lives of Udayan and his comrades that could embed the assassination in a political and emotional framework. On the other hand, and in sharp contrast, the policeman is located in an identifiable and sympathetic milieu. Prior to his death, we're given an intimate portrait of him as father to a young child. He is implicitly someone for whom policing was merely a job. Lahiri portrays his murder as an unambiguously grievous crime. The manner of Udayan's own execution, on the other hand, is noted only in passing and elicits little beyond a rote condemnation of police brutality. The text's real investment thus rests in the authorial judgment of the policeman's assassination.

Lahiri portrays Udayan's connection with the Naxalite movement with neither empathy nor conviction. As part of his political training, Udayan leaves for the countryside for a month to live and work with agricultural laborers. Here was an opportunity for Udayan's author to dwell on the motivations behind his political beliefs, rather than merely allude to rural poverty as a sociological phenomenon. Through Udayan's experiences, the narrative could have explored what it means to live under grinding feudal oppression, to be forced into a subhuman existence for generations, and to pass such a lack of options on to one's children. The author might have woven into the narrative the everyday texture of deprivation, injustice and humiliation, thereby humanizing and contextualizing the militant peasant uprisings against feudal landowners.

In fact, *Lowland* rarely embeds Naxalism in the experiences of the characters. The brothers learn of Naxalite activities through the news or from fellow passengers on a train. This approach creates a cinematic effect—a camera zooming out from its focus on private lives to a city caught in the whirlwind of political agitation. Thus, there is mention of Udayan and his comrades attending political study groups and of their militant activism, but little engagement with the lives of those young people or with what drew that generation to sacrifice their safety and immediate interests to make common cause with the rural poor. In its measured authorial voice, the novel notes the draconian counterinsurgency operations, during which nearly everyone under age thirty was treated as a suspect and the state sanctioned rampant torture of young activists, as well as the disappearance and killing of unarmed prisoners. But again, what was it like to experience all this?

It is for his activism that the police kill Udayan, but Lahiri directs scant focus toward the texture of his moral outrage or the impossible courage that must have fueled that activist politics. The narrative does not attempt to fathom why and how someone like Udayan would be drawn to the movement. How did he and others of his generation transcend the middle-class insensitivity to the plight of the rural poor? What were their own experiences of a crippling social and economic system? In what ways did political organizing channel their energies? What was it like for Udayan to be young in Calcutta in 1969 and to know that he was part of a worldwide movement for social justice? What little we learn of Udayan's character surfaces through the memories of Bijoli, his grieving mother, who reminisces about his intelligence, his sensitivity, his concern for the poor and the weak. Yet Bijoli's descriptions of Udayan's characteristics do not acquire much resonance beyond the distraught recollections of a bereft mother.

The trope of a mother reminiscing about her revolutionary son inevitably evokes comparison with Mahasweta Devi's *The Mother of 1084* (1974). There, too, the young son was a Naxalite killed in counter-insurgency operations. The mother's bereavement becomes her reason to connect with the world of Brati, her dead son; for her, it becomes essential that his ideals do not remain mere abstractions. Through the mother's empathetic quest, Devi's readers connect with Brati and with the deepest motivations of a young, idealistic generation. By the end of the book, the reader shares the author's searing denunciation of Brati's state-sponsored execution. This contrasts strikingly, however, with Lahiri's treatment of her protagonist. Shorn of a similarly empathetic reading of Udayan's character and the movement, his killing becomes a simple parable of crime and punishment.

Udayan's death is not Lahiri's only novelistic indictment of the "crimes" of the movement. The author reserves even more severe judgment for Gauri, who escapes Udayan's fate and moves to the United States, where she begins life anew with his brother and her daughter. Lahiri thereby places Gauri in her own familiar territory of immigrant experience. But Gauri is unlike Lahiri's other immigrant characters, for there is little authorial sympathy for her. The move to another country produces in Gauri neither curiosity for the new nor nostalgia for the old. It is this pervasive indifference, a fundamental inability to connect, that becomes her punishment for having taken part in the Naxalite movement. Initially Gauri strikes the reader as a remarkably interesting character. In her life experiences, her interests, her relationship with Udayan, her flouting of all familial expectations through her marriage, and her nascent involvement in the Naxalite movement, one senses considerable potential for compelling character development. That promise, however, remains unfulfilled.

Once Gauri marries Subhash and moves to Rhode Island, her character becomes increasingly opaque. Her single distinguishing characteristic is a resistance to all relationships. The hardships of her earlier life notwithstanding, her descent into a stubborn, decades-long emotional withdrawal is almost inexplicable. In the end, Gauri's long, successful though austere life, free of sustained emotional attachment, could be ascribed to authorial excess and left at that, were it not for another failure on this character's part: Gauri abandons her twelve-year-old daughter, Bela, with hardly any explanation and pursues her own life without regrets. The reader is forced to judge Gauri for the cruelty, if not the intentions, of her act. And decades later, when the mother learns from her unforgiving daughter that, in contrast to her own emotionally barren life, both daughter and husband have thrived in their own ways, the reader cannot help but find satisfaction in this emotional justice.

Why does Lahiri reserve such judgment for Gauri? Udayan is executed by the state, but Gauri, too, is punished by her author for her participation in the Naxalite movement. Gauri also played a part in the assassination of the policeman by Udayan and his comrades; it was her job to observe and report back on the policeman's daily routine. In fact, it is through her eyes that we see a man walking his little son home—a father-and-son companionship both quotidian and precious. Gauri's guilt, though unstated, emotionally paralyzes her. Udayan confesses to Gauri that after what he has done, he cannot bring himself to parent a child, and since their guilt is shared, Gauri's life becomes an acceptance of that punishment. Although she does give birth to their daughter, Gauri finds herself unable to forge a bond with her child. Udayan's words thus become a prophecy imposed on them both.

As *The Lowland* unfolds, we see that the story revolves around the indictment of that one militant act in which Udayan and Gauri were both involved. It is about the long-term consequences of the political assassination of a man who was also a father. After such crime, what forgiveness? By making the assassination the source of the narrative's moral and emotional logic, the novel reduces the movement itself to criminal acts. Lahiri's depiction of Naxalism is largely in tune with conservative historiography—a selective rendering that casts the movement as well intentioned but wrongheaded, and devastating in the way it played out. Lahiri's choice to highlight and explore for literary reasons an act of Naxalite violence, while providing little more than a conventional overview of the act's context, has the effect of depoliticizing, even criminalizing, the entire movement.

Without doubt, Lahiri is entitled to her critique of the Naxalite strategy of "annihilation," the targeting of state officials. My issue with the novel does not relate to her position on a particular strategy; rather, it is that, while locating the Naxalite movement at the heart of her narrative,

Lahiri does not provide a humanized reading of it. It is entirely possible
to be critical of aspects of a movement, even of a movement in its
entirety, while offering a contextualized, intimate portrayal of its origins,
justifications and dynamics. Chapter 7 of this book offers such an example:
A. Sivanandan's *When Memory Dies* (1997), a novel that provides a scathing critique of the later-stage militancy of the Liberation Tigers of Tamil
Eelam (LTTE), while at the same time presenting a deeply historicized
and sympathetic portrayal of the driving force behind the Tamil movement in Sri Lanka. In that novel, the political is explored through the
intimate life experiences of the characters; it is never a state-constructed
backdrop. Such an empathetic investment in the historical process is a
characteristic sadly lacking in *The Lowland*.

Lahiri has remarked that her motivation for the novel was an incident
that took place in her grandparents' neighborhood in Calcutta. In front
of their own family, two brothers who were Naxalite activists were
summarily executed by the police. For Lahiri, the poignancy of the
incident is located in its familial core; the political is incidental. In
her rendering, the familial and the political may intersect at times but
usually run on parallel tracks; she is unable to appreciate how the political can dwell within the realm of the affective. In exploring the different
contexts of the incident, she had to acknowledge the political, but she
seems to have felt little genuine curiosity regarding the motivations of
the executed brothers.

Since the political is of limited interest to Lahiri, the politics to which
she subscribes are grounded in an easy, and easily available, critique of
Left radicalism. Thus, Udayan, grappling with the perceived futility of
the movement as well as his own imminent death, questions Che Gue-
vera's belief that the "revolution is the important thing and that each one
of us alone is worth nothing."[11] In the established tradition of Left-
bashing, Lahiri's character becomes aware of the sanctity of the individual
over and above any political process. The author remains oblivious to
the possibility that for a character like Udayan, the cause of a revolution
could be inherently personalized and its experience not in contention
with other aspects of individuality. Similarly, Gauri, confronted with the
failures in her own life, is drawn to the news of Naxalite leader Kanu
Sanyal's suicide. Her dark fascination with the leader's final act is far

---

11 Jhumpa Lahiri, *The Lowland*, Bloomsbury, 2013, p. 334

more compelling than her interest or involvement in the movement ever was. Ironically, it is only in encounters with imagined messages of defeat and loss that the political resonates meaningfully with Lahiri's characters.

In sharp contrast to Udayan and Gauri, Bela—a second-generation immigrant and hapless victim of a loveless marriage—benefits from the writer's abundant empathy. While Gauri's motivations in abandoning her daughter remain obscure, Lahiri portrays Bela's crippling suffering carefully. The author's remarkable skills in depicting the nuances of pain and its aftereffects are at play in Bela's quest for emotional anchors. Rejecting the pseudo-stability of a world that has failed her, Bela embraces the counterculture lifestyle of an agricultural apprentice, a farmhand, living in a commune-like arrangement, with an unstable income and strong commitment to organic living. Underlying her choices, claims the narrative, there is a "certain ideology . . . a spirit of opposition."[12] Such oppositional ideology, which often originates in private angst and manifests mostly in lifestyle choices, has Lahiri's blessings. Bela's parents, however, are censoriously judged for advocating another ideology that seeks a far more fundamental transformation of exploitative structures. Lahiri's empathetic rendering of Bela's life exhibits her literary strengths. Unfortunately, Lahiri's empathy is limited to characters such as Bela and the universe she inhabits.

Lahiri's earlier writings may have been circumscribed by a narrow range of sympathies, but there at least she was deeply connected with her subject. To have drawn the character of Gogol in *The Namesake*, Lahiri surely had to be truly invested in the travails of immigration. The greatest failing of *The Lowland* is that while the Naxalite movement is a more or less academic matter to Lahiri, it is nevertheless the primary catalyst for the plot. In an interview with National Public Radio[13], the author expressed her reservations when she referred to the Naxalites as "basically kids" attracted by an ideology with a certain appeal. The mature, responsible Subhash echoes the authorial position when he voices skepticism that an "imported ideology could solve India's

---

12 Ibid, p.224

13 Lynn Neary, "Political Violence, Uneasy Silence Echo In Lahiri's 'Lowland,'" September 23, 2013, npr.org.

problems."[14] Whatever the merit of such a critique, Lahiri could have chosen to express her perspective through a literary and humanistic engagement with the political. Instead she simply patronizes and dismisses the movement, an approach that resonates well with liberal readers who embrace multiculturalism and shun "extremist" ideologies. Ultimately, Lahiri remains confined by a sensibility invested in cultural knowledge unencumbered by questions of power and ideology. It is a neoliberal sensibility that crumbles under the burden of a subject outside its author's ambit of sympathy.

Mukherjee: Legitimizing Neoliberalism

Neel Mukherjee's second novel, *The Lives of Others*, shortlisted for the 2014 Man Booker Prize, has been widely acclaimed for its dark realism, the range of its narrative sympathies, its psychological nuance, its compelling storytelling, and, as A.S. Byatt observed, for the writer's uncanny "capacity to imagine the lives of others."[15] Mukherjee's is an ambitious undertaking that seeks to expose both systemic injustice and the structure of feeling that enables the system, as well as the anguish of and the resistance by the oppressed. He paints an impressively broad canvas, with microscopic portraits of both the urban and the rural landscapes where the Naxalite movement was born and, for a time, flourished. The artistry on the canvas, however, is rather uneven. Portrayed through the letters of the Naxalite activist Supratik, the rural scene is rich in ethnographic documentation but devoid of interiority, whereas Mukherjee's remarkable talents in the portrayal of the affective realm are on display in his depiction of the multigenerational Ghosh family in Supratik's Calcutta home.

Supratik's grandfather Prafullanath, the grand patriarch, has built a lucrative paper business, now run by his two sons. While they live under the same roof, the actual living quarters of the family members—the patriarch and his wife, each of the sons and their families, an unmarried daughter, the widow of a dead son along with her children—represents

---

14 *The Lowland*, p. 28
15 A.S. Byatt, "*The Lives of Others* by Neel Mukherjee Review—Marxism and Tradition in 1960s India," *Guardian*, May 14, 2014, theguardian.com.

their material status within the familial system. For instance, while Prafullanath and his wife occupy the comfortable top floor, the widow and her children are relegated to the very bottom of the multistory house, their status more akin to that of the family servants. Thus, materiality is a central, but certainly not the only, register through which the complicated family drama plays out.

Commonplace matters of illicit romance, sibling rivalry, maternal broken hearts, envious and plotting sisters-in-law, deceitful brothers, and anguished children constitute the multigenerational saga of the Ghosh family. Mukherjee is, however, invested in exposing a particularly dark underside of familial life. One manifestation of this is the incestuous yearning of an unattractive spinster for her brother, a yearning she artfully makes public through her music on the night of his wedding as their mother watches in horror and fascination. There are also sharp acts of cruelty toward a toddler by the older siblings, not simply because they are jealous of the child's stronger claim to parental attention but because they derive pleasure from their experiments. A ten-year-old despises her mother so strongly that she fabricates horrendous tales about her and relays them to her teachers at school. Yet another child is drawn to torturing animals and humiliating the indigent.

Mukherjee is a skilled writer and never overplays his hand. None of the depictions of betrayals and cruelties, large or small, ring false. They are entirely believable and in fact offer a corrective to the more prevalent borderline sentimentalism often present in the depiction of familial dynamics—an attribute that usually passes for novelistic realism. The narrative offers piercing insights into the deep but mostly hidden costs of the stunted emotional universe so pervasive in Indian middle-class lives. Indeed, Mukherjee's investment in the dark areas of interpersonal dynamics, which enables him to excavate deep patterns of emotional responses that shape lives and cultures, is commendable.

There is, however, a glaring lacuna in the narrative that has managed, for the most part, to evade critical scrutiny. The deficiency in *The Lives of Others* is not that its portrayal of the dark underbelly of social and familial life falls short in any way. To the contrary, the portrayal is incisive and brilliant. The issue with this novel is that it does not get past that underbelly. In fact, the compromised nature of emotional lives, beneath which lurks moral corruption, if not amorality, constitutes the *entirety* of Mukherjee's portrayal. Although critics have almost unanimously praised the complex treatment of the social and the domestic in the novel, I contend that, the depth of its psychological insights notwithstanding, the narrative remains deeply flawed.

The narrative is notably devoid of instances of generosity and compassion, which are as much the raw material of inner lives as those dark aspects so well drawn by the author, and there is little allowance for the crippling contexts often responsible for the implicit violence in familial relationships. And, if the depictions of interpersonal dynamics tend to be somewhat unidimensional, this is even more poignantly the case with the author's depictions of the political. Again, the novel has received much critical acclaim for its engagement with the Naxalite movement and its juxtaposition of misery and exploitation with affluence. It is, as one critic opines, "a graphic reminder that the bourgeois Indian culture Western readers so readily idealise is sustained at terrible human cost."[16] The novel certainly centralizes the Maoist movement and the interlacing relationships that connect the oppressed with those who benefit from oppression. Further, there is not one iota of romanticism or exoticism attached to the representation of the rural scene; the rich portrayals of ethnographic detail are offered with no shred of sentimentality. Nevertheless, the realistic representation of an oppressive world, as I will try to show, is undermined by a disengaged narrative stance.

In the novel's prologue, Nitai Das, a landless laborer, finds his way home in the scorching sun after fruitlessly begging all day outside the landlord's house in hopes of feeding his family, who have starved for five days straight. On returning home, in a harrowing act, Nitai murders his wife and five children before ingesting poison himself. Even as the novel proper begins with an intricate portrait of the Ghosh family in Calcutta, of their many family intrigues and heartaches, the prologue serves as a backdrop, an undercurrent of other lives and other realities. The juxtaposition of Nitai's brutal life and death with the lives and family fortune of the Ghoshes forms the first narrative acknowledgment of the systemic injustice that frames the world of middle-class domesticity.

---

16 Patrick Gale, "*The Lives of Others* by Neel Mukherjee, Book Review: A Departure from the Comfy Indian Novel That Both Shocks and Impresses," *Independent*, May 15, 2014.

The more direct agent of narrative engagement with both deprivation and resistance is Supratik, scion of the Ghosh dynasty. The child of a prosperous family, he grows up amid both emotional and material security and enrolls in the city's most prestigious college in preparation for a successful life. But as for many in his generation, Supratik's young life in the Calcutta of the early 1970s takes a different turn. It was then that the Naxalite movement, started by landless peasants against their feudal lords, arrived in the cities, and it was the city youth who joined it in droves. Much like Udayan in *The Lowland*, Supratik is inspired by the idealistic battle against injustice and, to his family's chagrin, joins the movement.

It is not merely a corrupt system and the plight of the indigent that move Supratik. Like others of his generation, he rebels against the stifling domesticity of the Bengali middle class and its moral conscience, which lacked any reference outside the boundaries of its own class. His exposure to poverty, for instance, makes him cringe at the eating habits of his own family. And it revolts him that the rest of the family castigates some of its own members—his widowed aunt and her children—as a financial drain. In his rebellion against a corrupt moral and political order, Supratik joins the Naxalites and, as part of the training program, goes to the countryside to live and work with farmers and to organize them.

As discussed earlier, Lahiri's depiction of Udayan's experiences in the countryside is brief, sketchy and uncompelling. By contrast, the delineation of Supratik's life in the country among indigent peasants— offered entirely in the form of unsent letters written by Supratik and addressed to his aunt, the widow of his uncle, with whom he's in love— comprises a large part of Mukherjee's novel and is in fact detailed to a fault. The letters offer extensive descriptions of life in rural Bengal; the peasants' literally backbreaking labor, meager diet and spartan living conditions; the breathtaking beauty of the countryside; and the efforts of Supratik and his comrades to organize the peasants.

The choice of the epistolary form to portray "the lives of others" is not incidental. Supratik is young and emotionally immature, and although his feelings for his aunt run deep and their attraction is mutual, they share no real relationship. Thus, his letters, while highly descriptive, are lacking in reflection and display no traces of a deeper connection with his addressee. Compared to Lahiri, Mukherjee offers much more on the human and material conditions that gave rise to the Naxalite movement. But, as in Lahiri, the offering is devoid of the relational and the experiential. Supratik does not form meaningful relationships with the farmers, nor does he dwell on the inner world or experiences of those he tries to organize. The actual feudal peasant, though presented as an object of sympathy, remains a general category, never individualized, never possessing interiority. That privilege, it appears, is reserved only for the more identifiable city dwellers, not for others. It is understandable, then, that Mukherjee chooses the epistolary form to portray a world in which the burden of an impoverished representation could be placed on a particular character, rather than on the narrative itself.

On the other hand, there is a greater degree of interiority in the representation of labor unrest in the urban setting, even though these scenes also suffer from insufficient empathetic engagement. In conflicts between the Ghoshes' business interests and the rights of their workers, the narrative is under no delusion as to the self-serving, hypocritical position of the business owners. In one of the more lucrative paper mills owned by the Ghosh family, a worker loses his arm in an accident involving a factory machine. After paying for the worker's initial hospital care and offering sympathetic lip service, the Ghoshes fire the worker and hire a replacement. The narrative offers no justification for or understanding of the Ghoshes' actions, depicting them as motivated solely by their own immediate material interests.

What stands out, however, is that the narrative maintains the same ironic distance toward the workers who demand reinstatement of their injured colleague—an ostensibly objective portrayal of the resistance that exposes authorial biases and limitations. When their demand is denied, the workers use organized resistance to slowly ratchet up the pressure on management. After token strikes prove ineffective in making management relent, the workers conduct a *gherao* (a labor tactic of preventing management from leaving the premises until demands are met) against the manager, Ashok Ganguly. The ensuing conflict is portrayed thus: "Ashoke-babu remained imprisoned by this human cordon for fifty eight hours; his captors clearly worked on a shift-and-rota basis. At the end of the ordeal when Ashoke-babu collapsed, the men were still unwithered, shouting out their mantras with undiminished vigour . . . if the police had not arrived, the factory workers would have happily continued until Ashoke-babu died."[17] Ashoke-babu may not be a particular object of his author's sympathy; few characters in this narrative can claim such privilege. But he is particularized, a man doing his job and being persecuted by workers to the point of near-death, reminiscent of the policeman killed by Naxalite activists in *The Lowland*. In contrast, the workers are presented as a general mass, carried away by a seemingly mindless form of protest and callously heedless of the impact of their actions.

When the factory occupation comes to naught, the workers declare an indefinite strike, closing down the factory altogether. There are repeated references to the Communist Party of India (Marxist) being behind the workers' agitations there and elsewhere. The party is depicted as an agent organizing unionized workers in its own electoral interests, with the clear implication that the workers are mere stooges of larger political forces. As with the portrait of the peasants in rural Bengal, what is strikingly absent from this picture is a view of the events from the perspective of the workers themselves.

One character, Dulal, could have been a channel for such representation. Dulal is the son of the Ghoshes' family servant Madan; the family's regard for Madan led to their employment of Dulal in one of their factories. That favor notwithstanding, Dulal has become a union leader, someone who has irredeemably crossed over to the other side. We learn of the Ghoshes' dismay at this development, their indignation at the fact that someone who should have been grateful for their kindness has actually turned against them. But not once do we get to hear from Dulal himself. How did he feel about his father's lifelong servitude in the Ghosh household? How did he relate to his fellow workers? What motivated him to join the resistance? How did he navigate the expectations of his bosses, of which he must have been well aware, and reconcile them with his actual actions? To the Ghoshes he was a betrayer, but what were his self-image, his beliefs, his motivations, his anguishes?

No, Dulal is not humanized, and neither are his fellow workers. After a long time maintaining their strike, the numbers of workers marching outside the factory dwindle till they are "nothing but a thin raggedy slum" by virtue of their "self-willed impoverishment."[18] Unfortunately,

---

17 Neel Mukherjee, *The Lives of Others*, New York: W.W. Norton, 2014, p. 86.
18 Ibid., p. 87.

the narrative imagination expresses no interest or curiosity in how these workers, so familiar with material deprivation and the repercussions of insubordination, find the courage to carry out actions with such harsh consequences. Nor does it pause to dwell on the idea that the objective of the strike is not a pay raise or any immediate benefits, but rather the reinstatement of a fellow worker. Instead, the author's remark concerning the workers' "self-willed impoverishment" implies a pointless battle in the interest of dubious goals.

The narrative commentary on an exchange between Supratik and the domestic help, Madan, again upholds the conventional view that personal relationships should always be prioritized over generalized struggles for social justice. Madan takes it on himself to gently upbraid Supratik about his life choices:

> The world does not change, you destroy yourself trying to change it, but it remains as it is. The world is very big, and we are very small. Why cause people who love you go through such misery because of it . . .
>
>   Being kinder to one's near and dear ones—isn't that a bigger thing than doing good for the unknown mass of people?[19]

Supratik reminds Madan that for all his grandstanding on kindness to one's kin, Madan himself had been prepared to sacrifice his son, Dulal. Following Dulal's involvement in the strike, Madan had been prepared to work with the Ghoshes to punish his son in order to remain in his employer's good graces. Supratik also reminds Madan that it was at a time, following the closure of the factory, that Dulal and the other poor workers were unemployed and struggling to feed their families. Even though Madan is indeed guilty of colluding with his employers against his son, Supratik's attack on Madan is still cringeworthy coming from a privileged individual. Given his sympathy for the oppressed, Supratik should know that morality is not an absolute construct; for someone like Madan, the prospect of the loss of his employment is nothing less than an existential challenge.

But that is not the reason the authorial voice questions Supratik. It is something entirely different: "Supratik knows that somebody who is not

---

19 Ibid., p. 426.

a servant in their home can easily retaliate with the argument that Madan's advice to him, that one must pay heed to the private over the public, otherwise one is inviting disaster in, is coherent for both situations, Dulal's and Supratik's."[20] The message here is that the responsibility for the disaster caused by the strike—the loss of Dulal's and all the other workers' jobs—rests on Dulal himself. If instead of becoming politically active Dulal had remained loyal to his own father, and by extension to his father's employers, the disaster would have been averted. This passage reinforces Madan's advice that "one must pay heed to the private over the public, otherwise one is inviting disaster."[21]

By these means, the narrative commentary erases the Ghoshes' culpability for the strike and its consequences. Mukherjee may lampoon his rich characters for their moral failings, but he appears to simply decline to question the business logic that takes away the employment of a worker who loses an arm while discharging his duties. Nor is there any understanding or sympathy for the workers who organize against this injustice toward a fellow worker and continue to fight back, even at the cost of their own jobs. The author indicates no solidarity with such acts of courage. Instead, the reader is reminded that it is Dulal who is responsible for the workers' plight, because he dared to organize them, and that the workers' impoverishment is "self-willed."

Mukherjee's suspicion of the value of organized resistance reveals itself elsewhere, as well. Dulal is said to have sanctioned a "complete lockout of the mill"; subsequently, the workers are referred to as "lockout men."[22] It is common knowledge that a lockout is an act undertaken by *management* to bring about work stoppage or to deny employment. How does Dulal, a union leader, get to sanction a lockout? He does not. The author uses "lockout" as a synonym for "strike." In a novel seeking to centralize social unrest, it is telling that the author did not familiarize himself with the basic parlance of industrial conflict—yet another authorial slight, however unintentional, of the value of organized resistance.

Moreover, the narrative undermines Supratik's worldview by making him unworthy of the reader's empathy. He steals from the family in

20 Ibid., p. 425.
21 Ibid., p. 427.
22 Ibid., pp. 86, 87.

order to mobilize resources for the movement. But since the loss of a prosperous family's jewelry for a greater cause does not elicit much sympathy, that theft in itself is not the damning act. Rather, it is that Supratik needs to frame someone for the theft, and he chooses Madan. Later, Supratik wonders why he did not frame one of the family members instead. The glaring contradiction between his commitment to the oppressed and his betrayal of the one member of that class closest to him does cause him some disturbance. But it does nothing to undo the disastrous consequences unleashed for Madan, and it reinforces the narrative position that the ethics and morality guiding the politics of the oppressed cannot be trusted.

Supratik, like Udayan in Lahiri's novel, is murdered by the police in a counterinsurgency operation. But unlike Lahiri's, the depiction of police brutality here is detailed and vivid. There is no sugarcoating of a draconian state's crackdown on a youth uprising, nor any abstract sympathy for the law enforcement functionaries who carry out that mandate. In fact, the narrative cannot be faulted for shying away from any aspect of the gross injustices causing deprivation and powerlessness. The gruesome acts of murder and suicide by the landless peasant Nitai, the intricate portraits of feudal oppression and impoverished urban workers, the graphic descriptions of police torture of young activists: all these testify to a social structure unjust and corrupt to the core.

The issue with *The Lives of Others* is not that it fails to indict an inhumane system, but that it cannot envision anything outside of it. Having exposed the brutality of the social order, the narrative offers no redemption through either familial, communitarian or political counterforces. Noting the author's "nihilism," Amitav Ghosh takes the novel to task both for its failure to depict the warm and joyous aspects of middle-class Indian life, and for its stance on political resistance. In regard to the latter, Ghosh refers to the epilogue, which dramatizes a moment, forty years after Supratik's death, in which his only legacy is presented in terms of indiscriminate violence. A group of Maoist activists in the impoverished Indian state of Jharkhand manipulate the railway tracks in the dead of night to facilitate the derailing and devastation of a train carrying 1,500 passengers. The exchanges between the activists reveals that they owe their knowledge of this particular technique of derailing trains to the now-long-dead Supratik. Ghosh, taking exception to the import of the novel's epilogue, observes:

In other words, what Neel [Mukherjee] chooses to celebrate about Supratik's life is not the transmission of a spirit of resistance— something that is more than ever necessary at a time when the environment and the poor are being subjected to devastating violence in the name of "growth"—but rather a particular means of resisting: in this instance a technique of mass murder. This is troubling, for it was precisely the means adopted by the student-Naxals of the 1970s that doomed their movement . . . To endorse that nihilism – which is what the coda to Supratik's life suggests—is, to me, both incomprehensible and indefensible. It is the last thing one would wish upon those who find themselves compelled to resist the land-grabs and repression that are being inflicted upon them today.[23]

While I largely agree with Ghosh's critique, I do not believe Mukherjee "celebrates" or "endorses" the militant strategies of the Maoists. Rather, he condemns both their larger politics and their strategies. If Mukherjee sympathized with the cause of the Maoists, he would not have ended his narrative with the prospect of the impending brutal death and suffering of thousands of ordinary people, all brought about by the activists. While Mukherjee may be sympathetic to the inhumane deprivation and brutality that drives people to a militant politics, he believes all such politics to be a dead end.

In fact, the "nihilism" that Ghosh attributes to the Naxalites applies much more to Mukherjee himself. For Mukherjee, the work of people like Supratik and his comrades is always doomed to failure because of violent strategies and inevitable moral compromises. It is a politics that only ends up causing devastation, either through vengeful violence against oppressors and "collateral damage" to ordinary people, or by making the situation worse for the oppressed through strikes and other political actions. Mukherjee's is a bleak vision that, while recognizing oppression and injustice, rejects the notion that there can be any meaningful resistance or alternative to the order.

If Mukherjee's narrative vision were confined to comprehensive social and moral wretchedness, completely lacking in hopeful glimmers, it would qualify as a powerful dystopia. But that is not the case, for the

---

23 Amitav Ghosh, "Neel Mukherjee's *The Lives of Others*: A Review," *Amitav Ghosh* (personal blog), May 3, 2014, amitavghosh.com.

narrative does invest in a specific kind of possibility. In Lahiri's novel, even as some characters may be deeply flawed, there is an unambiguous moral center—the integrity of relationships—and such personal relationships are the source of hopeful possibilities. In Mukherjee's novel, however, that source has little power because of the pervasive and ingrained moral corruption that characterizes all relationships. The alternative offered by Mukherjee's narrative is thus a vision of individual success, untainted by either interpersonal or social dynamics.

That possibility of individual success is exemplified in Sona, Supratik's young cousin and the son of his dead uncle—a boy who, along with his mother and sister, had been relegated to the material and emotional periphery of the Ghosh household. The adolescent Sona, it turns out, is a mathematical prodigy comparable to the famous, largely untutored mathematician Srinivasa Ramanujan. Sona is an emotional recluse almost to the point of autism. But the parts of the novel that are devoted to Sona's lone pursuit in the world of numbers, his fortuitous encounter with a social pariah who too is a mathematical genius, and the discovery of Sona's incredible mind by his math teacher at a modest school constitute some of the most animated parts of the narrative. They are filled with possibilities so starkly missing elsewhere in *The Lives of Others*, and these possibilities are concretized in the first part of the novel's two-part epilogue. While the second epilogue lays out Supratik's legacy in terms of acts of terrorism by the deprived, the first defines hope. In that first part, Sona, who by virtue of the efforts of his math teacher was whisked away to Stanford University and nurtured there, receives the Fields Medal, the "Mathematics Nobel," at the young age of thirty.

This is a vision unable to appreciate how the success of an individual like Sona is never "a freak, a singularity, a flash in the pan,"[24] but must be contextualized within communitarian and familial life worlds. Still, there is a greater issue with Mukherjee's perspective. The best, or perhaps only, answer to the complex political, social and domestic dilemmas besetting an impoverished, postcolonial subject appears to be escape to the United States. That is the only imaginable setting where solace and nurture will be on offer. In fact, escape to the West is a hackneyed trope in mediocre postcolonial fiction. Even in real life, beset by material hardships, it is often conceived of as the only path to fulfillment. It is

24 Ibid.

unfortunate that a writer with otherwise-sharp critical sensibilities ends up embracing such an undiscriminating and commonplace resolution.

Then again, the authorial perspective has already rejected two other possible sources of resolution: the interpersonal and the political. Human relationships in this narrative, unlike in *The Lowland*, do not hold out much hope, because of their necessary failings and flaws. It is not coincidental that Sona, the sole source of hopeful possibility, is a solitary soul, unable to make emotional connections. This is a firm rejection of the relational; from this perspective, the only redemption available derives from individual talent, untainted by relationships. And the political, as discussed earlier, is equally strongly rejected as an alternative because it is characterized by moral corruption and is doomed to failure. As such, Mukherjee's rejection of both the interpersonal and the political forecloses on any portrayal of the possibilities inherent in the interconnectedness of the two spheres.

The novel's critical sensibility notwithstanding, the privileging of Sona's success amounts to a straightforward approval of neoliberal logic. There is a cogent critique of systemic injustices in the *descriptive* aspects of Mukherjee's narrative that sets it apart from a neoliberal perspective. However, the *normative* aspects that emerge from the narrative are aligned with a neoliberal worldview. The only source of hope and progress, in this view, is individual talent, which has little truck with the communitarian and none with the systemic. Sona's success and pursuit of happiness is the only possible alternative to all the ills that can beset the social and the domestic.

Conclusion

Lahiri and Mukherjee are part of a generation of Indian Anglophone writers who have steered the genre away from narrow investments under the shadow of colonialism, and toward expansive explorations of universalist themes. Both writers, however, subscribe to a universalism born of the dominant logic of neoliberalism. They reflect the ideological consensus of their era, which rejects the possibility of an alternative to the current regime. The writers choose to explore a period of socialist radicalism, only to then undermine the structure of feeling that fueled the reigning political energy of that era. They note systemic injustices but are unable to drum up any real empathy for the oppressed and are actively hostile toward organized resistance. And both narratives grapple with the militancy of Naxalite activism but ultimately remain captive within a perspective that effectively criminalizes the movement.

That "spirit of opposition" which Lahiri does endorse in Bela is characterized by lifestyle choices and an Obama bumper sticker, an "opposition" fully coopted by the neoliberal order. Mukherjee, for his part, refuses to grant any validity to even the angst generated by a consumption-oriented social order. Instead, he maintains equal ironic distance from oppressors like the capitalist Ghoshes and from the struggles of their oppressed workers. The ironic stance may seem to grant him an artist's "objective" vantage point, but it, too, is just as comfortable within the neoliberal order as is Lahiri's stance. Neither challenges the fundamental ideological premise that there cannot be an alternative to the present order.

The contrasting characters of Bela in *The Lowland* and Sona in *The Lives of Others*—the strongest recipients of authorial empathy—signify both a divergence and an underlying commonality in the narrative approaches. Bela's emotional universe points to Lahiri's faith in interpersonal relationships as the only arena of possible redemption. In a world that has supposedly moved past the illusions of collective struggles, Bela encapsulates a humanistic stance at peace with the neoliberal order. In Mukherjee's darker world, a pervading moral corruption contaminates almost all possible sources of redemption; thus, not only is resistance futile, if not immoral, but it takes place in a world where even human relationships are of minimal value. It is consistent with this stance that Sona, the one character who receives authorial empathy, is a recluse, unable to forge social relationships. But it is the character's mathematical genius—an attribute disconnected from social context— that offers the only generative possibility in the narrative. Through Sona, Mukherjee situates the only source of hope in *individual merit*: the legitimizing principle of neoliberalism.

PART TWO
The World in the Grain

5

Indigeneity as Myth and Message

If the four chapters of the first section examine the intrinsic limitations of the premises of postcolonial theory, this section highlights the possibilities and promises inherent in some central postcolonial literary texts. The texts I explore remain firmly anchored to their local contexts, but their commitment to forms of radical universalism flout the constraints of postcolonial theory. While all three of these chapters engage with questions of subject formation as it intersects with nations, nationalism and forms of militant resistance, the present chapter takes up the issue of indigeneity.

Indigenous studies emerged as a specialized area in the late 1960s and early 1970s, and its preoccupations have increasingly become central to postcolonial studies. Scholars of indigenous studies focusing on populations of original inhabitants in regions like the Americas, Australia and New Zealand, of diasporic indigenous communities as in Palestine, and of tribal populations as in India have explored the intersection of indigeneity with issues of colonialism, national formations, race, land rights and cultural identity. Much of indigenous studies is undergirded by a critique of development discourse that holds patterns of national economic growth responsible for the marginalization of indigenous populations. Indigenous people face onslaughts on their lands and ways of life in the name of an economic growth from which they do not benefit, thus generating what scholars of indigeneity have called a "development impasse."[1]

---

1 John Briggs and Joanne Sharp, "Indigenous Knowledges and Development: A Postcolonial Caution," *Third World Quarterly* 25:4 (2004), pp. 661–76, 661.

The familiar themes of the plight of marginalized groups within and by the nation, the critique of development, and the privileging of culture[2] have made the study of indigeneity the *"cause célèbre* of postcolonial studies."[3] This chapter explores the points of tension between the fields of post-colonial and indigenous studies, and makes the case that, their differences notwithstanding, a culturalist foundation common to the fields is a stronger unifying force. I offer a reading of a novella by Mahasweta Devi to highlight the limitations of a culturalist approach and to make the case for a materialist position on indigeneity grounded in culture and lived exper-ience. While the culturalist premise fails to address the genuine issues and dilemmas encountered by indigenous populations, the chapter concludes with a brief discussion of ecocriticism, a branch of postcolonial studies—that signals a rupture from the culturalism endemic in the discipline.

Spurious Opposition

The tension between postcolonial studies and the emergent field of indigenous studies is based on some substantive concerns but is primar-ily about disciplinary boundaries. Precisely because the preoccupations of scholars of indigeneity dovetail with postcolonial studies, it has generated the anxiety that indigenous concerns will be subsumed by the larger postcolonial field. Elizabeth Cook-Lynn, a proponent of indige-nous studies, points to the marginalization of the key issues of Native Americans in particular and of indigenes in general within discourses like postcoloniality. She contends: "For American Indians . . . and for the indigenes everywhere in the world, postcolonial studies has little to do with independence, nor does it have much to do with the actual deconstruction of oppressive colonial systems . . . Postcolonial thought in indigenous history, as a result of the prevailing definition, has emerged as a subversion rather than a revolution."[4] The disaffection

2 For an account of the state of the Native American studies discipline, see Jace Weaver, "More Light than Heat: The Current State of Native American Studies," *American Indian Quarterly* 31:2 (2007), pp. 233–55.

3 Bill Ashcroft, Gareth Griffiths and Helen Tiffin, *The Postcolonial Studies Reader*, London: Routledge, 2006, p. 214.

4 Elizabeth Cook-Lynn, "Who Stole Native American Studies?," *Wicazo Sa Review* 12:1 (Spring 1997), pp. 9–28, 14

with postcolonial studies among indigene scholars is rooted in the growth and aspiration of a discipline with a somewhat-different political trajectory than that of postcoloniality. The indigenous studies scholars saw themselves as less allied and more in competition with other reigning academic preoccupations like feminism, racial conflicts, immigration and calls for interdisciplinarity as the mode of addressing the multifarious issues with oppressed populations. For Native American studies scholars, the primary issue is of sovereignty for indigenous people, and that has little to do with the discursive subversion of dominant formations of race or gender; and because indigenous studies scholars have not yet been allotted proper *disciplinary* space within academia, they remain uninterested in interdisciplinary approaches. The aspiration of the field is to carve out a space devoted to the question of First Nation sovereignty, and to the study of native languages, land reform, the laws and treaties pertaining to the indigenous population, and the devising of "new epistemologies."[5] Further, indigenous studies scholars hold that this body of intellectual information and analysis should be organized by native scholars themselves.

Indigenous studies scholars offer a multipronged critique of postcoloniality illuminating that there is "nothing in that analysis for indigenous peoples."[6] In his discussion of why the postcolonial discipline is unable to address the issues of indigeneity, Jace Weaver claims that postcolonialists are primarily invested in the time *after* colonialism, and that the discipline remains indifferent to the question of internal colonialism within nation-states; he highlights what he views as a metropolitan sensibility of the postcolonial discipline that is disdainful of native cultures, silent on indigenous liberation struggles, and, via its poststructuralist critique, dismissive of identity as something "real, concrete, and centered."[7] For both Weaver and Cook-Lynn, the central issue with postcoloniality is that the discipline is grounded in anti-essentialism, a perspective that is in

---

5 Ibid.

6 Jace Weaver, "Indigenousness and Indigeniety," in *A Companion to Postcolonial Studies*, ed. Henry Schwartz and Sangeeta Ray, Oxford: Blackwell, 2005, p. 222. Robert Warrior is an exception to this broader trend; while sympathetic to the concerns of his fellow indigenous studies scholars, he argues for a robust engagement with some postcolonial theorists.

7 Ibid., p. 226.

conflict with the contending indigenous aspiration for sovereignty based on native identity.

Thus, while postcolonialists are viewed as dismissing the notion of a rooted identity as a relic of humanism, for indigenous studies scholars, the establishment of native identity is a foundational imperative. However, I believe indigenous studies scholars' resistance to postcoloniality, on account of the supposed incommensurability of anti-essentialism with native identity, is somewhat misconceptualized. Proclamations of the death of subjectivity by postcolonial scholars notwithstanding, the discipline is in fact very much wedded to the embrace of autochthonous identities. Both postcolonialists and scholars of indigeneity employ a culturalist framework to theorize the marginalized position of indigenous people. They read the oppressed position of the indigenous populations as resulting from the dominance of Western culture with its reliance on science. They claim that the scientific model of development, endemic to Western cultures, is detrimental to the interests and cultures of indigenous people. Both disciplines hold that the systemic marginalization of indigenous people stems from an aversion to ancient cultures. In this reading, the West, science and development are conflated, and all are guilty of cultural impositions on and marginalization of indigenous cultures. While it is true that until recently, indigeneity was not a central concern for the postcolonial field, the discipline has now clearly expanded to include indigenousness and indigeneity. Weaver's essay in which he takes issue with postcoloniality for its unsuitability as a paradigm for indigeneity in fact appears in an anthology on postcolonial studies.[8]

The keen interest in indigeneity by postcolonial critics is not surprising given the discipline's foundational stance grounded in anti-Enlightenment critique of development andthe privileging of marginalized groups. The inclusion of indigeneity by the postcolonial field as a necessary area of study among others, however, will not satisfy

8 Similarly, in the revised edition of her reader on postcolonial theory, Ania Loomba draws attention to the need for postcolonial criticism to engage with indigenous histories and struggles. See Gaurav Desai and Supriya Nair, *Postcolonialisms: An Anthology of Cultural Theory and Criticisms*, New Brunswick: Rutgers University Press, 2005; Bill Ashcroft, ed., *Postcolonial Studies: The Key Concepts*, London: Routledge, 2013; and Graham Huggan, ed., *The Oxford Handbook of Postcolonial Studies*, Oxford: Oxford University Press, 2013.

indigenous studies scholars who aim at the formation of their own discipline—one fully devoted to their specific agenda and whose principal if not sole practitioners would be indigenes themselves. The tension speaks less to intellectual differences and more to competitive aspirations, on the one hand, of a nascent discipline fashioned strictly along identitarian lines, and on the other, of an established academic field primarily invested in discourse analysis. The underlying culturalism of both fields, however, makes them birds of the same feather, even as they may like to fly separately.

Culture and Capital

The culturalist perspective shared by postcolonialists and scholars of indigeneity places the burden of indigenous predicament on a development model that is based on hegemonic Western scientific culture. They contend that the "ways of knowing the world and knowing the self in non-Western culture are trivialized and invalidated" by the dominant scientific model of development grounded in Western Enlightenment culture.[9] It is the fact of indigenous identity or its difference from mainstream culture, the argument goes, that relegates indigenous cultures to the periphery. In claiming a Western model of development based on science to be the central adversary of indigenous people, the culturalist perspective misidentifies the driving force of indigenous marginalization.

The contention that the dominant model of capitalist development is motivated by a fundamental hostility to indigenous cultures is not borne out by facts. The World Bank, an institution epitomizing the model of Western capitalist development, has, in fact, been increasingly engaged in the integration of local knowledges of populations at whom it aims its projects.[10] Proponents of the approach believe that local populations

---

9 Briggs and Sharp, "Indigenous Knowledges and Development," p. 664.

10 For instance, the World Bank describes its Indigenous Knowledge for Development Program, started in 1998, as a "response to clients, and civil society who called for a more systematic integration of the indigenous knowledge (IK) in the development process . . . its objectives include raising awareness about the potential use of IK in development, disseminating pertinent information, and integrating IK into Bank projects, and capacity building of local institutions." P. C. Mohan, *Indigenous Knowledge*

with lived experiences of their environments have developed a knowledge base that is essential for sustainable development. The trend is
notably instantiated in the World Bank's contention that it is necessary
to "learn about indigenous knowledge (IK) from . . . [developing] countries, paying particular attention to the knowledge base of the poor."[11]
World Bank literature on this "IK" framework lays out not just the
desirability but the necessity of integrating these knowledge systems
into the development process. It speaks to the effectiveness of IK, in
combination with the "empowerment of community groups," in countries like Mozambique, Nepal and Senegal in resolving refugee crises.
The literature highlights instances where traditional practices are rene-
gotiated by indigenous people themselves to efficiently facilitate drives,
such as the organization of a food distribution system, in ways that
modern technology could not. Their position is not just to take advan-
tage of the existing indigenous knowledge systems, but to "*protect* IK in
a way that fosters the further *development, promotion, validation, and
exchange* of IK."[12]

Now, the inclusion of indigenous knowledges by the emissaries of
global capitalism is certainly an instrumentalist move, and to the extent
that it furthers their fundamental economic agenda, it is part of a
general strategy to mobilize all available intellectual and material
resources. Put differently, outfits like the World Bank will adopt any
knowledge system, scientific or otherwise, as long as it advances the
goal of capitalist development. Because indigenous systems of knowledge in certain instances offer a valuable repository of information that
can be channeled for what's called sustainability (of capitalism), they
have embraced its utilitarian value. Contra culturalist claims, however,
this adoption shows that the motivating factor in dominant development models is not a hostility toward indigenous cultures, but global
capitalist growth. However, it is also the case that, institutional promotion of indigenous knowledges by institutions like the World Bank

---

for Development: Africa Region Findings and Good Practice, World Bank Indigenous
Knowledge for Development Program, Washington, DC: World Bank, 2001. The
program has a dedicated journal, *IK Notes*.

11 Briggs and Sharp, "Indigenous Knowledges and Development," p. 667.

12 Nicolas Gorjestani, *Indigenous Knowledge for Development: Opportunities and
Challenges*, World Bank Indigenous Knowledge for Development Program, Washington, DC: World Bank, 2000.

notwithstanding, such an inclusive approach toward traditional knowledges is not the norm. In fact, more often than not, indigenous
populations have little to offer to the trajectory of capitalist development, or constitute a hindrance in its path; therefore, such populations
are typically marginalized. But, note that the *driving* factor in the treatment of indigenous populations—inclusion or exclusion—is not
cultural. Rather, it is the logic of capitalist growth.

Instances of integration of indigenous systems of knowledge into
hegemonic Western institutions attest to the fact that the dominance of
existing power structures is not grounded in the "trivialization and
invalidation" of non-Western or indigenous cultures, as postcolonial
and indigenous studies scholars would claim. Rather, these power structures are robust enough to incorporate "other" perspectives and practices
within their own agenda of capitalist growth. Scholars of indigeneity
occasionally grapple with the question of whether cultural conflict is
indeed at the foundation of the marginalization of indigenous populations. In an article on "indigenous knowledge and development,"
geographers John Briggs and Joanne Sharp, after discussing the appropriation of indigenous knowledge by institutions like the World Bank,
arrive at the right conclusion regarding the reason for such institution-
alization of IK:

> Although there seems to be an implicit assumption in much of the
> literature that capitalism and Western science are inextricably bound
> to each other, it may well be that, if alternative knowledge systems
> offer potentially higher returns in capital than Western science, then
> capitalist interests will inevitably embrace such knowledges. Hence
> we have a possible explanation for the World Bank's recent interest in
> indigenous knowledge.[13]

The authors succinctly decouple science—the knowledge system that,
for postcolonialists, is at the core of Western culture—from capitalism
in trying to explicate the reason for the World Bank's embrace of indigenous knowledges. The reasoning here is that if institutions like the
World Bank were *fundamentally* invested in science and a scientific
worldview, it would rule out an inclusive approach toward indigenous

---

13 Briggs and Sharp, "Indigenous Knowledges and Development," p. 673.

knowledge. Their eager embrace of IK reveals that what really motivates them is capitalist growth, rather than a particular worldview. Of course, theirs is an instrumental approach where the "embrace" of IK will always be limited and circumscribed based on the extent of its utility. But again, even such an instrumental appropriation of IK reveals that dominant institutions like the World Bank are driven *primarily* by capitalist interests—not by an assertion of cultural supremacy based on science, Enlightenment values and the denigration of indigenous cultures, as the postcolonialists and scholars of indigeneity would have it.

If the postcolonial analysis of indigeneity is premised on an undifferentiated notion of "development" as responsible for the relegation of indigenous cultures to the periphery, it then follows a familiar trajectory: the elevation of cultural difference. Since the central conflict is posited in cultural terms—western versus indigenous—the recourse becomes a privileging of indigenous culture, or a discourse of historical difference. Without the necessary grounding in economic and political contexts, such an upholding of indigenous difference or indigenous cultures and traditions paves the way for the exoticization of indigeneity in postcolonial discourse.[14] It is reminiscent of Fanon's invective against the cosmopolitan intellectual who places "a high value on the customs, traditions and the appearances of his people; but his inevitable painful experience only seems to be a banal search for exoticism."[15]

While the World Bank's receptivity toward indigenous knowledge problematizes the idea of an *essentialized* cultural conflict between dominant capitalist structures and indigenous populations, the fact remains that there *is* a central conflict at work between indigenous and other oppressed people, on the one hand, and the interests of the dominant system, on the other. Indigenous people have been on the losing end of capitalist development, and their cultures are marginalized to the point of extinction. Their way of life, their traditions, their everyday battles must be foregrounded, but in a way that does justice to the lived reality of indigenous people without mobilizing it toward either dominant

---

14 In this sense, differences in motivations notwithstanding, the World Bank's instrumentalization of IK for its own economic agenda ironically aligns with the postcolonial privileging of indigenous culture to justify its narrative of otherness.

15 Frantz Fanon, *The Wretched of the Earth*, trans. Constance Farrington, 1963; repr., New York: Grove, 1965, p. 177.

economic interests or particular discursive narratives.[16] A sensitive mate-rialist reading both rejects the exoticization of indigenous culture *and* resists the trap of reducing culture to an aspect of the economic. Post-colonial literature, unlike postcolonial theory, does offer instances of such readings—ones that deeply engage with indigenous cultures while situating them within a dynamic relationship with their material contexts.

The Myth as a Message

Spanning over half a century, Mahasweta Devi's illustrious writing career was primarily invested in the struggles of tribal populations, and it offers instances of precisely such a rooted materialist reading of indi-geneity. She documented the histories of the Indian tribal populations, while also championing their political cause. In texts like *Aranyer Adhikar* (1977), and *Chotti Munda Ebong Tar Tir* (1980) she unearths the rich history of tribal resistance based on her long engagement with tribal people and collection of oral histories. Much of Devi's writing stems from a righteous fury against the stupendous exploitation of a people who have been relegated to the status of "suffering spectators of the India that is traveling towards the twenty-first century."[17] And her anger is fueled by her deep love for the people with whom she lived and worked for decades in solidarity with struggles and in defense of their ancient and marginalized cultures.

One of the most "instructive aspects" of Devi's work, as Henry Schwarz rightly observes, is the absence of discussions of colonization or of the independence movement; Devi has steered clear of those discourses and instead chosen to remain engaged in her life and work with the lived reality of marginalized populations. According to Schwarz,

---

16 Some postcolonial environmental critics note the danger in the appropriation of the rhetoric of difference by transnational capitalist entities. Neel Ahuja, for instance, reminds postcolonial ecocritics to "remain attentive to the ways in which rhetorically figuring the indigene as essentially culturally different and as always-already endan-gered by modernity has a history of contributing to genocide." Neel Ahuja, "Rhetorics of Endangerment: Cultural Difference and Development in International Ape Conserv-ation Discourse," in *Postcolonial Green: Environmental Politics and World Narratives*, ed. Bonnie Roos and Alex Hunt, Charlottesville: University of Virginia Press, 2010, p. 129.

17 Mahasweta Devi, "The Author in Conversation," in *Imaginary Maps: Three Stories by Mahashweta Devi*, trans. Gayatri Spivak, New York: Routledge, 1995, p. xi.

Devi's fiction offers compelling portraits of tribal culture without a shred of exoticism, focusing instead on "class, gender and ethnic difference in ways that go far beyond the ideology of the state in order to question the official story of national integration following independence."[18] While such an approach may appear exceptional within the postcolonial literary canon, it is in fact typical when considered in the context of regional literatures not necessarily translated into English or other metropolitan languages. As Auritro Majumder notes, it is an outlook that "combin[es] indigenous history, clinical analysis, as well as a decided orientation in favor of 'grand narratives' of emancipation rather than against."[19] Devi's work is, in fact, connected with a long vernacular tradition of radical women's writing.[20]

Devi describes her novella *Pterodactyl, Puran Sahay and Pirtha* (1989) originally written in Bengali and translated into English by Gayatri Spivak in her collection, *Imaginay Maps* (1995), as "an abstract of my entire tribal experience."[21] It is set in the 1980s in a fictive place, Pirtha, located in the actual central Indian state of Madhya Pradesh. *Pterodactyl* is the story of one of India's more than 600 tribes which comprise over 84 million tribal people.[22] The novella, while extremely specific in its ethnographic documentation, achieves a high form of abstraction in its encapsulation of the experiential world of the tribal people, portrayed through the prism of an outsider—Puran Sahay, an urban journalist.

The figure of the journalist, who searches for publishable facts while traveling into the interstices of the tribal world, allows the author to dwell on what is arguably the central theme of the story: the distance that separates the mainstream from the marginalized tribal population. Puran's journalistic ethic exposes the lack of any substantive commitment in mainstream journalism even though there may be engagement with facts of subaltern exploitation and misery:

---

18 Henry Schwarz, "Postcolonial Performance: Texts and Contexts of Mahasweta Devi," *Sussex History of Art Research Publication* 2 (November 2002).

19 Auritro Majumder, "Can Bengali Literature Be Postcolonial?," *Comparative Literature Studies* 53:2 (2016), pp. 417–25, 423.

20 Nivedita Sen and Nikhil Yadav correctly observe that in her presentations of Devi's works, Spivak extracts her texts out of local literary traditions so as to align Devi's writings to postcolonial conventions.

21 Devi, "The Author in Conversation," p. xx.

22 For a general overview of the Indian tribal population, see Chaturbhuj Sahu, *Indian Tribal Life*, New Delhi: Sarup & Sons, 2001.

As a journalist his reporting of the massacres of the harijans at Arwal has received praise, and he too like others, has fallen into disfavor with the Government in Patna. He wrote about the killing in Banjhi with a razor-sharp edge: "Red Blood or Spark of Fire in Black Tribal Skin?" And then water scarcity in Nalipura. Enteric fever epidemic in Hataori. The blinding of prisoners in Bhagalpur . . . he is untroubled by the maelstrom of political moves in Bihar or the pre-historic warfare of castiesm. He gives money to all political parties. He has support everywhere. The newspaper is a business to him. If reporting caste-war keeps his paper going, so be it . . . The illustrated magazine called *kamini*, devoted to women and the film world, brings in most money. Right beside a balance sheet on suicide are recipes on the "For the Home" page. Right beside the world travels of an international Guru is the statement of the sex-bomb star: "Motherhood is woman's greatest wealth." This sort of a mixed chow-mien dish.[23]

Puran's want of passion in his profession also pervades his personal life; His inability to commit to a woman with whom he has been involved for many years speaks to a tendency to drift with the flow, without any sense of purpose. Devoid of the wherewithal to offer responses to situations outside the narrow confines of his worldview, Puran is the everyman of modernity. By offering her urban educated reader the view of a tribal inhabitation through the prism of a dispassionate urban journalist, Devi ensures that her readers identify with Puran's challenges in his encounters with the tribal world.

Puran agrees to visit Pirtha in response to an invitation from an old friend, now a government officer in the region. The friend requests that Puran survey and report the near-famine conditions of the region. For Puran, the map his friend shows him does more than enough to signal the strange relation of the region to the rest of the country:

The survey map of Pirtha Block is like some extinct animal of Gondwanaland. The beast has fallen on its face. The new era in the history of the world began when, at the end of the Mesozoic era, India broke off from the main mass of Gondwanaland. It is as if some prehistoric

---

23 Mahasweta Devi, *Pterodactyl, Puran Sahay and Pirtha*, in *Imaginary Maps*, p. 96.

creature has fallen on its face then. Such are the survey lines of
Pirtha.[24]

The geographic strangeness of Pirtha is signified by its near inaccessibil-
ity and the repeated use of animal imagery to describe its physical
features. The peculiarity of the physical landscape of Pirtha is, however,
only a minor marker of its difference. Puran hears from his friend that
there was another journalist, Surajpratap, who like him had arrived
from the city to write about Pirtha. But after his Pirtha encounter, that
journalist suffered a mental breakdown and lost his job.

It was Surajpratap who had drawn attention to an image of another
animal in the context of the region. Puran's friend shows him a picture,
taken by Surajpratap, of a painting drawn by a boy in Pirtha; the picture
was never released to the press. At the sight of the picture, Puran
wonders aloud: "What is it? Bird? Webbed wings like a bat and a body
like a giant iguana. And four legs? A toothless gaping horrible mouth."[25]
The story that follows is, at one level, Puran's unraveling of the mysterious connection between Pirtha and the pterodactyl—the prehistoric
animal on which the painting is based.

Once in Pirtha, Puran learns that the tribals have supposedly seen a
strange flying animal and that the vision haunts them. Bhikia, a tribal
boy, paints a picture of the animal on the wall of his hut, and the tribals
pay obeisance to the painting as they would to the symbol of an ances-
tral soul. That the painting corresponds to a prehistoric animal was a
fact that could hardly be known to the tribals themselves. It is in the
magical realist presence of the pterodactyl that the narrative locates the
essence of tribal existence. Puran, addressing Bhikia's painted image of
the prehistoric animal, wonders:

> Was some communication established between your prehistoric eyes
> and his [Bhikia's] eyes, so that he (illiterate, never having read a book,
> with no knowledge of the history of the evolution of the planet)
> grasps that to keep your affair secret is tremendously urgent. The
> world of today cannot be informed about you. "Today" does not know
> the "past," the "ancient." "Today," "the present times," "civilization,"

---

24 Ibid., p. 99.
25 Ibid., p. 102.

becomes most barbaric by the demands of getting ahead. Yet he doesn't know that "today" desecrates the ancient people's burial grounds by building roads and bridges, cutting down forests. They won't let you go if they know of your existence, that is why he is protecting your visit like the sacred ashes of a funeral pyre or the bones of the dead. He has found some contact. He is a tribal, an aboriginal, you are much more ancient, more originary than his experience, both your existences are greatly endangered.[26]

Puran wonders why it is to "a half-man, a rootless weed" like himself that the message of the pterodactyl reveals itself.[27] Puran, the hollow man of modernity, for the first time in his journalistic career, actually has a glimpse into the spirit of the people about whom he is reporting. The "prehistoric eyes" of the pterodactyl reflect both the ancient past and the endangered present of the people of Pirtha, and critics have variously read the pterodactyl as the silent witness to the pile of civilizational destruction (much like Benjamin's angel of history),[28] or as a critique of the Green Revolution, referring to the period when agriculture was industrialized starting in the mid-1960s under Indira Gandhi, and an "uncanny eruption of the untimely inherent to the world ecology."[29] Beyond the broader significations of the rich metaphor, it also always connects to the immediate materiality in Pirtha. The hollow rhetoric of national development, of progress, has only offered two choices to the tribals: extinction, or survival by joining the mainstream where their "social position will be on the ground floor and their sense of ethnic being will no longer be distinct." Bikhia knows that at a time when his people are forced to sacrifice everything they hold dear, the pterodactyl, an embodiment of what they believe to be their ancestors' soul, will also leave them:

[He] is witnessing that their ancestors' soul embodied itself and flew in one day, and now it's leaving its form and returning. If it were truly that? Would it have told all the tribals of the burial grounds in the extinct

26 Ibid., p. 156.
27 Ibid., p. 60.
28 See Neil Lazarus, "Epilogue: The Pterodactyl of History?," *Textual Practice* 27:3 (2013), pp. 523–36.
29 David Farrier, "Disaster's Gift," *Interventions* 18:3 (2016), pp. 450–66, 456.

settlement, lying underneath the bridges and paths, the new settlements and fields of grain, that our descendants are disappearing? Their existence is freshly endangered . . . Bikhia's eyes are like the still flame of a lamp, he wants to see his fill of the noble death of the noble myth.[30]

If the novella is about the connection between Pirtha and the pterodactyl, it is equally invested in foregrounding the *disconnect* between Pirtha and the modernized, developed parts of the nation. Thus Puran, glimpsing the truth of tribal existence through Bikhia, knows only too well that he could never write a report on this experience. He does not have the language to explain to an outside world, terrorized with the possibility of finding a real pterodactyl, that the prehistoric animal in Pirtha was both a "myth and a message."[31]

This trope of disconnect, of the failure of language, runs through the narrative. In fact, Puran's first experience with this impossibility of communication is not in his encounters with the tribals but in his conversation with his friend, the government officer. The officer, who has his own enduring and intimate association with the tribals, finds it hard to communicate his understanding to Puran: "He [the officer] is moving his hands, trying to explain, as if there's a tremendous communication gap between him and Puran, a tremendous (mental and linguistic) suspension of contract. Are the two placed on two islands and is one not understanding the most urgent message of the other, speaking with vivid gestures on the seashore?"[32] The journalist in Puran recognizes this particular kind of communication gap, as he has encountered it before in his work with other subaltern groups:

This asymptote is a contemporary contagion. A man in Mahanadi had split open the head of a guy who had poisoned his water buffalo and had received a life sentence. How valuable is a buffalo that you are going to jail for twenty years? Asked this, the man, collar-bone shaking and foaming at the mouth, had made an effort to explain to Puran what a buffalo meant in the life of a villager. A water-buffalo is a priceless good to a well-to-do farmer.

---

30 Devi, *Pterodactyl, Puran Sahay and Pirtha*, p. 180.
31 Ibid., p. 195.
32 Ibid., p. 102.

Puran had not grasped the desperation behind his urgent and troubled message. Although he did turn the man's words into a most compassionate small news item, "For the Sake of a Buffalo."[33]

Puran is yet to learn that his trite conceptual framework and cynical journalistic formulas will not work here, as the social terrain of Pirtha is entirely different from that of modern India. A people living in perennial starvation, largely excluded from even the rhetoric of "progress and development," the tribals have evolved their own way of responding to the outside world that may well be inexplicable to Puran. The officer openly expresses his skepticism regarding Puran's capacity to appreciate the vastly different world of the tribal: "How will I make you understand that it is not possible for these tribals to think reasonably, to offer explanations? You will understand them with your urban mentality? You will fathom the Indian Ocean with a foot-ruler?"[34]

Puran tries hard to disguise his marks of class difference while living among the tribals in their utterly impoverished conditions. He refuses the offer of a proper bed accorded to him as a guest, choosing instead to sleep on a grass mat like other tribals. But such gestures of solidarity, he realizes, will always fall hopelessly short: "He sees that's not enough. He feels inadequate realizing that he can't reach these people "by eating little or sleeping on grass mats. There is a great gulf."[35] Through an appreciation of this "gulf," it dawns on Puran that, for all his investigative journalism about people in excruciating distress, he had never allowed himself to actually experience anything. After each one of his journalistic reports, he had returned to his dispassionate and commitment-free universe.

The chasm of difference, evolved over thousands of years and sharply accentuated by a modernizing nation, stands in the way of Puran's attempts at meaningful communication with the people of Pirtha. Shankar, one of the Pirtha tribals, has a bit of formal education and acts as an interpreter between Pirtha and the outside world. It is also Shankar's job to escort Puran around Pirtha and help him with his work. But even with Shankar, Puran realizes, communication is not something to be taken for granted.

---

33 Ibid., pp. 102–3.
34 Ibid., p. 104.
35 Ibid., p. 140.

Shankar speaks the same language that Puran does. But Puran discovers that the comprehensive meaning of language is not restricted to words but also extends to the experience encapsulated in those words:

> Shankar goes on talking with his eyes closed. Alas! He speaks Hindi; Puran . . . also speak[s] Hindi, but how can one touch the other? Shankar says his say in Hindi, but the experience is a million moons old, when they did not speak Hindi. Puran thinks he doesn't understand what language Shankar's people spoke, what they speak. There are no words in their language to explain the daily experience of the tribal in today's India.[36]

Puran learns, for instance, that in Ho, a tribal language, there are no words for "exploitation" or "deprivation." The interrelated concepts of exploitation and deprivation, unknown to the internal social codes of many such tribes, have never entered their lexicon either. "In a class divided society [running on] parallel lines," Puran ruminates, "language too is class-divided."[37]

The magical realist pterodactyl and numerous realist markers of deprivation signify a theme familiar to the postcolonial scholar: subaltern *difference*. In this reading, Puran must not only accept but honor the impossibility of communication with the tribal. The only possible way of reaching out to the tribal subaltern is through an acceptance of what is supposedly their singular and untranslatable experience. Baron Haber, for instance, holds that

> Puran learns from his encounter with the pterodactyl, this ancestor spirit, the impossibility of fully understanding and occupying the adivasi [tribal] perspective. He learns to pause, to give space, and to resist any discourse that "proves" every cultural, spiritual, or biological entity to be "the same." This respect for difference and spatial singularity is precisely what any plan for global sustainability needs to develop as a first step towards a more just and sustainable earth.[38]

---

36 Ibid., p. 118.

37 Ibid., p. 163.

38 Baron Haber, "'We Destroyed It Undiscovered': Slow Violence, the Gothic, and Neocolonialism in Mahasweta Devi's *Imaginary Maps*," *Darkmatter*, April 13, 2016, darkmatter101.org.

However, contra Haber, Devi is at pains to reject any suggestion that her depiction of tribal experience is a plea for untranslatability or singularity. In an interview with Gayatri Spivak, who translated the novella, Devi specifically rejects the notion of ethnic singularity and notes that her position should not be viewed as a celebration of distinct and autonomous ethnicities.[39] Neil Lazarus is right in noting that the text's motif of the "soul of ancestors" is an engagement with what has been "indefinitely deferred" in postcolonial discussions: the "*content* of the subaltern consciousness."[40] Instead of an assertion of subaltern difference, Lazarus rightly signals, Devi explores the actuality of tribals' responses to their systemic isolation and deprivation.

Even as the narrative underscores the necessity of communicating the message of systemic degradation of the tribal population, it unambiguously rejects certain dominant modes of communication. For instance, an NGO-funded film is being made on the famine in Pirtha for an international audience in order to garner worldwide moral and financial support for the region. The narrative is fiercely critical of such hollow gestures of outreach, which amount to little more than a resort to international charity. The tribals resist the filmmakers, not wishing to be exhibited for their abject poverty and humiliation: "Will you make me say that we are surrendering? . . . Everything finally becomes a deal, even giving food to the hungry. At this moment we're eating his food, in exchange he wants to capture us in film. His dictionary cannot include the self-respect of the hungry."[41] But such resistance turns out to be futile. The film is made for the supposed welfare of the tribals, regardless of their own feelings about it:

> Now the pictures are taken. The women cover their faces with the torn end of their cloth. The men turn their faces away. The scene of an old woman holding a skeleton baby in arms taking lentil-rice in her bowl, is captured very well and when the tape recorder is held close you can catch the rattle in the old woman's throat and the mumble as well as the child's chirping wail.[42]

---

39 Devi, "The Author in Conversation," p. xvii.

40 Neil Lazarus, *The Postcolonial Unconscious*, Cambridge, UK: Cambridge University Press, 2011, p. 155.

41 Devi, *Pterodactyl, Puran Sahay and Pirtha*, p. 168.

42 Ibid., p. 169.

The realism of such portrayal denies agency to the subaltern and evades issues of structural causes of poverty. Conversely, the seamy underside of the politics of international charity exposes the utter failure of the national government to address the economic and cultural marginalization of indigenous people.

Devi understands well the impasses of a politics of myth making, of reification, of cultural identity in the name of difference. Her narrative exposes the politics of tribal culture's exoticization—as untranslatable difference—to be *complementary* to the systemic oppression of tribals, rather than opposed to it. A politics of difference, regardless of whether such difference is projected for the consumption of a benevolent international audience or to untutored domestic spectators, allows for isolation and oppression. Thus, Puran knows better than to report anything about the story around the ancestors' soul, precisely because such a report would be an easy sell for an audience used to exoticizing the tribal. He understands that the popularization of such stories leads to the marginalization of others about the perennial starvation conditions of the same people.

As hard as the communication barriers are, the pterodactyl is not just a myth, but also a *message*. And that message has little to do with the singularity of tribal culture; nor is it about the mere divulgation of material deprivation to a liberal audience. Instead, the narrative draws attention to the mechanics of tribal exploitation enabled by the nexus of political and economic forces geared to work only for elite interests. While the state might pass a few laws in the interest of the tribal population, widespread corruption and a lack of adequate administrative mechanisms ensure the isolation and disempowerment of the tribal. The ownership of arable land, for instance, makes all the difference between sustenance and starvation for an agricultural community. In recognition of this fact, the state passed laws making it illegal for non-tribals to acquire tribal land. The law ensures that in a dispute involving land ownership, a tribal will have the assistance of special officers charged to look out for tribal welfare. In reality, however, such assistance remains a hoax: upper-caste non-tribals buy land under a fake tribal name, and the tribal owner of the land receives nothing. Such exchanges operate through back channels involving high-ranking bureaucrats.

Devi's focus on the actual functioning of the system shows how political legislation remains meaningless without any political will for

implementation. Thus, the safeguards and rights provided in the constitution and subsequent legislation have made hardly any difference to the
predicament of the tribal:

> What is theirs by right? The constitutional rights of 7.76 percent
> of the population of India ... They have not yet been informed of
> this ...
>
> What an immense deal of labor and money is spent to keep up this
> directive of non-information. How many subtle heads work hard.
> How many political knots are tied.
>
> What was theirs by right. The Adivasis will enter the twenty-first
> century, ignorant of this in their shadowy habitation.[43]

Since the rhetoric of nation formation has made little difference to the
life of the inhabitants of Pirtha, they respond in kind. The state reaches
out to the tribal people by inundating them with posters disseminating
the official line on issues ranging from birth control to communal amity.
For the tribal in Pirtha, however, the message lies not in the words of
the poster, but in the quality of the paper that is used: "Yesterday the
Sarpanch [chief] arrived and distributed bundles of posters. 'End separatism, keep communal harmony intact, and renounce the path of
violence.' Dimag's wife was saying, This paper is not good, too thin."[44]
The quality of the paper matters because of its multiple uses to the
impoverished tribal. The statist discourse is here literally reduced (or
elevated) to its material worth:

> Harisharan had brought for the Sarpanch today posters proclaiming
> that "Leprosy can be cured if caught in time. Go to the nearest leprosy
> hospital." The paper is good, the posters large-sized. The crowd has
> opined that it is a help that the government is giving such paper.
> Pasted on grass frames such paper will keep out the wind. The women
> say they can lay their babies down on it. You can sift the relief food
> grains on it. It is useful in many ways.[45]

---

43 Ibid., p. 110.
44 Ibid., p. 153.
45 Ibid., p. 174.

Statist benevolence in the form of messages about communal harmony or government hospitals does not come close to addressing the depth and scale of material deprivation in Pirtha. The unrelenting focus on tribal poverty is the flip side of the myth of the pterodactyl. If the pterodactyl—as "myth and message"—foregrounds the spirit of an ancient people at the brink of forced extinction, the narrative urgently highlights the inextricable connections of cultural extinction with material deprivation.

Conclusion and Other Directions

I noted earlier that both indigenous and postcolonial scholarship locate the cause of marginalization of indigenous people primarily within the cultural realm. They argue that because indigenous cultures are incompatible with the model of development undergirded by Western science, such cultures are marginalized and oppressed. And thus, postcolonial and indigenous studies scholars foreground the historical difference of indigenous cultures. I have argued against locating the source of indigenous oppression in cultural difference, and against the related reification of the lived experience of indigenous people. In fact, such cultural reification is ironically similar to the treatment of indigenous culture by corporate and other dominant interests.

In the West, it is primarily Spivak's detailed theoretical interventions that have established the tone for readings of Devi's oeuvre.[46] Spivak conceptualizes indigeneity as a form of subalternity and believes that Devi's literary writing, with its meticulous ethnography, allows for a meaningful appreciation of indigenous experience. Spivak's views on indigeneity and subalternity have been influential for indigenous theorists like Robert Warrior, who has credited postcolonial theory for helping "Native Studies understand subalternity as constitutive of the

---

46 See "The Author in Conversation" and "Afterword," in Devi, *Imaginary Maps*, pp. ix–xxii, 197–212; Gayatri Spivak, "Woman in Difference: Mahasweta Devi's 'Douloti the Bountiful,'" *Cultural Critique* 14 (Winter 1989–90), pp. 105–28; "A Literary Representation of the Subaltern," in *Subaltern Studies*, vol. 5, New Delhi: Oxford University Press, pp. 91–134; repr. in Spivak, *In Other Worlds: Essays in Cultural Politics*, New York: Methuen, 1987, pp. 241–68; "'Draupadi' by Mahasweta Devi," *Critical Inquiry* 8:2 (Winter 1981), pp. 381–402.

Native American and indigenous world."[47] In both fields—postcolonial
and indigenous studies—there is an imperative to not merely conceptualize indigeneity but also theorize possible trajectories for resistance and
transformation.

If, for Spivak, the "witnessing love" in Devi's work paves the way for
"slow attentive mind-changing," Warrior calls for an "indigenous subaltern studies group" and the need to develop a project that "will not just
involve theory, but will be theory." And, like Spivak, Warrior issues a
reminder of the necessity of "paying attention" to the subaltern.[48] Given
that the disciplines of postcolonial and indigenous studies overtly
embrace a political imperative of social transformation, it is instructive
that eminent scholars of the fields steer away from indigenous revolutionary politics and the call for structural transformation embedded in
the works of writers like Devi, in favor of reading groups and slow
"mind changing."

I have argued that, the territorial struggle between postcolonial and
indigenous studies notwithstanding, both fields share the underlying
commonality of subscribing to a culturalist premise, and therefore, both
suffer from its pitfalls. Theorists of the fields are unable to meaningfully
shed light on the actual sources of indigenous oppression, and despite
their claims to radical politics, they remain similarly incapable of envi-
sioning transformative possibilities.

Significantly, however, there is a branch of postcolonial critique that
marks a refreshing break from the culturalism endemic in the discipline: postcolonial ecocriticism. The field has been carved out by
scholars who have centralized postcolonial concerns within the
broader field of ecocriticism by paying specific attention to issues like
the distinction between Northern and Southern environmentalisms,
and the question of neocolonialism and development, as well as by
highlighting ecofeminism and ecosocialism.[49] Arguably, it was

---

47 Robert Warrior, "The Subaltern Can Dance, and So Can Sometimes the Intellectual," *Interventions* 13:1 (2011), p. 89.

48 Ibid., pp. 93–4.

49 See, for instance, *Postcolonial Green: Environmental Politics and World Narratives*,
ed. Bonnie Roos and Alex Hunt, Charlottsville: University of Virginia Press, 2010 ; *Postcolonial Ecologies: Literatures of the Environment*, ed. Elizabeth DeLoughrey and George
B. Handley, New York: Oxford University Press, 2011; *Global Ecologies and the Environmental Humanities: Postcolonial Approaches*, ed. Elizabeth DeLoughrey, Jill Didur and
Anthony Carrigan New York: Routledge, 2016; Graham Huggan and Helen Tiffin,

Ramachandra Guha who laid the foundation of postcolonial critique
within ecocriticism with his rebuttal of Norwegian environmentalist
Arne Naess's philosophy of "deep ecology."[50] Arguing against Naess's
philosophy, which is premised on the belief in the *intrinsic* worth of
nature and all living beings, Guha contends that, deep ecology's claims
of universality notwithstanding, its biocentric principles do not serve
the interests of the global South. For Guha, neither Naess's promotion
of the preservation of wilderness nor his dehistoricized privileging of
indigeneity accounts for the needs and experiences of the South,
especially those of its poor populations: "Deep ecology," Guha claims,
exhibits a "lack of concern with inequalities *within* human society."[51]
Instead, he argues, there needs to be an environmentalism that primarily addresses the exploitation of nature and people in the global South.
With Spanish economist Joan Martínez-Alier, Guha has called for an
"environmentalism of the poor"—one that highlights not only the
policies resulting from the nexus of transnational capital and national
governments, but also the resistance of the disempowered classes in
the global South.[52] The field has since responded to these concerns
with a robust body of literature that weaves together multiple strands
but largely converges on some fundamentals, including the capitalist
exploitation of people and environment in the global South, and the
struggles against it.

Interestingly, when venturing into issues relating to ecocriticism,
preeminent postcolonial theorists have chosen to ignore a central
insight of some postcolonial ecocritics: the structural incompatibility
between capitalism and ecological justice. Robert Young, for instance,
highlights the case of Nigerian environmental activist Ken Saro-Wiwa,
who was executed by the military after he led a campaign against

Postcolonial Ecocriticism: Literature, Animals, Environment, New York: Routledge, 2015;
and Upamanyu Mukherjee, *Postcolonial Environments: Nature, Culture and the Contemporary Indian Novel*, UK: Palgrave Macmillan, 2010.

50 Ramachandra Guha, "Radical American Environmentalism and Wilderness
Preservation: A Third World Critique," *Environmental Ethics* 11:1 (Spring 1989). See *The
Ecology of Wisdom: Writings by Arne Naess*, ed. Alan Drengson and Bill Devall, Berkeley:
Counterpoint, 2010.

51 Guha, "Radical American Environmentalism," p. 72.

52 Ramachandra Guha and Joan Martínez-Alier, "Introduction," *Varieties of Environmentalism: Essays North and South*, ed. Ramachandra Guha and Joan Martínez-Alier,
London: Earthscan, 1997, p. xxi.

environmental degradation in the Niger Delta—an outcome of the operations of crude oil extraction perpetrated by the multinational petroleum industry, and Royal Dutch Shell, in particular.[53] After a detailed study that shows how the deaths of Saro-Wiwa and his compatriots were a desirable outcome for Shell, and outlining the company's direct responsibility for the executions, Young, strangely enough, concludes his piece by calling for the necessity of corporate ethics and responsibility. It is as if Shell merely went astray and there are no structural reasons why the interests of companies like Shell are fundamentally inconsistent with a responsibility toward the communities and environments where they operate.

In contrast, Arundhati Roy suffers from no such illusions regarding corporations or governments when she writes on the Narmada Valley Project in India and its deleterious impact on the lives of hundreds of thousands of poor people. It is a government irrigation project, built with the active involvement of the multinational dam industry, that has given rise to a "war for the rivers and the mountains and the forests" between the inhabitants and the government, and has become what Roy calls "India's Greatest Planned Environmental Disaster."[54] In the context of the displacement of millions of tribals from their lands to pave the way for the Narmada project, Roy observes that the "ethnic 'otherness' of their victims takes some of the pressure off the Nation builders. It's like having an expense account. Someone else pays the bills. People from another country. Another world."[55]

Like Roy, through her literary and political work, Devi makes it impossible to cast away indigenous populations as "ethnic others" simultaneously celebrated and marginalized. Postcolonial ecocriticism, with its steadfast focus on both indigenous exploitation and resistance, is more aligned with Devi's perspective than the kind of culturalism more prevalent in the field. Devi's *Pterodactyl* is specifically remarkable because it shows that the rejection of culturalism is not inconsistent with the foregrounding of culture. Culture, when appreciated as *constitutive* of the material and of the quotidian life world—as in the figure of

---

53 Robert Young, "'Dangerous and Wrong': Shell, Intervention and the Politics of Transnational Companies," *Interventions* 1:3 (1999), pp. 439–64.

54 Arundhati Roy, *The Cost of Living*, London: Flamingo, 1999, pp. 52, 44.

55 Ibid., p. 44.

the pterodactyl—does not lend itself to otherness and exoticism. Thus, it is precisely because Puran realizes that a representation of the ptero-dactyl in dominant discourse will lend itself to culturalism, or to the prying apart of the material from the cultural by a dismissal of the former and a privileging of the latter, that he decides to tell the story only of material deprivation.

Radha Chakravarty rightly notes the "vital link" between the aesthetic and the political in Devi's writings;[56] I would add that there is a similar link between the cultural and the political. The tribals' deep investment in the folklore of a past when they lived with dignity and respect, for instance, is at once embraced by the narrator and yet understood in materialist terms:

> These people are fully in exile. They have not received anything from modern India . . .
>
> How can he [Shankar, as a tribal] abandon the past? They don't know if the past is legend or history, and no researcher comes to separate the two. And who is going to tell us what is legend and what history from the perspective of these totally rejected tribals? Where is the boundary between history and story?

The boundary between history and legend is deeply entangled in tribal culture because there is no other history that they can call their own. "Modern India" has only given them "posters for family planning."[57] The tribal has never been included in the process of decolonization and has been denied a space in national history. It is only natural, then, that the tribal takes pride in her own legend/history that offers a sense of past and of shared belonging.

But an acknowledgment of the richness of tribal culture—"a conti-nent that we kept unknown and undiscovered"—is not the only goal, because Devi's is not simply a politics of recognition. Devi, like post-colonial ecocritics, makes a demand for equal access to resources and rights, and a plea to end a "death farce" in the name of the kind of

---

56 Radha Chakravarty, *Feminism and Contemporary Women Writers: Rethinking Subjectivity*, London: Routledge, 2008, p. 11.
57 Ibid., p. 146.

development that oppresses entire populations.[58] If postcolonial cultur-alism is characterized by the anxiety that a materialist frame always marginalizes culture, then Devi's rooted, nuanced and compassionate narrative shows such anxiety to be unfounded.

---

58 Ibid., p. 177.

6

The National and the Universal

Nations and nationalism remain subjects of abiding interest in political and cultural theory. Within postcolonial studies, one of the most fecund lines of analysis has been a vigorous critique of the nation, both as a category of analysis and a form of political domination. If the acceleration of neoliberal globalization has fueled the discipline's move away from a national to a global imaginary, the broad approach within postcolonial studies in the theorization of nations and nationalism has been underpinned from the outset by the poststructuralist suspicion of grand narratives as conceived in the Western Enlightenment tradition. There are two components to this view, related but distinct. The first identifies nationalism as an ideology emanating from the West and therefore unsuited to the actualities of the erstwhile colonized world. The second objection stems from a concern that the nation secures its hold through homogenization, marginalizing identities that resist its mold. As a result, the discipline's current preferences emphasize alternative practices and identities that counter the totalizing drive: migrancy, hybridity, deterritorialization and other destabilizing phenomena.

The critique of nationalism did not begin with postcolonial theorists. An earlier generation of anti-colonial thinkers, many of whom were socialists, offered wide-ranging analyses of the dangers and dead ends of nationalist ideology. Amílcar Cabral warned that national liberation movements too often end with a "fictitious political independence," whereby the "material effects" of the nationalization of certain resources, together with the "psychological effects" of being ruled by a native elite, profoundly demobilizes working-class consciousness.[1] In the context of the national liberation of European countries under Nazi domination, C.L.R. James argued for the necessity of prioritizing a worker's government. M.N. Roy held that the national bourgeoisie, when put in charge of the nation, could not be trusted to play a progressive role. Similarly, Frantz Fanon contended that a "bourgeoisie that provides nationalism alone as food for the masses fails in its mission and gets caught up in a whole series of mishaps."[2] For that generation of anti-colonial thinkers, rejection of nationalism was grounded in a deep investment in struggles of national liberation, which cleared the ground for an *appreciation* of the contradictions of nationalist ideology.

What sets the postcolonial critique of nationalism apart from that of the socialist tradition are the *grounds* on which it engages the nation. If for Rosa Luxemburg, for instance, the danger lay in the nation's tendency to obscure class domination,[3] for postcolonial critics the problem lies in its homogenization, *tout court*—in its suppression of "difference" generally, whether related to class or not. And while socialists hold that it is the contradictory role of the national bourgeoisie that is responsible for the failure of national objectives, postcolonial critics highlight what for Homi Bhabha is a "conceptual ambivalence" in the very formation of the Western idea of the nation, as contrasted with the heterogeneities it attempts to contain. The national project fails because it never marks a break from the colonial ideology it supplants, and it thus remains what Partha Chatterjee calls a "derivative discourse."[4] Similarly, other critics point to the conflict between the homogeneity implied in the conceptualization of the nation and the way it actually functions to "elide and obscure . . . important constitutive differences."[5] Noting how the nation's suppression of underprivileged constituents was manifested in the gendered rhetoric and practices within the South African

---

1 Amílcar Cabral, "The Weapon of Theory" (1961), in *Revolution in Guinea: Selected Texts by Amílcar Cabral*, New York: Stage 1, 1969, p. 105.

2 Frantz Fanon, *The Wretched of the Earth*, trans. Constance Farrington, 1963; repr., New York: Grove Press, 1965, pp. 164–5.

3 See Rosa Luxemburg, *The National Question: Selected Writings*, New York: Monthly Review Press, 1976.

4 See Partha Chatterjee, *Nationalist Thought and the Colonial World: A Derivative Discourse*, Delhi: Oxford University Press, 1985.

5 Bill Ashcroft, Gareth Griffiths and Helen Tiffin, *The Empire Writes Back: Theory and Practice in Postcolonial Literatures*, London: Routledge, 1989, p. 152.

160

anti-apartheid movement, Anne McClintock opines that "all national-isms are . . . dangerous."[6]

There is no gainsaying that nations, while deriving legitimacy from the claim to represent all societal constituencies, *do* primarily serve ruling-class interests. The experience of postcolonial nations attests to this phenomenon, and the betrayal of egalitarian ideals is especially glaring given the idealism of the recent anti-colonial struggles. What postcolonial theory never satisfactorily addresses, however, is *why* national projects fail, beyond pointing to their roots in Western thought and to their "grand" or universalist aspirations that necessarily trample on local and concrete issues.

The disjuncture between the rhetorical inclusivity of nationalist ideology and its actuality of oppressive exclusions is not limited to the global South; indeed the phenomenon is common across the world. And the issues of oppressions and exclusions within nations cannot be analyzed merely as an ideological byproduct of nationalism without accounting for the operation of capital—both in the North and the South. The emancipatory and egalitarian ideals of national projects fail not because they are too Western and universalist but because they are class projects. In postcolonial contexts, the national bourgeoisie, as the new ruling class, does not share common interests or aspirations with large sections of the population. Rather, it maintains its supremacy through simultaneous rhetorical incorporation of heterogeneous inter-ests and active suppression of those very interests consistent with the project of bourgeois nation building. The postcolonial castigation of nationalism usually elides the concept's history, its contested character and its continuing centrality and relevance, even in the period of neolib-eral globalization.

Local or Universal

The bedrock commitment to difference, and its attendant valorization of local particularities, is evident in postcolonial approaches to national literature. Perhaps the most important debate on the place of the nation

---

6 Anne McClintock, "Family Feuds: Gender, Nationalism and the Family," *Feminist Review* 44 (Summer 1993), pp. 61–80, 61.

in postcolonial literature was the one triggered by Fredric Jameson's essay "Third-World Literature in the Era of Multinational Capitalism."[7] The fact that, even three decades after its publication, critics continue to stake out positions on the essay speaks to the articulation of some of the most abiding questions on cultural criticism raised by Jameson. Initially the essay occupied a tenuous place in cultural studies, criticized by many as mischaracterizing the nature of literature issuing from the global South.[8] In recent years, however, scholars have offered a more favorable reading of Jameson's argument, aiding in the essay's rehabilitation.[9] In order to appreciate the affiliations and the pitfalls of the discipline, it is instructive to discuss the changing fortunes of the piece on "national allegory."

The crux of Jameson's argument is that the rightful questioning of nationalist ideology in the first world is not a politically desirable trend to be followed in the context of the third world. The rejection of nationalism, he contends, opens up the possibility of the negation and/or representational appropriation of "third world" realities by North American postmodernist culture. Thus, nationalism is necessary if the "radical difference" of the third world, in the spheres of politics and culture, is to

---

7 Fredric Jameson, "Third-World Literature in the Era of Multinational Capitalism," *Social Text* 15 (1986), pp. 65–88.

8 See, for instance, Aijaz Ahmad, "Jameson's Rhetoric of Otherness and the 'National Allegory,'" *Social Text* 17 (1987); Gayatri Spivak, *A Critique of Postcolonial Reason: Toward a History of the Vanishing Present*, Cambridge, MA: Harvard University Press, 1999, pp. 109–10; Frederick Buell, *National Culture and the New Global System*, Baltimore: Johns Hopkins University Press, 1994; Sara Suleri, *The Rhetoric of English India*, Chicago: University of Chicago Press, 1992; R.M. George, *The Politics of Home: Postcolonial Relocations and Twentieth Century Fiction*, Cambridge, UK: Cambridge University Press, 1996.

9 See, for instance, James Christie, "Jameson among the Contras: Third-World Culture, Neoliberal Globalization, and the Latin American Connection," *Mediations* 29:1 (Fall 2015), pp. 43–67; Avram Alpert, "We Are Cannibals, All: Fredric Jameson on Colonialism and Experience," *Postcolonial Studies* 13:1 (2010), pp. 91–105; Imre Szeman, "Who's Afraid of National Allegory? Jameson, Literary Criticism, Globalization," *South Atlantic Quarterly* 100:3 (2001), pp. 803–27; Neil Lazarus, "Fredric Jameson on 'Third-World Literature': A Defence," in *The Postcolonial Unconscious*, Cambridge, UK: Cambridge University Press, 2006, pp. 89–113; Ian Buchanan, "National Allegory Today: The Return to Jameson," *New Formations* 51:1 (2003), pp. 66–79; Julie McGonegal, "Postcolonial Metacritique: Jameson, Allegory, and the Always-Already-Read Third World Text," *Interventions* 7:2 (2005), pp. 251–65; Marjorie Levinson, "News from Nowhere: The Discontents of Aijaz Ahmad," *Public Culture* 6:1 (1993), pp. 97–131.

be maintained. "All third world" literary production, Jameson holds, embodies the "radical difference" of that world, and in that sense "all third world texts are necessarily . . . *national allegories*."[10] Aijaz Ahmad argues that Jameson's assessment is neither true nor desirable.[11] He questions Jameson for subscribing to a categorization of the globe wherein the first and second worlds are described in terms of their political and economic systems, while the third world is designated only in terms of its experience of colonialism. Ahmad contends that the political and cultural ethos of the postcolonial world cannot be reduced to the colonial experience of a nation, and that writers from that part of the world do not necessarily subscribe to emblematic notions of the nation.

Ahmad's forceful critique spearheaded a decade of attacks on Jameson that focused on the unviability and undesirability of a characterization of a vast heterogeneity of literatures from several continents under the singular rubric of national allegory. Ahmad's Marxist criticism was aimed at Jameson's imposition of the overarching trope of the national on the postcolonial world, and his elision thereby of the social and political actualities of that part of the world. But the initial round of critics influenced by Ahmad ignored his larger framework; in fact, Ahmad makes the case that there are not three worlds, but one world characterized by capitalism and uneven development. The critics focused only on the parts where Ahmad foregrounds the heterogeneity of the postcolonial world in order to question Jameson's theory of national literature. Since the nation was consigned to be a universal category within postcolonial theory, the critics vigorously contested Jameson's claim that all third world literature could be read as national allegory. Jameson had, after all, mobilized a universal category to delineate the vast diversity of postcolonial literature. Ahmad's "Marxist critique of 'Third-Worldism,'" in Neil Lazarus's cogent summation of the critical trend, had mutated into a "Third-Wordlist critique of Marxism."[12]

In fact, Jameson never committed the sin of universalization. On the contrary, he was fully participating in the postcolonial attack on

---

10 Jameson, "Third-World Literature," p. 69.

11 Ahmad, "Jameson's Rhetoric of Otherness," *Social Text* 17 (1987), p. 325.

12 Lazarus, "Jameson on 'Third-World Literature,'" p. 99.

universalism, albeit with a twist. Jameson's argument *does* diverge from the postcolonial consensus that casts the nation as a universalizing organization sustained at the expense of postcolonial heterogeneity. Instead, he contends, in parts of the world that have experienced colonialism, the nation performs a different function, a function that is actually quite the opposite of what is claimed by postcolonial critics. For Jameson, the nation *is* the repository of cultural particularity, and a national consciousness inevitably frames literary production from that part of the world. Further, this national consciousness embodying the specificity of the third world is the only force powerful enough to withstand the onslaught of another universalism—that of American postmodernism. Jameson mobilizes the universal/particular binary very much along the lines of postcolonial criticism, where the universal is the dominant formation and the particular is subject to repression. However, in Jameson's version, the nation becomes not a manifestation of the universal, but the *locus of cultural specificity*, and therefore a site to be defended.

The critical trend of postcolonial attacks on Jameson has since changed, and in the past fifteen or so years, in an effort to reclaim Jameson's essay for the field, there have been several challenges to the initial round of criticisms of the essay, especially of Ahmad's critique. This is not surprising: if Jameson was initially attacked for obliterating the particularities of numerous literary traditions and held guilty of committing the primal sin of the discipline—universalization—it did not take postcolonial critics long to realize that his positions were in fact much more in sync with postcolonial thought than defenders of the discipline had previously thought. Imre Szeman, for instance, clarifies that while "Jameson has been criticized throughout his career for his insistence on totality as a central concept in social and political criticism,"[13] postcolonial critics should not be worried about the notion of totality implicit in the concept of national allegory, because here it stands for the "good" kind of nationalism. The essay is thus increasingly valued for speaking to the discipline's preoccupations with issues of national and cultural identity. And critics now realize it was in fact Ahmad who was the outlier with regard to the discipline. However, the new round of criticism, while offering an occasional fresh insight on

13 Szeman, "Who's Afraid of National Allegory?," p. 805.

Jameson's literary interpretations, fails to make a persuasive case against the challenge issued by Ahmad.

A recurring theme in defenders of Jameson is that the "Third World" essay was aimed at a "first world audience" unschooled in the cultures of other parts of the world. Therefore, Jameson's intervention was, as Julie McGonegal claims, not so much about defining "what Third World texts intrinsically are," but about "how interpretations of Third World texts actually happen—in other words, how social and economic conditions shape the entire process of literary production, publication, dissemination and, perhaps most importantly, reception."[14] Similarly, Neil Lazarus contends that in reading Jameson, it is necessary to take into account the fact that he was primarily writing for US students and scholars—trained to privilege only the Western canon, and exhibiting an "inability to grapple with cultural difference."[15] Reaching such an audience, the argument goes, necessitates a schematization of the world so as to foreground the significance of an undervalued part of the world. This echoes with earlier defenses of the essay by critics like Benita Parry, who argued that to claim "radical difference" for a part of the world was not an act of othering but a response to an "ethical imperative" that is the burden of first world scholars.[16]

But critics do not merely defend the schematization the world as an expedient tool for an untutored Western audience; rather, they posit the intrinsic political value of the category of the third world. If Ahmad points to the depoliticization of the postcolonial world by categorizing it primarily in terms of the *experience* of colonialism, while the first two worlds are described in terms of their political and economic systems, critics attempt to invalidate Ahmad's position by arguing that his critique does not account for the operation of capital in the third world. James Christie, for instance, contends that a critique of neoliberalism is impossible without highlighting the exercise of "US power and the developments in the overseas domination in the third world which took place within it."[17] In this reading, in rejecting the "three worlds" thesis, Ahmad negates the ways in which the supremacy of the first world is

14 McGonegal, "Postcolonial Metacritique," p. 258.
15 Lazarus, "Jameson on 'Third-World Literature,'" p. 103.
16 Benita Parry, *Postcolonial Studies: A Materialist Critique*, New York: Routledge, 2004, pp. 130–1.
17 Christie, "Jameson among the Contras," p. 44.

intimately connected to the violent imposition of "capitalism and the repression of popular movements and governments in the developing world.

In a related line of defense, Lazarus and Szeman argue that the concept of third world in Jameson acts as an oppositional category to celebratory postmodernist claims on the triumphs of transnational capital. It is a reminder that a part of the world remains unincorporated by the alleged "richness and excitement of the new free market all over the world."[18] In another iteration of the concept of third world as resistance, Szeman, referring to Jameson's other writings on globalization, argues that Jameson subscribes to an idea of the nation that remains central to a dominant strain of Left politics because the nation is the focal point where "truly progressive and innovative political response to globalization" and the notions of alternative collectivities are concretized: "Other 'national situations' offer models of different forms of collective and social life—not, it is important to add, in the form of 'traditional' or 'pre-lapsarian' modes of social being, but in the form of 'rather recent and successful accommodations of the old institutions to modern technology.'"[19] And thus the idea of national allegory in the "Third World" essay, Szeman holds, actually stands for the idea of the kind of Marxian utopia generally prevalent in Jameson's work.

None of the defenses holds up to closer scrutiny. The problem with the defense that Jameson was writing for a first world audience is that his central conceptualization of the distinction between literatures from different parts of the world is not merely a rhetorical trope to educate US students about cultural specificities. Jameson, by his own admission, is advancing a "cognitive aesthetic of third world literature" as national allegory; it is an ambitious theoretical project aiming to formulate a novel apparatus for studying postcolonial literature. Since Jameson's intended audience is surely anyone and everyone engaging with his chosen area, its composition makes no difference to his argument.

Second, when critics like Christie claim that Ahmad is unable to appreciate the working of capitalism because he denies how the third world is produced by Western capital, they demonstrate a failure to understand what is at the heart of the critique of the "three worlds"

---

18 Quoted in Lazarus, *The Political Unconscious*, p. 108.
19 Szeman, p. 821.

theory. While, unlike Christie, Ahmad does not postulate a neocolonial thesis that views capitalism as a "violent imposition" on the global South, his argument is not that the South is outside the circuit of capital; in fact, Ahmad would claim that it is precisely Jameson's schematization that diverts attention from the operation of capital under native bour- geoisies in the South and the resistance that it generates. Highlighting "the existence of stable and widespread classes of capitalist society within [the Indian] post-colonial bourgeois polity,"[20] Ahmad notes that the country has

> all the characteristics of a capitalist country: generalised commodity production, vigorous and escalating exchanges not only between agriculture and industry but also between Departments I and II of industry itself, technical personnel more numerous than that of France and Germany combined, and a gross industrial product twice as large as that of Britain. It is a very miserable kind of capitalism . . . But India's steel industry did celebrate its hundredth anniversary a few years ago, and the top eight of her multinational corporations are among the fastest growing in the world, active as they are in numer- ous countries, from Vietnam to Nigeria.[21]

The division of the world to which Jameson subscribes is based on whether its inhabitants are subjects or objects of their history. Capital- ism and socialism, the bases, respectively, for the categorization of the first and second worlds, imply in a Vichian sense that history is the product of human making; colonialism, in contrast, signifies an experi- ence of history merely as an object or imposition. And, even when critics like Christie point to a neoliberal world order, they view the South as a *recipient* of such an order where it has been "imposed." An appreciation of the global operation of capital in fact necessitates a rejection of the three worlds theory.

Among Jameson's defenders, Lazarus actually appreciates well the inherent problems with the schematization of the world in such terms. In defending Jameson, Lazarus imbues the three worlds categorization with significations that are not present in Jameson's own analysis. If, for

---

20 Ahmad, "Jameson's Rhetoric of Otherness," p. 23.
21 Ibid., p. 7.

Ahmad, Jameson employs an untenable method for categorizing parts of the world, Lazarus argues that the categorization signifies more than that for which Ahmad gives it credit. The "experience of colonialism" in Lazarus's reading does not reduce the postcolonial subject to a political Caliban; instead it foregrounds postcolonial resistance.

The question, however, is: To what extent is the resistance to colonialism a part of *Jameson's* analysis? For Lazarus, in colonial societies, some form of nationalism may be a necessary "site of liberation struggle," a stage in the path of revolutionary restructuring toward socialism. But it is not a tenable defense to argue that such an analysis is an implicit part of Jameson's categorization of the third world. If by "resistance" we mean active struggle, nowhere in the "Third World" essay does Jameson discuss anti-colonial or anti-imperial resistance as *the* (or even *a*) defining characteristic of that part of the world. The opposition to what he calls "American postmodernism" simply rests in the idea and the experience of the national.

Szeman and Jameson are right to subject to critique the premature postmodernist dismissal of the power of nations, and to acknowledge its crucial role in transformative politics. But in invoking the "progressive and innovative political response to globalization," there needs to be distinction between nations and states, even as the two concepts often function in tandem. Left demands that represent a struggle against capitalist globalization are aimed at states, not nations. Now, a national consciousness may be strategically invoked in order to concretize such demands, as in, for instances, references to a French radical culture or British pride in the National Health Service. But a Left politics has to be based on the knowledge that it is the political machinery of the state—as distinct from the imagined community of the nation—that, in providing national health care or public housing or public education, represents a power that can work against the logic of neoliberal capital. Jameson's privileging of the national construct eschews this distinction and in fact locates resistance merely in a third world national consciousness.

Second, to the extent that the idea of nation may represent a contested and alternative ideal, it is not enough to characterize the nation simply as a "different form of collective or social life" without delineating its content. After all, a conservative politics also offers the vision of an alternative collectivity. Szeman tellingly quotes Jameson's approval of the "successful accommodations of old institutions to new technology" as a desirable national model. Of course, such "accommodation" presents absolutely no threat to the forces of capitalist globalization; in fact, it represents cultural *adaptation* to capital. Finally, the question arises as to why, to the extent the idea of nation may indeed represent an alternative Left ideal, its applicability is restricted to the third world?

Lazarus would argue that the "first world" or the "West" in Jameson is an epistemic concept that stands in for postmodernism or the "cultural logic" of late capital,[22] and therefore, that he must locate resistance elsewhere. The question, however, that Ahmad asked still remains unanswered: Why is it that Jameson, a self-professed Marxist, needs to define the world through categories that are ultimately geographic? After all, regardless of the epistemic significance of a category like "first world," the fact remains that aspects of late capital are also present in Japan or China, and its "cultural logic" is quite ubiquitous across the globe. Similarly, if resistance to imperial oppression is the idea that Jameson had wanted to foreground in his conceptualization of "third world," then there is no reason to preclude, for instance, working-class resistance to the same imperial powers in their home territories. Such inclusions would, of course, invalidate the underlying rationale of Jameson's categorizations.

Jameson, like many postcolonial theorists, is fiercely critical of the operations of capital. His is certainly a clearer realization than those of other practitioners in the postcolonial field of how late capitalism, with increased inequality, offers only a future of "incorporation rather than inclusion." It is not the analysis of capitalism, but what he upholds to be

---

22 Lazarus's defense is notable for its attempt to "rescue" Jameson from his own postmodernism. Based on Jameson's other works, Lazarus argues that the West functions as a particular postmodern perspective, a view of the world from a "specifically delimited and historically determinate vantage point" with which Jameson engages. Lazarus, "Jameson on 'Third-World Literature,'" p. 111. Lazarus belabors the point that Jameson merely describes—albeit in excruciating detail—the contours of such a postmodern or Western perspective where the world has been homogenized by transnational capital; Jameson, he argues, never identifies with such a position. Of course, Jameson is much more beholden to postmodernism than Lazarus would have it. But what is curious is that Lazarus needs to repeatedly disentangle Jameson's critique of capital from his passages signaling the triumph of capital; the latter, Lazarus patiently reminds us, are only *descriptive* of the postmodernist mindset. The point is taken, but with the caveat that Jameson's anti-capitalism should not require such a painstaking defense as Lazarus provides.

a *response* to the injustices of capital, that positions him firmly within the postcolonial field. It is not resistance to capital, or even to imperialism, that Jameson offers as the opposing force to oppression of different kinds. The category that Jameson privileges, very much consistent with postcolonial theory, is that of *difference*.

The "Third World" essay ends on an instructive note. After laying out his argument for a theorization of third world literature based on difference, Jameson evokes a couple of lines from an Ousmane Sembène novel that he has discussed earlier. The narrator's reference in the novel is to an underdeveloped part of the country, but Jameson offers the description as both a response to the entire third world and an exhortation to remember what's valuable in it: "We may well feel, confronted with the daily reality of the other two-thirds of the globe, that 'there was nothing at all attractive about it in fact.' But we must not allow ourselves that feeling without also acknowledging its ultimate mocking completion: 'Its life was based on the principles of community interdependence.'"[23] Now, "community interdependence" may be a worthwhile ideal, but it can acquire a specific resonance based on how it is employed. For Jameson, the ideal marks the difference of the third world, a difference that in the context of Sembene's text is intricately connected to a feudalist framework. So, what is privileged here is the country or the third world because its inhabitants live by the principle of community interdependence. If the reason for privileging "radical difference" in the form of "community interdependence" is that it acts as a bulwark against neoliberal capital, Jameson, as a Marxist, must know that such feudal ideals, however worthy, cannot by themselves resist the onslaught of capital. Postcolonial critics have attempted to rescue the concept of "third world" by imbuing it with the notion of resistance and revolutionary aspirations. But what we have in Jameson is simply a romanticization of a pre-capitalist past as third world difference.

It is not surprising that, the initial critical ire notwithstanding, Jameson's essay is now reclaimed by postcolonial critics, given that it is very much in line with the reigning orthodoxies of the field. It repudiates universalism in the name of difference and locates that difference in aspects of a pre-capitalist past. Jameson, while aware of the pitfalls involved in the articulation of difference, nevertheless holds that the

---

23 Jameson, "Third-World Literature," p. 86.

recognition of the radical difference of other cultures is the only available politically acceptable choice:

> It is clear to me that any articulation of radical difference . . . is
> susceptible to appropriation by that strategy of otherness which
> Edward Said, in the context of the Middle East, called "orientalism." It
> does not matter much that the radical otherness of the culture in
> question is praised or valorized positively, as in the preceding pages:
> the essential operation is that of differentiation, and once that has
> been accomplished, the mechanism Said denounces has been set in
> place. *On the other hand, I don't see how a first-world intellectual can
> avoid this operation without falling back into some general liberal and
> humanistic universalism.*[24]

It is indeed quite remarkable that for Jameson, the only alternative to
"some general liberal and humanistic universalism" is to accept the
Orientalist premise. Marxist cultural analysis, Jameson implies, applies
only to what he calls the first world, not to postcolonial reality. I would
like to reiterate that Jameson stands with postcolonial theorists in his
affirmation of the universal/particular binary, where the universal is the
homogenizing, dominatory force and the particular needs to be
defended and privileged. Thus, the initial attack by postcolonial critics
on the "Third World" essay was based on a misreading, corrected in
more recent interpretations. In contending cultural difference to be the
only possible opposing force to the kind of liberal universalism associated with the logic of colonialism and capital, Jameson has placed
himself squarely within the postcolonial field. Both Jameson and the
postcolonialists subscribe to a premise that posits the universal and the
particular as in a conflictual relationship where the latter needs to be
defended against the former. If for postcolonialists the nation is a manifestation of the dominatory universal, for Jameson it is the repository of
the particular.

My argument in this chapter is that, contra Jameson and his defenders, most of postcolonial literature does not bear out the premise of a
universal/particular opposition, regardless of whether the nation is cast
as the universal or the particular. Through an examination of texts from

---

24 Ibid., p. 77, emphasis mine.

Palestine and Egypt, I argue that the literature articulates a universalism that either postcolonial critics disavow or that someone like Jameson, by his own admission, simply cannot see.[25] In the texts I discuss, universal needs, aspirations and dilemmas assume local form and a local voice, but they are recognizable precisely because they describe situations that resonate well beyond the site in which the particular story is located. The local is thus the site in which the universal takes form—with its own specificities, of course, but always relatable, always in conversation with its incarnations elsewhere. While firmly rooted in cultural difference, the literature shows that the universal resides within the particular.

The first text I consider, a memoir built around the Palestinian liberation struggle, points to a glaring absence within postcolonial studies. In a discipline grounded in challenges to colonial order and discourse, one nonetheless finds barely any engagement with Palestine[26]—the most prominent contemporary instance of colonial occupation. This absence speaks, in part, to the discipline's almost-exclusive focus on Anglophone and, to a lesser degree, Francophone literature from South Asia, Africa and the Caribbean at the expense of literatures in non-European languages. In the case of Palestine, another factor contributing to its minimal presence in postcolonial studies might be that the regional dynamics foreground elements that are not counted among the discipline's core emphases. The second text under discussion is a novel set in contemporary Egypt. As is more typical of postcolonial texts, its preoccupations are gender, class, diasporic challenges and the fate of traditional rituals and relationships in a modernizing world. Many of these struggles emerge from and converge into national identity and nation formation, but here the national is more of a gateway to the universal, rather than an instance of the local in opposition to the universal.

---

25 Jameson observes, "I don't see how a first-world intellectual can avoid this operation [of Orientalizing third world literature] without falling back into some general liberal and humanistic universalism." Ibid.

26 Bashir Abu-Manneh's *The Palestinian Novel: From 1948 to the Present*, Cambridge, UK: Cambridge University Press, 2016, is a notable exception that offers a remarkable synthesis of the seventy-year trajectory of Palestinian literature.

The National as Universal

Waïl Hassan is right in observing that one of the "ironies of postcolonial studies is that [while] colonial discourse analysis began with several theorists who studied colonialism in the Arab world: Albert Memmi (in Tunisia), Frantz Fanon (in Algeria), Edward Said (in the Levant) . . . [their work led] to the development . . . [of postcolonial theory] that rarely takes Arabic literary and cultural production into account."[27] Postcolonial studies, primarily invested in literary discourse from the British Commonwealth and, to some extent, in the erstwhile French colonies, tends to exclude regions that have undergone a different experience of colonialism. The problem, however, is not merely one of inadequate representation. It is conceptual. The Palestinian experience, in particular, with its history of occupation and its struggle for nationhood, challenges the discipline's vilification of nationalism. It demonstrates that nationalist ideology can perform a variety of historical functions, thus exposing the fallacy of the standard postcolonial line on the nation as a dominatory formation.

The acclaimed poet Mourid Barghouti's memoir, *Ra'aytu Ram Allah*, published in Arabic in 1997 and translated into English in 2000 as *I Saw Ramallah*, challenges fundamental assumptions of postcolonial studies regarding universality and national identity. In 1966, Barghouti left his village—Deir Ghasannah, near Ramallah in Palestine—to complete the final year of his undergraduate degree at Cairo University. While he was in Cairo, the twenty-two-year-old Barghouti's family was exiled from their homeland following the 1967 Arab–Israeli War, after which the Israeli army prevented Palestinians from returning home. Not until thirty years later, after the Oslo Accords, was he able to visit his homeland. *I Saw Ramallah* chronicles the writer's thoughts and feelings upon returning to a land once intimately his own and yet foreign, now under occupation. The lyrical memoir was warmly received in the Arab world, earning Barghouti the prestigious Naguib Mahfouz Medal for Literature the year it was published and the Palestinian Prize for poetry in 2000. Beautifully translated in English by the Egyptian writer Ahdaf Soueif

---

27 Waïl S. Hassan, "Postcolonial Theory and Modern Arabic Literature: Horizons of Application," *Journal of Arabic Literature* 33:1 (2002), pp. 45–64, 45.

and given an adulatory foreword by Edward Said, the book earned a similarly enthusiastic reception in the West.[28]

In his foreword, Said calls the memoir "one of the finest existential accounts of Palestinian displacement that we now have."[29] Said has extensively documented the historic injustices of the Occupation and how it has forced generations to live in exile. But there is a crucial difference between Said's and Barghouti's approaches to the condition of exile. Even as Said is attentive to both the injustice and the melancholia of exile, he has also repeatedly *embraced* the exilic condition because he values the outsider perspective and the resultant independence. In her reading of Barghouti, Anna Bernard takes Said to task for inscribing *I Saw Ramallah* with his own stance on exile. For Said, she argues, Barghouti's memoir is "not so much a document of 'repatriation' as a voyage of self-discovery,"[30] and he privileges what he believes is Barghouti's articulation of a "permanent state of detachment."

Bernard correctly suggests that Said's reading is motivated by the privileging of exile as an idealized intellectual condition. In his eagerness to find an echo of his own take on exile, Said ends up missing Barghouti's "critique of the idealized exilic perspective that runs throughout the narrative."[31] Barghouti's distinction between those who have been displaced by the Occupation and those who are actually living under it speaks to his refusal to idealize exile. To present the Palestinian situation under the banner of exile is to marginalize the lived realities of the millions who live *in* Palestine; the narrative is especially attentive to this aspect when it chronicles the devastation wrought by the Occupation in Barghouti's native village. Said's reading is also insufficiently sensitive to the fact that even when the narrative dwells on the myriad consequences of the Occupation on Barghouti's own displaced life, it is always underpinned by a sense of injustice at living a life imposed, not chosen.

---

28 See Avi Shlaim, "Earth and Stone," *Guardian*, April 16, 2004; Peter Clark, "Despair of the Heart," *Times Literary Supplement*, April 19, 2002, p. 28; Tom Paulin, "The Poetry of Displacement," *Independent*, March 19, 2004; "*I Saw Ramallah* by Mourid Barghouti," *Kirkus*, April 1, 2003.

29 Edward Said, "Foreword," in Mourid Barghouti, *I Saw Ramallah*, 1997, repr., New York: Anchor, 2003, p. vii.

30 Anna Bernard, *Rhetorics of Belonging: Nation, Narration, and Israel/Palestine*, Liverpool: Liverpool University Press, 2013, p. 79.

31 Ibid., p. 69.

While Bernard draws an insightful contrast between Said and Barghouti, I believe she overlooks a strong area of concurrence between them.
It is true that for Barghouti, the agony of displacement and his outrage
at its injustice are too strong to be compensated by any wisdom supposedly produced by the situation. In that sense, he does not value the
"detachment and independence" that Said believes to be inextricably
tied to the condition of exile. However, Barghouti, too, upholds the
detached stance of the poet and the intellectual—except that, in his case,
the stance in not a by-product of exile but rather a more clearly
connected feature of the older idea of positing the artist/intellectual as
separate from and superior to the collective:

> I was never convinced enough to join any political party and I have
> never joined any faction of the Palestine Liberation Organization.
> Perhaps, for someone who has lost his country, that is a vice rather
> than a virtue. Not only that I have resisted open and implicit invita-
> tions from those factions and parties. And I have paid varying prices
> for my abstention.[32]

Observing street demonstrations, Barghouti remains distant from, even
overtly critical of, such action. He speaks of his inability to shout slogans,
regardless of how convinced he may be of their supposed value. But he
does not stop with descriptions of his own aloofness. He also implicitly
mocks acts of collective resistance as "comic" exhibitions where people
chant "rhythmic slogans," reminding him of a Sergei Eisenstein film in
which chanters transform into giant open mouths. He tells the reader
that the spectacle of waving arms and raised fists has made him laugh.[33]
Here, then, is a straightforward lampoon of mass action as a mindless
spectacle, unworthy of serious consideration.

Setting up the intellectual and aesthetic priority of the solitary artist
over mass political struggles, Barghouti notes that political work is not

---

32 Barghouti, *I Saw Ramallah*, pp. 41–2. Undoubtedly, Barghouti's politically
detached stance greatly contributed to the celebratory reception of the memoir in the
West. Avi Shlaim's review in the *Guardian*, for instance, lauds the text for going beyond
the "partisanship and polemics" that usually characterizes literature on Palestine. Similarly, Tom Paulin's review in the *Independent* praises Barghouti for "being Outside any
political faction . . . temperate, fair-minded, resilient and uniquely sad."

33 Ibid., p. 176.

for him because "he reacts to the world with feelings and intuition."[34] In
this respect, the apparent divergence notwithstanding, he falls in with
Said's general view on the relation between aesthetics and politics. As a
result, while Bernard is right in her observation that Barghouti does not
subscribe to the idealization of the exilic condition the way Said does, it
is also true that there exists an underlying similarity in their positions.
Both writers ultimately embrace an idea of the intellectual as separate
from, and superior to, the masses.

However, the commonality between Said and Barghouti runs deeper
than their adherence to the notion of the detached intellectual. In spite of
their privileging of idealized notions of intellectual activity, it is the political that frames their own intellectual work. Whatever their beliefs, the
sheer urgency of the national question is so powerful that neither can
escape it. Thus, while Barghouti might be amused by street demonstrations, he struggles with his responses, precisely because of the political
convictions that do unite him with the demonstrators. To reject the aspiration for a nation because of the view that the nation is a homogenizing
or dominatory category is never an option for either Said or Barghouti.

And, while Barghouti might assert his independence from all shades
of what he considers groupthink, he does not eschew politics altogether.
He understands only too well that to contemplate a life outside of politics is untenable, especially for those who are on the receiving end of
historic injustices. In one of the most lyrical passages, he lays out the
meaning of the political:

> Can the defeated be let off politics? . . . How can our Arab francophone
> and anglophone critics believe this? . . . Politics is the family at break-
> fast. Who is there and who is absent and why . . . Where is your illusion
> laid bare by the newspaper lying on the cane chair at your side? . . .
> Who ruins your sweet inconsequential things with the awe of his
> authority and his driver and his servants and his happy bodyguards? . . .
> Politics is the number of coffee cups on the table, it is the sudden
> presence of what you have forgotten, the memories of what you are
> afraid to look at too closely, though you look anyway. Staying away
> from politics is also politics. Politics is nothing and it is everything.[35]

34 Ibid., p. 182.
35 Ibid., p. 43.

Politics delineates a landscape where hard lines have been drawn between the victors and the victimized, the colonizer and the colonized. To stake a position outside the lines of conflict is to embrace absurdity. Barghouti does occasionally try to imagine the shape of the Other as it might look outside the lines of division. Driving down the Palestinian roads with Israeli settlements on the sides, he is immediately struck by the solidity of their presence, but he reminds himself that his is a perspective "from a distance":

> I wonder what their lives look like on the inside? Who lives in this settlement? Where were they before they were brought here? Do their kids play football behind those walls? Do their men and women make love behind those windows? Do they make love with guns strapped to their sides? . . . Are they really afraid of us, or is it we who are afraid?[36]

Yet such speculations about the psychological landscape of the enemy do little to erase the materiality of power. As one of the colonized, Barghouti cannot shake off the knowledge of what the settlements symbolize: "These are not children's fortresses of Lego or Meccano. These are Israel itself; Israel the idea and the ideology and the geography and the trick and the excuse. It is the place that is ours that they have made theirs."[37]

The injustice perpetrated by colonizers' action is compounded by the pain inflicted by their rhetoric. Barghouti, the man of letters, is especially cognizant of the specific harms wrought by the colonizers' perverse claim to be the true victims. He notes in particular his pain and anger when, in a speech at the White House, Israeli prime minister Yitzhak Rabin yet again cast Palestine as the aggressor and Israel the victim of a war in which it continued to suffer. It is a narrative, Barghouti eloquently notes, that is made possible only by "alter[ing] the order of things":

> It is easy to blur the truth with a simple linguistic trick: start your story from "Secondly." Yes, that is what Rabin did. He simply neglected to speak of what happened first. Start your story from "Secondly," and

---

36 Ibid., pp. 29–30.
37 Ibid., p. 29.

the world will turn upside-down. Start your story with "Secondly," and the arrows of the Red Indian are the original criminals and the guns of the white men are entirely the victim. It is enough to start with "Secondly" for the anger of the black man against the white to be barbarous. Start with "Secondly," and Gandhi becomes responsible for the tragedies of the British . . . It is enough to start with "Secondly," for my grandmother, Umm 'Ata, to become the criminal and Ariel Sharon her victim.[38]

Barghouti then takes it on himself to redirect attention to the original crime. He holds the Occupation criminally responsible for turning the concrete into the abstract. Generations of exiled Palestinians have been robbed of the quotidian intimacy of their relationship to their homeland. They have no access to the "colors, smells and sounds" of everyday life, of belonging. The longing and the struggle for Palestine then draws on received notions, on memories, on ideas of the land: abstractions. The Occupation, Barghouti laments, has "succeeded in changing us from the children of Palestine to the children of the idea of Palestine."[39] If the Occupation has changed the concrete into the abstract, then the writer's job has become to effect the converse. It is this job of concretizing Palestine into a land of lived experiences that Barghouti embraces in his memoir.

To concretize, to focus on the particular, carries risks, a salient one being the risk of exoticization. Palestine, even when sympathetically referenced in the Western press, is often portrayed only in its particularities, a situation of interest only for its specificity, but without universal implications. In a sense, *I Saw Ramallah* follows the logic of particularity; in painstaking detail it chronicles the many cultural, historical and geographic facets of the land. As Barghouti traverses the spaces of his childhood and youth, images come rushing to him of a time when the self and home were still inseparable, and these images take varied shapes: figs washed by the dew, grandmothers squatting in front of ovens, the newly arrived jar of olive oil from Abu Seif's press, shawarma at Abu Iskander's restaurant, the local bookstore that, to the owner's chagrin, he treated as a library.

---

38 Ibid., p. 178.
39 Ibid., p. 63.

However, the text never *merely* particularizes Palestine and, therefore, never exoticizes it. The Occupation may be a particular historical
event, but it acquires resonance because it invokes the universal feeling
of injustice. The specificities of Palestine lovingly charted in the narrative are always undergirded by universal concerns of pain, love, loss and
anger. In this Barghouti again echoes Said, a thinker, as Jan Selby rightly
notes, whose positions on nationalism are outside the mold of postcolonial thought.[40] For Said, Selby observes, progressive nationalisms
are "founded on universal principles, being at their best when they see
individual national histories 'as an aspect of the history of all subjugated
men and women.'"[41]

From the very moment Barghouti steps foot on the rickety bridge to
cross the Jordan River and commence his travels through the towns and
villages of Palestine, the dominant feelings are of pain and fury at a
political reality that denies him his natural claim to his homeland. At the
entry point, he looks at the Israeli soldier in charge of border crossings
and ruminates on the ironic inversions of the Occupation: "His gun
took from us the land of the poem and left us with the poem of the land.
In his hand he holds earth, and in our hands we hold a mirage . . . The
others are still the masters of the place."[42]

It is the very concreteness of the memories that leads to the author's
remarkable realization that the "places we desire are only times but
conflict is over place."[43] The Occupation thus forces Palestinians to live
in another time, in the past; it freezes time and thus denies the fluidity
and forward movement intrinsic to it. It reduces lived experience to a
"bouquet of symbols," an abstraction.[44] There is a temptation here that
is also a trap—to romanticize the past and celebrate the symbols. Even
as Barghouti takes solace in memories of another time, he fully refuses
the temptation to reify them:

They [Israel] moved forward as fast as they could and made sure that
we keep moving backwards . . . I have always believed that it is in the

---

40 Jan Selby, "Edward W. Said: Truth, Justice and Nationalism," *Interventions* 8:1
(2006), pp. 40–55.
41 Ibid., p. 49.
42 Barghouti, *I Saw Ramallah*, p. 13 and p. 38.
43 Ibid., p. 88.
44 Ibid., p. 182.

interests of an occupation, any occupation, that the homeland should be transformed in the memory of its people into a bouquet of symbols. Merely symbols. They will not allow us to develop our village so that it shares features with the city . . . Let us be frank: when we lived in the village, did we not long for the city? Did we not long to leave small, limited, simple Deir Ghassanah for Ramallah, Jerusalem, and Nablus? Did we not wish that those cities become like Cairo, Damascus, Baghdad, and Beirut? . . . The Occupation forced us to remain with the old. That is its crime. It did not deprive us of the clay ovens of yesterday, but of the mystery of what we would invent tomorrow.[45]

Moreover, Barghouti does not shy away from fundamental queries that have the potential to challenge his emotional stance. Why, he asks himself, the attachment to the land, to this specific piece of land? He asks the question after rejecting poetic and political idealizations of the land to focus instead on its materiality, which is "touchable as a scorpion . . . visible as the prints of a shoe."[46] The answer does not hark back to intimate memories of belonging and loss but instead to a more visceral memory of injustice: "We sing for it only so that we may remember the humiliation of having it taken from us. Our song is not about some sacred thing of the past but about our current self-respect that is violated anew every day by the Occupation."[47]

The moral and intellectual arc of *I Saw Ramallah* is difficult to reconcile with the characterization of nationalism and universalism that dominates postcolonial studies. Barghouti's memoir documents the ubiquity of the aspiration to nationhood among the colonized and, further, highlights the universal drives that underpin the particular aspiration. Perhaps paradoxically, in its affirmation of the nation, the narrative insists on the limitations of a category defined by borders: "I hate borders, boundaries, limits. The boundaries of the body, of writing, of behaviour, of states. Do I really want boundaries for Palestine? . . . Now I want boundaries that later I will come to hate."[48] Yet, for now, is

45 Ibid., pp. 147, 69.
46 Ibid., p. 6.
47 Ibid., p. 7.
48 Ibid., pp. 38–9.

another option possible? The narrative confronts that question and, in answering it, highlights the universal drive for resistance. The aspiration for sovereignty in the form of nationhood must be honored because the "others are still the masters of the place."[49]

Similarly, Said reads the seemingly contrary pulls of the national and the universal in Fanon, who had "committed himself to combat both imperialism and orthodox nationalism" while arriving at the insight that universalist liberation is a *process*.[50] Whereas in postcolonial theory the nation is either vilified as an instance of universalist domination or celebrated as epitomizing particularist resistance, Barghouti, like Said and Fanon, eschews both positions. Erasing the duality between the universal and the particular, Barghouti observes that for the Palestinian poet, the poem's "horizon expanded . . . to embrace the universal, the human, as well as the intimate and the personal."[51]

The Cultural as Universal

Ahdaf Soueif, the translator of Barghouti's memoir, established her mark as an Egyptian novelist enriching the small corpus of Anglophone Arab literature.[52] Unlike Palestine, Soueif's late-twentieth-century Egypt is not in a fight for its national soul in an anti-colonial war, and so her preoccupations are of a somewhat-different order. Her characters navigate issues of gender violence, of class identity, of diasporic angst, of the age-old conflict between traditional mores and modernity. But, underlying all their experiences is a cultural identity that is also a national identity. The fact of being Egyptian is so fundamental in her texts that it requires no overt gestures. A national consciousness looms large in Soueif's *In the Eye of the Sun* (1992), but just as in Barghouti, it is never a silo or a fragment. Rather, it encapsulates the universal.

49 Ibid., p. 38.

50 Edward Said, *Culture and Imperialism*, New York: Vintage, 1993, p. 274.

51 Barghouti, "The Servants of War and their Language," *AUTODAFE*, 3/4 (2003) p. 43

52 Soueif's novel *The Map of Love* was shortlisted for the Man Booker Prize in 1999. *In The Eye of the Sun* enjoyed a strong critical reception as well. See, for instance, Frank Kermode, "Asyah and Saif," *London Review of Books*, June 25, 1992, pp. 19–20; Leila Ahmed, "A Woman Caught Between Two Worlds," *Washington Post*, June 13, 1993; and Hilary Mantel, "Double Identity," *New York Review of Books* 40:15 (September 23, 1993), pp. 28–9.

If Barghouti's is a commendable engagement in Arabic with the concreteness of the Palestinian experience while remaining grounded in a universalist ethos, Soueif's achievement, written in English, is arguably greater.[53] "Her companions in this enterprise," as Said reminds us, "are other post-colonials using English (as a world-language) to reconstruct, revise and repossess experiences formerly either suppressed or denied them by colonialism."[54] Writing in a colonial language, an author navigates a peculiar set of pressures that create a far-stronger gravitation toward cultural exoticization.[55] Soueif's novel beautifully rises to the challenge of steering clear of the temptations of such exoticization as well as those of a banal cosmopolitanism that sometime passes for universalism.

In the Eye of the Sun centers around the life and times of Asya al-Ulama, a daughter of university professors in Cairo, from the mid 1960s to the early 1980s. Along the way, Asya travels to England to study for a doctoral degree and to other places more briefly, thereby offering insights on cultural encounters. Throughout, Asya's upper-middle-class life is densely intertwined with the lives of her extended family and her friends. The political destiny of Egypt in this period frames the entire

---

53 For an interesting discussion on the reception of Souief's work, see Waïl S. Hassan, *Immigrant Narratives: Orientalism and Cultural Translation in Arab American and Arab British Literature*, New York: Oxford University Press, 2011, pp. 159–79.

54 Edward Said, "*Aisha* by Ahdaf Soueif," *London Review of Books*, July 7, 1983.

55 The narrativization of native culture under the colonial gaze is never an easy process, and the results are often problematic. If Orientalist scholarship exoticized the East, it is not uncommon for literary texts from erstwhile colonies to do the same, albeit for somewhat different reasons. The very practice of writing in the colonizer's language, the often-deracinated social position of the writers, and the need to cater to an audience largely untutored in the represented culture all add to the pressure to produce an exoticized product. There is a robust critical conversation on the issue in the context of South Asian Anglophone literature. See, for instance, Meenakshi Mukherjee, "The Anxiety of Indianness: Our Novels in English," *Economic and Political Weekly*, November 27, 1993, pp. 2607–11; Bethan Benwell, James Procter and Gemma Robinson, *Postcolonial Audiences: Readers, Viewers and Reception*, New York and London: Routledge, 2012; Sarah Brouillette, *Postcolonial Writers in the Global Literary Marketplace*, New York: Palgrave Macmillan, 2007; Nivedita Majumdar, "Commodifying Culture: Language and Exoticism in Indian English Literature," in *Indian Writing in English and the Global Literary Market*, ed. Lisa Lau and Om Dwivedi, New York: Palgrave Macmillan, 2014, pp. 63–80; Vikram Chandra, "The Cult of Authenticity," *Boston Review*, February/March 2000, pp. 42–9; Amit Chaudhuri, "East as a Career," *New Left Review* 40, (July/August 2006), pp. 111–26.

narrative: while Asya remains primarily focused on relationships and work, the broader political culture is always noticeably present in her world. And even though that world is pervaded by numerous markers of traditions from a feudal past and from Islam, Asya also belongs to the cultural elite of an Egypt shaped by Gamal Abdel Nasser's secular nationalism.

In the bildungsroman of Asya, the political is depicted as a vital constituent of subject formation. Throughout, the narrative is interspersed with vignettes of changing power configurations, within both Egypt and the Arab world in general. Some commentators, having chosen to read the text as "essentially a private novel," hold that the political "never really penetrates the texture of the narrative."[56] What such commentary misses is that, while the novel indeed focuses on the subjective, it is the larger political milieu that is constitutive of Asya's subjectivity. She is animated by a nationalist spirit reflective of Nasser's Egypt. For her, the 1967 war retains its intensity because of the multipronged devastation it wrought; she movingly records Nasser's final years and death, and voices strong judgment against Anwar Sadat's subsequent repression and return to fundamentalism. If nationalism remains a steady presence in the social consciousness of the central characters, the novel also acknowledges the nation's heterogeneity. Asya's encounter at her British university with Mahrous, a fellow Egyptian student, highlights the wide socioeconomic as well as cultural gap between the Egyptian urban elite and the rural underprivileged.[57]

Soueif never strains to emphasize her cultural authenticity, precisely because she is secure in her grounding in the culture. This confidence surfaces in the depiction of Asya's years pursuing a PhD at an unnamed "redbrick" university in the North of England. The rendering of her experiences there, I believe, is among the finest portrayals of homesickness to be found in postcolonial literature. The colonial country holds

---

56 Rasheed El-Enany, "A Maze Made of Soft, Shaded Paths," *Independent*, August 8, 1992.

57 Leila Ahmed is right in pointing out that the author fails to show any awareness of Asya's class biases. Even though the narrative does exhibit a cognizance of class *disparities*, it also betrays a conservative stance. While the narrative's humane liberalism includes in its fold several minor but well-drawn characters from the underprivileged social rungs, Asya's own privileged class position in an impoverished country is never quite interrogated.

neither glamor nor charm for our postcolonial subject. Instead, what strikes her repeatedly is the coldness, certainly of the weather, but also of the life of a solitary graduate student. In a wintry, windy town with little communal life, at a university struggling with budgetary cuts (no graduate common room, no department library), working under a reserved and socially inept supervisor, all Asya can call her own is a little cubicle of a room in a ravenous dormitory. She seeks solace in repeatedly calculating the time of day in Egypt, in a way familiar to new immigrants everywhere, wondering what the people at home are doing at that moment.

Yet, for all her homesickness, Asya finds little comfort in connecting with other Egyptian students. In fact, the insularity of their concerns and pursuits alienates her. Writing to her mother, she complains that these students insist on remaining parochial:

> They've all got their radios propped up at an angle with the aerials sticking out of the window (in this cold!) so they can listen to Voice of the Arabs through horrendous crackling, of course—and contrive to pass the days as though they were not really here. I mean, of course here is completely deadly, but still—they're sort of *insistent* on their Egyptianness.[58]

Asya's background—an extended family that belongs to Egypt's elite, parents who were university professors, cultural capital, exposure to the wider world—sets her apart from most of the other Egyptian students at her university. Consequently, even as the northern British town feels "completely deadly," she does not embrace the comfort of a parochial nativism. As Said notes in his laudatory commentary on the novel, it is because Asya is so "securely Arab and Muslim [that] she does not need to make an issue of it."[59]

Much later, Asya's visit to New York offers yet another refreshing take on cultural encounters.[60] She is overjoyed by the lively, crowded city,

---

58 Ahdaf Soueif, *In the Eye of the Sun*, London: Bloomsbury, 1992, p. 352.

59 Ibid., p. 410.

60 For an interesting reading of the novel that highlights how different spaces shape Asya, see Nadine A. Sinno, "The Power of Place and Space: (Re)Constructing Identity and Selfhood in Ahdaf Soueif's *Eye of the Sun*," in *Representing Minorities: Studies in Literature and Criticism*, ed. Larbi Touaf and Soumia Boutkhil, Newcastle upon Tyne,

with its informality and untidiness and people who are mostly loud but also genuinely interactive. Writing to her friend, Asya unwittingly hits on the reason the city appeals to her:

> It's terribly like Cairo that way, with people yelling at each other and making jokes and blowing their horns, but I haven't seen an actual fight yet. It's like Cairo in other ways too (I know it sounds silly, but it's true) most of the cars have dents in them one way or the other—and there's a general untidiness about the place: bits of paper blowing around, little piles of rubble here and there, puddles and pot-holes and some people in a great big rush and others standing in their doorways picking their noses. And people *look* at you: men look at you in the street, which they never do in England, and I had a whole chat with a woman in Bloomingdale's about which earrings she should buy.[61]

New York appeals to Asya because it reminds her of Cairo. However, the comparison in no way diminishes the impact of cultural difference. She finds pleasure in New York because it is novel and different (how could it not be?) but also because she can relate to it. Cultural rootedness does not act as a barrier to a full experience of difference; in fact it enhances the experience. Too often, the East–West theme in postcolonial texts gets bogged down by common tropes that end up reifying constructs of home or of the foreign culture. Here, by contrast, through the representations of both the North of England and New York, remarkably different though they are, the narrative offers a fulsome treatment of cultural encounter that is experiential and genuine.

There is, arguably, no greater marker of cultural identity than female sexuality, and Soueif's novel is centrally invested in the subject. The portrayal of women and sexuality in postcolonial texts must always negotiate a difficult terrain because of the connection between colonial ideology and women's status. A primary justification for colonial conquest, still very much in vogue in our neocolonial times, is the lamentable position of women in such countries; colonial rule, the justification goes, would civilize the culture and enhance the place of women. For writers like Soueif, the challenge is to depict patriarchy and

---

UK: Cambridge Scholars, 2008, pp. 194–206.
    61 Soueif, *In the Eye of the Sun*, p. 718.

its multifaceted impact without feeding into colonial rhetoric regarding women. *In the Eye of the Sun* elegantly negotiates this challenge by maintaining steadfast integrity in the portrayal of intimate experiences. The author well understands that the experience of patriarchy is always mediated through myriad social relationships. Colonial ideology denigrates the intricate fabric of culture by first isolating a single aspect, such as patriarchy, and then painting the entire culture with the same brushstrokes used to depict that one element—a well-tested colonial method of othering and conquering. Soueif's novel challenges colonial othering without shying away from an intimate portrayal of cultural realities.

In one of many powerful scenes in the narrative, Asya's closest friend, Chrissie, faces the wrath of her father because of her alleged transgressions. The action under scrutiny is that Chrissie, a college student, was seen walking on the street with a man, a fellow student. The scene unfolds at Chrissie's home with Chrissie and Asya first reasoning with Chrissie's mother, trying to explain to her that the man was Chrissie's colleague and that he was in distress and needed to speak with her. The mother's response is instructive in that while she understands the insignificance of what transpired, she also knows that was beside the point. How, she wondered, could Chrissie flout the clear injunction that as a young woman, she could not be seen publicly with a man to whom she was not related? Mostly, however, Chrissie's mother is deeply afraid of her husband's response. She tries to mediate the matter by turning to her son, hoping to soften his position, since, as the male heir, his thoughts on how they might relate the matter to the father carry weight. At the mother's request, Asya tries to reason with the son, who nevertheless, true to his position in the patriarchal setup, remains unrelenting. As anticipated, on learning of Chrissie's misdemeanor, the father is furious at Chrissie, verbally assaulting her and declaring she will not be allowed to continue her education. The mildest stirring of protest from Chrissie ends with a physical assault by her father. Asya, witness to the scene, leaves for her own home, fervently hoping Chrissie's father will not carry out his threat to remove her from college.

Only in the context of the larger narrative does the scene acquire its true meaning. Depictions of the everyday oppressiveness of patriarchy can range from condemnation to acceptance, but Soueif approaches her subject with a complexity that, while exhibiting elements of both, cannot be reduced to either. Her sympathies are evident in the portrayal of the event, revealing the unmistakable strain of brutality within patriarchal domesticity as observed through the perspective of Asya, a young woman who herself is subject to unreasonable (though comparatively less stringent) demands of decorum. And yet this scene cannot simply be extracted from the larger context without doing injustice to its narrative logic. First, even though Asya herself is not subject to the same level of patriarchal surveillance as her friend, she does possess plenty of cultural familiarity with such issues and thus is not especially surprised or shocked at what happens to Chrissie. In addition, because of her friendship with Chrissie, Asya has an affectionate relationship with Chrissie's family. And, as Asya had hoped, it turns out that Chrissie's father does not punish his daughter by terminating her education, as he had threatened to do. Furthermore, we later see Asya extending the expected forms of courtesy to the father, signaling that there has been no break in her relationship with her friend's family. Yet none of these complexities mitigate the prior vivid portrayal of domestic violence. As a result, patriarchy is here both culturally situated *and* subjected to critique.

The author's approach to the confrontation at Chrissie's home is echoed in many of the narrative's other manifestations of patriarchy. One notable example is the protracted misery that Asya's husband, Saif, puts her through when he learns of her infidelity. Grappling with loneliness and marital frustrations, Asya engages in an affair with a fellow student at her university. After Saif learns of the affair, while understandably upset, he loses the reader's sympathy because of his relentless, vengeful haranguing of Asya, which extends to multiple physical assaults. Saif, otherwise urbane and suave, is revealed as subject to primitive patriarchal instincts when he feels his rights are under attack. As is the case in Chrissie's conflict with her father, the injustice of Asya's experience is clearly depicted, but the reader is also privy to her own mediated response to her suffering. Even when confronting the worst from Saif, Asya manages to make it bearable by reminding herself that Saif's actions emanate from the pain she has caused him.

While Asya's responses may be meant to mitigate, at least to some extent, the reader's judgment of Saif and other male characters, the fact remains that Asya herself is shaped by patriarchy. Such a portrayal of patriarchal relations through the lens of a sympathetic character may seem problematic, but I think Soueif's critique of patriarchy in *In the Eye of the Sun* is effective precisely *because* it is offered from the perspective of a character grounded in a patriarchal cultural milieu.[62] Amin Malak has written on the ways in which Arab women writers "reveal an acute awareness of their own distinct and delicate exploration of a troubling terrain."[63] While Malak's emphasis on the centrality of an enlightened Islamic tradition for Arab women writers is not borne out by Soueif's more secular nationalist bent, Malak is right in highlighting that for women writers of the region, religious and national identity cannot be ridiculed or rejected but must be engaged.

Even as they highlight patriarchal oppression, Arab women writers such as Nawaal El Saadawi are keenly aware that the condemnation of specific questionable cultural practices can further the agenda of other-ing and conquering.[64] For a novelist, a decontextualized critique of patriarchy—or, for that matter, any cultural issue—is never a real choice. Soueif persuasively depicts patriarchy not as an isolated, abstract system but as part of a totality, interwoven with the larger fabric of social rela-tions. Her portrayal of Asya's sexuality in its interplay with patriarchal ideology is especially noteworthy in this context, as female sexuality is a largely uncharted area in Arab Anglophone fiction. Soueif's rendering of Asya's sexuality is mindful of Anastasia Valassopoulos's cautionary note: for Arab women writers, to discuss sexuality "in and of itself offers little more than a reactive reaction (isn't it great that Arab women are writing about sex?). Instead, is it not what is learnt, revealed, accepted and repudiated in this frank elaboration on sexuality that should be our focus?"[65]

Through her painful sexual experiences, Asya comes to the realiz-ation that, contra received notions, emotional and physical fulfillment are often at odds with each other. At eighteen, she falls in love with the brilliant and debonair Saif Madi. Her parents will not let her marry him

---

62 Chandra Mohanty highlighted the pitfalls of representing non-Western women in Western feminist scholarship as a monolithic category without reference to their roles and relationships in the family and community. See her "Under Western Eyes," *Bound-ary 2* 12:3 (1984), pp. 338–58.

63 Amin Malak, "Arab-Muslim Feminism and the Narrative of Hybridity: The Fiction of Ahdaf Soueif," *Alif: Journal of Comparative Poetics* 20 (2000), pp. 140–83.

64 See Nawal El Saadawi, *The Hidden Face of Eve: Women in the Arab World*, 1977; repr., London: Zed, 2015; and *Women at Point Zero*, 1975, repr., London: Zed, 2007.

65 Anastasia Valassopoulos, *Contemporary Arab Women Writers: Cultural Express-ion in Context*, London and New York: Routledge, 2007, p. 126.

immediately, and so she waits four years to do so. Saif, for his part, is
very much in love with her, but even though he is caring and indulgent,
he is unable to relate to her as an equal, often addressing her as "prin-
cess," "pussycat," and so on. During a fight, Asya accuses him of being
unable to grasp the implications of his own preferences:

> [Asya:] "You don't really see any connection between things, do you?"
> "What things?"
> "Well, say between this song and anything . . . or books. Even the
> ones you like . . . all the women in the books you like—Sartre and
> Camus and all that—they don't really exist. Not as people. They're
> only there to wait for the men. To love them and be loved back or
> not—mostly not, to be beaten up or killed; to appear as a face on the
> wall of Meursault's cell."[66]

To her deep chagrin, Asya finds herself unable to respond to Saif sexu-
ally despite her love for him. Saif repeatedly realizes that even though
she desires sexual intimacy, her body resists him. It is a mind/body
split: her body acknowledges the mismatch with Saif while her mind
refuses to do so. He accepts the painful state of affairs between them
and tells her that he loves her enough to have her live with him like a
sister. His way of accounting for Asya's sexual response is to tell himself
she is too delicate, even ethereal, to want sex, and so he assumes the
grand, self-abnegating stance of renouncing sex with her altogether.
This, of course, only makes matters worse for her, deepening her
frustrations.

Asya ends up having an affair at her university with a man toward
whom she feels only a mild fondness. As matters unfold, her lover,
Gerald Stone, turns out to be uncouth, possessive, and, his political
grandstanding notwithstanding, a deluded "sexual imperialist," as Asya
puts it. To her, Gerald presents in every way a study in contrast to the
elegant Saif. But it is to Gerald that her body responds—a state of affairs
whose irony she sees only too well:

> At times like this, when it's just over, it is as if a great, stormy sea had
> receded, and in the bed where a moment ago the waves were crashing

---

66 Soueif, *In The Eye of the Sun*, p. 345.

and seething and foaming, there is space . . . her body is content;
actively consciously content . . . but it is her mind that amazes her:
where do all those vast spaces come from that open up inside her
head? . . . Oh, if only, if only "Sex" and "Romance" were one—imagine
feeling like this and knowing that if she opens her eyes it will be Saif's
deep brown eyes that she meets.[67]

Here we see a culturally anchored sexuality: Asya's frustrations, attrac-
tions and guilt are all articulated in a culturally specific language and
sensibility. Indeed, how else could it be? It is the whole person—cultural
imprintings, beliefs, expectations, unconscious assumptions, memories,
culturally formed hopes and even practices—that engages in intimacy.
And yet Soueif shows—through Asya's mind/body split—that while
sexuality is a prime marker of cultural difference, it is also the medium
of the universal.

After enduring the agony of extricating herself from both her
marriage and her affair, Asya returns to the unchanging facets of life:
her family and her country.[68] The final part of the novel presents Asya's
moving reunion with everything she has always known and valued but
now, more mature and more aware, wants to reaffirm. However, true
to the spirit of the narrative, there is no simple cultural solace to be
had. Asya returns to Sadat's Egypt, an unfamiliar and frightening
place, with its political persecutions and its free rein to religious
fundamentalism. Her brother-in-law is imprisoned and tortured for
the sole crime of being part of a rather-innocuous leftist organization.
Asya returns to her alma mater as a professor, where she is struck by
the number of veiled women and bearded men, many more than she
had ever seen during her student days. When she and her sister Deena
visit a rural area and find themselves surrounded by veiled women and

---

67 Ibid., p. 564.
68 The author here draws a parallel between the trajectory of Asya's own life and
that of Egypt's political fortune. Asya leaves for England in 1967, just as Egypt "enters a
period of increased social mobility, consumerism and collaboration with the
West . . . Asya leaves on a historical cusp represent[ing the end of a chapter] both of her
life story and of a dominant (pan) Arabist construction of Egypt." Her return similarly
marks a new chapter in both her personal and national lives. Lindsey Moore, "Voyages
Out and In: Two (British) Arab Muslim Women's Bildungsroman," in *Culture, Diaspora,
and Modernity in Muslim Writing*, ed. Rehana Ahmed, Peter Morey and Amina Yaqin,
London and New York: Routledge, 2012, pp. 68–84, 72.

their families, Asya tries to spin it in a positive way, whereas her more politically conscious sister objects to the glib cultural generalizations Asya voices:

> [Asya:] "The thing is they [orthodox Muslims] spook me, and I know if ever they have their way we'd all be finished—at least, I would—but I do have a kind of sneaking admiration for them. I mean, they've sorted out some kind of an answer to what's happening all around us—all the manifestations of the West that they see here are no good for them, for the way of life they want to hold on to, the values they feel comfortable with, even to their standard of living. And their answer is genuine, it's not imported or borrowed from anywhere—"
>
> "How genuine is it, though? " Deena had asked. "I mean it's essentially an urban phenomenon—"
>
> "But don't most of the young men come from the countryside?"
>
> "Yes, but they only get like this when they move to the cities—no, I don't see it catching on here like in Iran."[69]

As I noted earlier, Jameson calls for a recognition of the "radical otherness" of the third world as a way of genuinely appreciating non-Western cultures. In the above exchange between Asya and her sister, what is it that amounts to the "radical otherness" of Egypt? Perhaps it is the expressions of religious practices that Asya calls a "genuine . . . not imported or borrowed" answer to the "manifestations of the West." It does fit exactly Jameson's call for the foregrounding of cultural particularities that supposedly have the power to resist the onslaught of the logic of late capitalism.[70] But Soueif does not allow for such exoticized celebrations.

---

69 Soueif, *In The Eye of the Sun*, p. 755.

70 In an interesting twist, Anglophone writers who adopt the strategy of representing cultural particularities end up being *symptomatic of late capitalism*, rather than resisting it. Graham Huggan, for instance, places the formation of the postcolonial exotic in the larger context of late capitalism and its culture of commodity fetishism. Connecting key aspects of the postcolonial exotic with commodity fetishism, like "mystification (or leveling out) of historical experience; imagined access to the cultural other through the process of consumption; reification of people and places into exchangeable exotic objects," Huggan observes that these processes "help [postcolonial] books and their authors acquire an almost talismanic status" (Graham Huggan, *The Postcolonial Exotic: Marketing the Margins*. London: Routledge, 2001, p. 19). Huggan's analysis thus undermines Jameson's contention that third world cultural production is

Deena corrects Asya, educating her as to the larger context in which the turn to conservative practices had erupted. There is nothing "genuine" about the phenomenon, because religious fundamentalism in this part of the world, much like in the West, is crucially a *political* rather than a *cultural* phenomenon. Deena also notes that she does not see the turn to fundamentalism "catching on here like in Iran." The third world cannot be homogenized.

Conclusion

And so, we return to the nation itself—largely vilified in postcolonial theory because of its putative exclusionary role, though at times privileged, as in Jameson, because the specificity embodied in a nation can become the locus for the contestation of oppressive ideologies. Both positions proceed from a critique of universalism as a category mobilized in the interests of oppressive, homogenizing agendas that appropriate the culturally particular or concrete. Because the particular is under threat from the logic of the universal, the argument goes, it needs to be defended and privileged. Jameson acknowledges that upholding national cultures as an instance of the particular necessitates an orientalist narrative , but, echoing the premise of postcolonial theory, he contends that such an Orientalist approach must be embraced because the only alternative is a meaningless liberalism. Barghouti and Soueif, however, show that those are not the sole alternatives.

I Saw Ramallah underscores the imperative of Palestinian nationalism but presents a justification based on universal principles. The desire and the struggle for Palestine gain resonance in Barghouti's text because they speak to universal notions of oppression and resistance. In Soueif's novel, the national is experienced through an intimate exploration of the cultural experience—a realm that emerges as an instance of the universal—beautifully demonstrating how literature, perhaps more than any other discourse, effortlessly locates the universality that underlies the culturally specific. Barghouti and Soueif remind us that an abstract universalism is just that—abstract. Our universality must be sought in

---

an opposing force to late capitalism by demonstrating how "successful" postcolonial literature is often driven by the logic of the capitalist market.

the particular and the specific. Conversely, a discourse of particularity that eschews the universal becomes hollow and exoticized. Together, these two postcolonial texts belie postcolonial theory, demonstrating that the universal and the particular are not in contradiction.

7

The Radical Universalism
of A. Sivanandan

Michael Ondaatje's novel *Anil's Ghost*, as I showed in chapter 3, exemplifies the shortcomings of a cultural framework that pits the local against the universal. By adopting that framework, Ondaatje and his defenders reinsert the very Orientalism that they seek to overturn. Ondaatje's failure, emblematic of the larger contradictions in the postcolonial field, raises the important question of whether it is possible to appreciate the specificity of the postcolonial context without falling into the Orientalist trap. A. Sivanandan's *When Memory Dies* addresses this challenge with great integrity and "extraordinary poetic tact."[1]

Published in 1997, *When Memory Dies* was Sivanandan's first novel, though the writer was already a well-regarded figure in the British intellectual and political establishment. A Tamil from Sri Lanka (then Ceylon), he had studied at the University of Ceylon and also worked as a teacher. Sivanandan moved to London in 1958 in the wake of ethnic riots in his country targeting Tamils and, in his own words, "walked straight into the riots of Notting Hill."[2] For him, it was a "double baptism of fire."[3] In 1964 he began his work as chief librarian at the Institute of

1 John Berger, "Back to the Future: The Roots of Our Future Are Planted in Our Past. But What Happens when We Choose to Obliterate Our Memories?," *Guardian*, February 13, 1997.

2 Ambalavaner Sivanandan, *Communities of Resistance: Writings on Black Struggles for Socialism*, London and New York: Verso, 1990, p. 9.

3 Ibid., p.9

Race Relations (IRR), a British anti-racist think tank, where in 1972 he was the principal organizer of an internal struggle between the membership and staff, on the one side, and the institute's management, on the other. The campaign succeeded in forcing the resignation of the majority of the institute's board, and Sivanandan became the new director in 1972. Under his leadership the IRR transformed itself from a policy-oriented establishment that advised the government to an anti-racist research organization that worked with community organizations and victims of racism. For more than forty years, Sivanandan headed the IRR, while serving as founding editor of its journal *Race and Class* and continuing to write actively and prolifically on institutional racism, class analysis of race, the political economy of immigration, and globalization, especially as the latter pertains to the global South, political organizing and grassroots struggles.

The writer's credentials notwithstanding, scores of publishers rejected the manuscript of his novel before the newly established Arcadia Books decided to publish it. The book, steering clear of contemporary trends in postcolonial fiction, apparently did not conform to publishers' idea of what a novel about the subcontinent should look like. Yet upon publication, the novel received two prestigious awards and proved a commercial success. Nevertheless, it remains a marginal work in postcolonial studies, garnering nowhere near the attention lavished on, for instance, *Anil's Ghost*.

Historicizing Memories

Linda Hutcheon identifies the dismantling of coherent subject positions as a key element of postmodernism and, based on this definition, correctly takes writers like Michael Ondaatje and Salman Rushdie to be exemplars of "postmodern poetics." She contends that the most effective means of "question[ing] the existing order" is to undermine the notion of a unified subjectivity and foreground the ideological construction of all subject positions and historiography.[4] *When Memory Dies* offers a meticulous contestation of colonial and nationalist constructions, a powerful

---

4 Linda Hutcheon, *A Poetics of Postmodernism: History, Theory, Fiction*, New York: Routledge, 1988, p. 200.

"questioning of the existing order." Yet, in contradistinction to Hutcheon's position, its strength lies precisely in its *retention* of the integrity of a radical subject position, one that is historical and historicized. The narrative does seem to abide by certain formal conventions of the postcolonial form, such as a diasporic narrator who constructs the story of the land he has left behind, and the narrator's lament that the colonized past does not afford a unified, verifiable story. The novel begins with the contention that "there is no story to tell, no one story anyway, not since that day in 1505 when the fidalgo Don Laurenco de Almeida, resplendent in gold braids and epaulettes and hat plumed with all the birds of paradise, landed on our shores and broke us from our history."[5] However, the familiar opening move, which the novel shares with much of postcolonial fiction, is deceptive. *When Memory Dies* not only dispenses with postcolonial conventions but also assumes a form that runs against the genre.

The near impossibility of constructing a history in the destructive aftermath of colonialism is far from the defining trope of the narrative; it is an acknowledgment of a historic hardship, but no more than that. The novel, as Qadri Ismail insightfully notes, is really about the "*necessity* of writing history after colonialism."[6] Once the commitment is made in the opening pages to a historical reconstruction from "bits and shards of stories,"[7] the novel steers away from well-trodden narrative modes of nostalgia or anguished incomprehensibility or exoticization in the telling of the tale. Those modes—all too familiar in diasporic, postcolonial fiction—are usually adopted by writers grappling with subjects that do not offer an easy engagement. Encountering that difficulty, the writers choose to shape the narrative by centralizing their own predicament. Sivanandan does not take this path.

The choice to utilize highly controlling narrators or multiple points of view in postcolonial fiction is a response to the daunting task of constructing real and imaginative alternative archives from raw material that is ruptured and fragmented. Narrative strategies that renounce the notion of a unified subjectivity allow writers to register their distrust of

---

5 A. Sivanandan, *When Memory Dies*, London: Arcadia, 1997, p. 5.

6 Qadri Ismail, *Abiding by Sri Lanka: On Peace, Place, and Postcoloniality*, Minneapolis: University of Minnesota Press, 2005, p. 184.

7 Sivanandan, *When Memory Dies*, p. 5.

both historiography and of the imagination in the wake of colonialism. However, by foregrounding merely the cooptation of subaltern experience and agency in elite metanarratives, much of postcolonial fiction remains limited, abdicating what is arguably its most significant task: the reinsertion and reanimation of subaltern subjectivity. It is in this context that *When Memory Dies* stands apart, in its commitment to both subalternity and subjectivity.

For Sivanandan, history and the subject are indeed fragmented, but to produce narratives that merely showcase such fragmentation is to remain trapped within that unacceptable reality. The achievement of Sivanandan's text is not so much its acknowledgment of subaltern agency, but that it elevates the subjective and experiential dimensions of agency. Part history, part imaginative reshaping, *When Memory Dies* constructs an alternative record in response to both the onslaught of colonialism and the limitations of narrow nationalism. Here, subjectivity is the key to the construction of an alternative account that endeavors to painstakingly salvage experiences of both oppression and resistance, and in so doing, to build an alternative historical imaginary.

The novel is a saga of epic proportions, charting the history of the author's home country, Sri Lanka, over the course of nearly a century. Beginning at the turn of the twentieth century, the story of three generations meticulously reveals the processes of the nation's colonial and postcolonial history from a subaltern perspective. The narrative is divided into three sections, each depicting the fortunes of the country at a particular historical moment through the story of a protagonist coming of age. Book one is the story of Sahadevan, spanning the early 1920s to around 1930. In Book two, the life of Sahadevan's son, Rajan, takes us through the political history of the country from the 1930s to the 1950s. Finally, through the life experiences of Rajan's stepson, Vijay, the contemporary history of the country up to the early 1980s unfolds. The most remarkable feat of the novel is the way the logistics of complex historical phenomena—colonialism, communalism, class warfare, terrorism—are always depicted through the intimate life experiences of its characters. In showing sympathetic characters as active historical agents, the novel implicitly challenges colonial and elite historiography by both presenting a people's history and showing history as a process.

Fragmentation

Throughout, the narrative provides incisive documentation of the ravages of colonialism in its myriad forms. Rajan, the young narrator, benefits from his education at a Catholic college, a "privilege" that required financial and familial accommodations. Even as he remains an outsider in an institution infused with colonial trappings, he is pulled in different directions. St. Lucia's, the church next to his college, elicits awe in him for its grandeur, but he cannot bring himself to enter it because it also evokes feelings of betrayal, "not mine but theirs, but mine, too, if I went in."[8] These contradictory feelings have been bequeathed to him by his father:

> I tried to make sense of the irrational, contradictory things he [Rajan's father] got me to do, like making me take private tuitions in Tamil while insisting that I do well in English so as to pass my exams and get a decent job, or forcing me to go to temple every Friday evening while sending me to a school that made me kneel at assembly every weekday morning.[9]

Rajan, like his father, Sahadevan, will never know the luxury of a unified subjectivity. Theirs is the plight of the colonial subject who will always have to negotiate contrary pulls of respect and revulsion, of expediency and authenticity.

Tissa, a close friend of the narrator's father, is steeped in an anti-colonial trade union culture but nevertheless loses his political edge during a visit to England. Tissa looks past the insularity of British culture, where his own country, though a British colony, is known only for its association with the Lipton tea gardens. He justifies this igno-rance by telling himself that Ceylon was, after all, a much-smaller country than England, and he is awed by the version of English history embodied in Buckingham Palace, Westminster Abbey, Parliament, the churches, the streets. Tissa is enraptured to experience firsthand everything he had studied about the mother country. On returning

---

8 Ibid., p. 151.
9 Ibid., p. 143.

home, he enthusiastically describes the speakers of different persuasions speechifying at Hyde Park: "There's real freedom of speech there, you know, Saha, unlike here." Saha's telling response to his friend, a reality check, reinserts the actuality of colonialism: "And why do you think that is?"[10]

The narrator's son, Vijay, also grapples with what it means for a people to have a common, unified history. Going through the classics of English literature, he compares a country with a history "spread so wide that they could talk of Northanger Abbey or Howards End or Hyde Park and the whole world would understand" to his own country: "We had no history, or we had several, mostly not of our doing, or we had forgotten that part of it which was." Then again, in the letters from his father, who is now an immigrant in England, Vijay sees that a coherent history could carry hidden costs. Rajan writes to his son of his anguish and his anger at his own country with its ethnic warfare that forced him to leave, that "separated him from his finer feelings, kept him from his duties and sent him off to a country which had history, but no beauty, not the beauty of ordinary people in their daily relationships. 'And we have lost our beauty in trying to find a history.'"[11]

The continual oscillation between authenticity and expediency, between respect and revulsion, between beauty and history, the continual prospect of losing hold of a coherent self—these are certainly the painful imprints of colonialism. But the realization that these imprintings have taken place forms only one strand of this rich narrative. Postcolonial fiction has documented the legacy of colonial fragmentation, but Sivanandan's narrative shows that the legacy is not intrinsic to colonialism alone. Colonialism—like other oppressive regimes— tears ordinary people apart because it pits fundamental human needs against each other. People are constantly forced to choose between safety and the fulfillment of basic material needs, on the one hand, and the equally fundamental human drive for justice and the fruits of peace, on the other.

The characters experience fragmentation from multiple sources. Saha is torn by his deep sense of duty toward his impoverished family and the need to participate in the trade union movement. Doing so

---

10 Ibid., p. 103.
11 Ibid., p. 282.

could jeopardize his job and thereby harm his family, who are dependent on him: "It is the same injustice that gets to me, it is what makes me want to fight. But if I fight too hard and lose my job, who will look after my father and my sisters?"[12] The narrative thus documents how oppression in different forms tears apart one's subjectivity. It denies wholeness to the psyche by forcing people to remain conflicted and struggling.

Resistance

Sri Lanka's history of resistance is woven into the lives of the characters, which are informed by an astute sensibility conscious of how the politics of colonialism, class and race both interact and conflict with one another. The history of working-class struggles, often actively suppressed, becomes buried in public memory; the narrative is primarily invested in resurrecting that memory. Saha is educated in a colonial institution and acquires no knowledge of the country's history of labor resistance until he comes to live with SW and Prema. There he learns of SW's lifelong work as a labor organizer and his attempts to stem the tide of communal acrimony nurtured by the British to undermine the labor movement. To the Sinhalese couple, Saha's Tamil ethnicity is irrelevant. He is treated like a son

Saha comes to understand that the history of his country as taught in his missionary school was a history sanitized of any mention of workers' resistance. "There were rebellions going on all the time," SW would tell him, "but your school history books wouldn't tell you that, would they? . . . Soon no one will know the history of our country . . . No history, no heroes."[13] Against SW's indictment of a colonial order destructive of working-class power, Saha tries to reconcile the memory of Brother Joseph, a missionary who tirelessly worked for poor fisherman. It takes him time, but Saha figures out that the two can indeed be reconciled, because what SW gave him were tools to understand the system, not the individual.

Slowly Saha learns the workings of the web that connects class interests with colonialism and its missionary institutions. SW apprises him

---

12 Ibid., p. 67.
13 Ibid., p. 40.

of a history in which missionaries aided the colonial state by selling out local Catholic rail workers in order to break a strike: "Your friends, the priests, the mission schools, the churches? They forced the Catholic workmen to go back to work, and then when the government was looking for ringleaders, to sack them or to send them off to godforsaken parts of the country, the Church forced those workmen to give the names of the trouble-makers to the government."[14] SW himself was one such "troublemaker." The "bosses' men" had broken both his legs with a crowbar to keep him from joining the strike. While that rail strike of 1912 was a signature event of the colonial period, labor resistance continues its trajectory into the postcolonial period. For Rajan's generation, the general strike, or *hartal*, of 1953 leaves its mark, both for its lessons of mobilization and for the resulting insights into the nature of the state.

The dual theme of working-class mobilization and its betrayal persist into the postcolonial period. Rajan is witness to the brutal suppression of the 1953 *hartal* by a heavy-handed state machinery—except that this time it is a postcolonial state doing the suppressing. The *hartal* was the first mass political action in the postcolonial era against an elected government. It was a nationwide action, organized primarily in protest against the economic policies of the government and, in particular, the rising cost of rice. From a distraught friend, Rajan hears how the state came down on the workers: "'Twelve of our people were killed, by our government.' He emphasized the 'our.' 'We expected it from the British, but this . . .'"[15]

The same betrayal is experienced again by Rajan's stepson, Vijay - the next generation. Vijay is part of the People's Liberation Front, a Left organization of farmers, students and workers formed in 1964 in response to disillusionment with the official Left parties. As with previous events, the novel references the actual violent repression of the 1971 uprising led by the Front, during which the army was used against the population and more than 10,000 people connected to the organization were killed, with twice that number incarcerated. Vijay's dear friend Padma, a committed activist, is killed by the state, and the incident becomes a "past which clung to him like a stigma."[16]

---

14 Ibid., p. 39.
15 Ibid., p. 172.
16 Ibid., p. 252.

In each of the three books of *When Memory Dies*, the characters experience a key event relating to workers' resistance; taken together, these three episodes demonstrate significant continuity between the colonial and postcolonial states. One of the events occurs in the colonial period—the rail strike of 1912—and two take place in the postcolonial era—the 1953 general strike and the 1971 uprising by the People's Liberation Front. Each of the three was a mass event that mobilized large sections of the population by drawing on experiences of economic and social oppression. And each of these actions was brutally repressed—the first one by the British, and the other two by the postcolonial state. Moreover, after repressing the 1971 mass uprising, the state, inspired by the old colonial strategy of divide and conquer, established affirmative action policies aimed at appeasing the majority Sinhalese population. Because the transfer of power from the colonial to the postcolonial rulers did not mark a shift in the class character of the state, labor resistance in both eras became a target of attack and an occasion to sow further divisions among workers.

The novel's searing critique of the native ruling class has led some critics to question Sivanandan's anti-colonial commitments. In his otherwise-insightful analysis, for example, Qadri Ismail contends that the novel depicts a tension between labor resistance and anti-colonial politics. Ismail cites a key passage describing the labor organizer SW:

> He was a fierce old man, with over forty years' service in the railways and still very active in union work. The rumor was that he had been one of the prime movers of the rail strike in 1912, but people remembered him for the charges of racial and religious bigotry he had laid against his employers before the Royal Commission of Inquiry the following year. Ironically, though, it was his own reference to the commissioners as *para suddhas* (bastard whites) that had drawn the public's attention to his evidence and made him a national hero.[17]

Ismail draws attention to the above passage to highlight the disconnect between SW's primary political work as a union organizer and his narrower place in public memory, specifically for standing up to the bigotry of his British employers. It is the latter move that made SW a

---

17 Ibid., pp. 21–2.

"national hero," while his more painstaking work organizing rail workers goes largely unrecognized. This leads Ismail to conclude that in "*When Memory Dies*, working class politics and anticolonialism may be incompatible or that, at the very least, the text identifies a tension between the two."[18]

While I accept Ismail's premise that the text identifies the distinctive motivational powers of anti-colonialism and working-class politics, I do not accept that it depicts an antagonistic relationship between the two. For Sivanandan, SW's class politics and anti-racism are not only compatible but embody a complementarity that is essential for any meaningful anti-colonial movement. The text, however, does identify a tension between two political perspectives, but it is not between working class politics and anti-colonialism as Ismail holds. The tension, indeed the incompatibility that the narrative highlights is between labor resistance and bourgeois anti-colonialism.

The narrative traces the legacy of SW's labor organizing in the context of an actual historical trajectory—one that witnessed the ascendance of a nationalism complicit with ruling-class interests. The labor leader Goonesinha exemplifies a movement coopted by bourgeois nationalism. SW's nephew, Tissa, works with Goonesinha, and SW tries to warn Tissa that the man has no organic connection with labor and is mobilizing labor unions only to further his personal ambitions. Even as the difference over Goonesinha threatens to sour relations between uncle and nephew, it is SW's political instincts that prove correct. In the end, Tissa becomes bitterly disillusioned by Goonesinha's obvious complicity with the colonial regime. Goonesinha signals the political formation of an ascendant postcolonial ruling class complicit with the bourgeoisie. The anti-colonialism of the native ruling class, while crucial to the consolidation of the postcolonial regime, is of little value to the struggles and aspirations of common people. In the narrative's logic, anti-colonialism is meaningful only when it is an expression of the interests of ordinary working people.

Given the character of the postcolonial state, it is hardly surprising that in response to the 1971 uprising, instead of instituting economic policies that would address the root causes of the unrest, the government established programs that would benefit the majority Sinhalese

---

18 Ismail, *Abiding by Sri Lanka*, p. 188.

population at the expense of the Tamils. The strategy harked back to a colonial maneuver: keep the population divided so as to decimate its power. Thus, the state instituted Sinhalese affirmative action programs in university admissions and government jobs, drastically reducing economic opportunities for the Tamils while appeasing the majority Sinhalese community. In another major act of appeasement, it enshrined Buddhism, the religion followed by the Sinhalese population, in the constitution as the only religion to be fostered and protected. It is this institutional racism against the minority population that sowed the seeds of Tamil terrorism.

The Beginning of Terror

Struggles against the fragmentation generated by oppressive regimes take many forms. Sivanandan's narrative invites us to explore the Sri Lankan Civil War as one such form of resistance. His approach to the war marks a departure from dominant conventions, as in, for example, *Anil's Ghost*, which casts the war as grounded in innate ethnic divisions and as a classic instance of terrorism. In the discussion of the latter in chapter 3, I argued that instead of challenging conventional views of the conflict, the novel draws on the hoariest Orientalist assumptions about it. In sharp contrast to such writing, the characterization of the war in *When Memory Dies* represents a postcolonial alternative, depicting an imaginative archive of historic specificity and the agency of postcolonial subjects.

The roots of the civil war go back to the colonial period, with its history of nurturing divisions between the ethnic populations. By the time of independence in 1948, the separate nationalisms were deeply entrenched. As I discussed earlier,[19] in response to mass movements for economic and social justice, the Sinhalese ruling class mobilized a race-based nationalism to appease the majority population. In 1955, the country abandoned the two-language policy and adopted an official Sinhala-only policy, along with affirmative action policies favoring the Sinhalese—a reversal of the usual minority emphasis in affirmative

---

19 See the section, "The Context" in chapter 3 for a brief historical overview of the events that lead to the growth of Tamil militancy.

action policies elsewhere—a move that was only further strengthened after the 1971 uprising. The institutional racism of the state, which established drastic inequities in educational and employment opportunities, had a tremendous adverse impact on the Tamil population and paved the way for the decades-long civil war.

Sivanandan's novel, however, does not merely chronicle the history of the ethnic war; it also illuminates the other history, that of a peaceful multiethnic society destroyed by communal politics. Pluralism is constitutive of the lives and relationships of all the major characters. Meaningful differences among the novel's characters, as Minoli Salgado rightly observes,[20] are always ideological, never ethnic. The many relationships between Tamil and Sinhalese characters are represented so organically that the reader can easily overlook the difference in the characters' ethnicities.[21]

Nevertheless, the narrative does not lose sight of cultural differences and the myriad ways in which they shape the characters' experiences. As a Tamil, Saha has little experience of communities other than his own and finds his preconceptions challenged when he visits Tissa's Sinhalese family in their village:

> Tissa's coastal village, with its coconut palms, flowering rhododendrons and green vegetables, its tiled roofs and cemented verandahs, was nothing like his own. And yet there was a familiar warmth and hospitality and an easy-going acceptance of him that he had not known since he had left Sandilipay . . . By the time Sahadevan returned to Colombo a week later, his ideas about Southern folk had

20 Minoli Salgado, "Writing Sri Lanka, Reading Resistance: Shyam Selvadurai's *Funny Boy* and A. Sivanandan's *When Memory Dies*," *Journal of Commonwealth Literature* 39:1 (2004), pp. 5–18.

21 Saha, who has firm Tamil roots, comes into intellectual adulthood in the home of the Sinhalese lifetime labor organizer SW and his wife, Prema. He finds a second home with them, and they take it on themselves to educate him on the country's working-class history. Their nephew, Tissa, remains Saha's closest friend, even though there are emotional and ideological tensions between them. Saha's son, Rajan, marries Lali, a Sinhalese woman, who is pregnant with Sena's child, another Sinhalese. Rajan, deeply in love with Lali, adopts the child. Lali, even though a Sinhalese herself, is murdered by a communal Sinhalese mob while trying to protect Rajan. The child, Vijay, is the son of two fathers, one Sinhalese and the other Tamil. Vijay is mostly raised by his paternal grandparents, a Sinhalese couple, who share a close tie with Rajan. While Vijay marries a Sinhalese woman, the real love of his life is a working-class Tamil woman, Meena.

already begun to change. They were not as uncaring and self-indul-
gent as he had previously assumed. Though they had cause to be;
their land was kinder to them, their hardships less fraught. Perhaps
that explained their outgoing natures and their easy acceptance of
life's vicissitudes. His own folk by contrast were impassive and dour,
their relationships were principled, their kindness more harsh. They
gave as the Southerners gave but, unlike them, they knew the cost of
their giving.[22]

Saha's reflections concern not merely cultural difference but, more
profoundly, how the interwoven threads of the material and the cultural
produce that difference in the first place: "their land was kinder to them,
their hardships less fraught." While the differences gain resonance, they
are never essentialized, and the characters connect across cultural lines:
"and yet there was a familiar warmth and hospitality."[23]

Despite Saha's reflections on the connecting threads of the communities, the narrative never minimizes the power of such social differences.
Thus, when his son, Rajan, marries a Sinhalese woman, he is compelled
to distance his son and daughter-in-law from the family because the
Sinhalese connection could hurt his daughters' marriage prospects in
the Tamil community. At a crucial turn in the narrative, however, Saha
breaks with social decorum and acts in sync with his deeper convictions. Amid growing communal tension, Saha has a visitor, an established
Tamil intellectual named Visvappa, who "explains" Sinhalese bigotry to
Saha and Rajan as stemming from a lack of culture and civilization; he
refers to the Sinhalese as a people without poets and writers. Unlike
Sinhalese, he points out, their shared language, Tamil, was spoken not
only by some people in Ceylon but all over the world. Initially Saha tries
to politely draw attention to the contradictions in his visitor's racist
reasoning, but when he finds himself unable to get through to him, he
lashes out, abdicating social decorum:

---

22 Sivanandan, *When Memory Dies*, pp. 20–1.

23 In an interesting reading that highlights the significance of the North–South
divide in the novel, Pavithra Tantrigodha rightly points out that the author resists
"hegemonic territorial reconfigurations along racial and class lines." See her "'Dangerous Geographies': The Erasure and Recalibration of the Contested Space of the Nation
in Times of War and Peace in Sri Lankan Fiction," *Interventions* 19:6 (2017), pp. 872–90.

"You really have taught me something ... Here I was getting mad about this Sinhala-only business and it dividing our people and all that ... but you, you have put me right." He was angry, there was no mistaking it now, cold, cold, angry, but the man didn't even see it. "You have shown me that it is precisely because Sinhala is spoken only in Ceylon that Ceylon must preserve Sinhala." Visvappa's mouth fell open. "And it is people like you—who make communalists of us all."[24]

Saha's exchange with his visitor sheds light on how the institutional racism of a majority community breeds a racist response from the minority. Thus, Visvappa reacts to Sinhalese racism by constructing a competing narrative of Tamil superiority. And Saha's angry response exposes the racist logic applicable to both majority and minority communalism.

The narrative focuses in equal measure on both the cynical cultivation and the insidious cultural consequences of race-based politics. In a country where the large majority are members of a particular race, the politics of racial identity can be institutionalized under the cover of democracy. Indeed in a democracy, no majority can be assumed to be permanent, because it shifts based on each particular issue or program. However, if race is made the single defining issue, there comes to be a race-based majority—a recipe for fascism. Para, Vijay's astute uncle, explains this turn of politics to Vijay's wife, Lali, who in turn explains the insidious logic to Vijay:

"I asked uncle Para where all this was going to end, and he answered: 'war.'"

"War? What war?"

"Communal war, between Sinhalese and the Tamils, that is what he said. He said it was already there, written into the constitution."

"Into the Constitution?" I could not believe my ears.

"Into the voting system: one man one vote."

"Rubbish," I laughed.

"Is it? What if you turn one man one vote into one Sinhalese man, one vote?"

"Well, what?"

---

24 Sivanandan, *When Memory Dies*, p. 206.

"You have a ready-made majority—and that is what Banada has done."

"Good Lord, I never looked at it like that."

"And that is what politics is going to be fought about in the future, he said. That is the legacy the British left us . . . divide and rule, only this time Banada will do it democratically with the vote."[25]

A politics unable to extend beyond ethnicity is one that undermines solidarity; it is a politics, as Sivanandan remarks in his essay on the New Times intellectual movement, of "identity, not of 'identification.'"[26] Lal, Vijay's brother-in-law and perhaps the most conscientious political agent in the novel, laments that the logic of race-based politics has ensured that "there will be no Sinhalese in parliament standing up for the Tamils now."[27] This is no small loss, for it signals the end of issue-based democracy.

Lal shows the limits of an ethnicized politics. His friend is a member of a party that intends to institutionalize Sinhalese dominance by claiming that the minority Tamil population has been disproportionate beneficiaries of upward social mobility. When his friend points out that the Tamils make up only one-tenth of the population yet hold almost half the administrative positions, Lal's response is instructive:

"So all the Tamils own half the government?" asked Lal scornfully. "What rubbish you talk! It's a small handful of Tamils . . . a small English-educated upper class like the Sinhalese upper class. What about the thousands of workers and peasants and toddy tappers and fishermen and . . . And where do the plantation Tamils come into your argument? You know your trouble, don't you? You are confusing race and class, like your whole bloody party, so you can keep your class while shouting race."[28]

The narrative is profoundly sympathetic to the gross injustice perpetrated on the ordinary Sri Lankan Tamil as a direct consequence of

25 Ibid., pp. 221–2.

26 A. Sivanandan, "All That Melts into Air Is Solid: The Hokum of New Times," *Race and Class* 31:1 (1990), p. 23.

27 Sivanandan, *When Memory Dies*, p. 185.

28 Ibid., p. 202.

ethnic politics. Such a politics has made Tamils second-class citizens in their own land and signaled that it is in their interest to leave the country. But, as Lal again poignantly points out, while the tiny minority of educated Tamils are able to leave the country, that option is unavailable to working-class Tamils: "But where can the ordinary people go? And the estate Tamils? Where are they to go? This is their country, it is their sweat and blood that built it. That's not words, you can see it in their coolie-line rooms. You can touch it."[29] It is this sense of alienation and injustice that gives rise to the militant Tamil movement. It needs to be stressed that in a global political context, where the phenomenon of terrorism is routinely drained of political and social meaning, it is a singular achievement of this novel that it situates the birth of Tamil militancy in an understandable, if not favorable, light. Indeed, in its inception, the movement captured the sense of betrayal and rage experienced by the Tamils, but mostly it expressed their demand for justice. Para reminisces about the day when "the boys"—a phrase often used for the Tamil fighters—finally came out of hiding so people could know who they were. The community gathered to see the fighters and were proud to find that it was not only their young men but also their young women who had joined the ranks in the cause of liberation. The narrative presents the resort to terrorism in the struggle for justice as a last desperate means, adopted by the youth to redress steadily mounting Tamil disenfranchisement and exclusion. Para insightfully sums up the motivation of the young Tamil fighters: "The British took away their past, the Sinhalese took away their future. All they have is the present. And that makes them dangerous."[30]

Sivanandan accords to Tamil militancy a deeply contextualized and strongly sympathetic reading, as born out of a demand for justice. However, true to its dialectical approach, his narrative also unequivocally rejects the militants' methods and direction, even while it endorses their cause. It shows the deterioration of an idealistic movement motivated by social justice into a top-down organization governed by dogma. Vijay tries to show the contradiction in the methods adopted by the movement to a young friend: "That way liberation never comes, and you know it. Socialism is the path to liberation, not just its end." Vijay also

---

29 Ibid., p. 203.
30 Ibid., p. 334.

offers telling commentary on the "suicide pill"—something that has come to symbolize Tamil terrorism in general:

> It was such a symbol of waste, of no-hope, of death as a way of life. It had such a finality about it. Maybe it was alright at the beginning when it symbolized a heroic refusal to inform, at least it implied choice; but now that it had been raised to dogma, belief, ideology, it symbolized the end of choice. And the end of choice was the beginning of terror.[31]

Among both mainstream critiques and postcolonial fiction renderings of Tamil militancy, a majority focus simply on the violence while remaining oblivious to the origin and dynamics of the movement. "The end of choice is the beginning of terror," declares Vijay. In contrast to ahistorical and Orientalist approaches, that one sentence invokes the entire history of an era and how it plays out in the individual consciousness. It contextualizes and explains the resort to terrorism without justifying it. Indeed, it is a portrayal remarkably nuanced in both its sympathetic identification of the causes of the movement and its denunciation of its trajectory.

The Writer's Politics

If *When Memory Dies* exhibits a sustained attention to local struggles, informed by an universalist commitment, the same simultaneous commitment is evident in Sivanandan's political work. Some of his essays, such as "From Resistance to Rebellion," analyzing Black protests from 1940 to 1981, have been widely influential; "Racism Awareness Training" and "Race, Class and the State" have repeatedly drawn attention to the "structured racism" of the state that popular discourse often obscures.[32] In his seminal "The Liberation of the Black Intellectual," Sivanandan focuses on the experiential dimension of racism and the

---

31 Ibid., p. 403.

32 A. Sivanandan, "From Resistance to Rebellion: Asian and Afro-Caribbean Struggles in Britain," *Race and Class* 23:2–3 (1981), pp. 111–52. "Racism Awareness Training," "Race, Class and the State: The Black Experience in Britain," *Race and Class* 17:4 (1976), pp. 347–68.

particularity of Black oppression while calling for a reframing of traditional theories to address them.[33] Apart from his engagement with issues
of race and immigration in the UK, Sivanandan's intellectual trajectory
is marked by his interventions in the debates on globalization and on
power struggles in the global South.

Sivanandan's long engagement with the politics of race and immigration has allowed for a certain misappropriation by postcolonial theorists,
some of whom have read his perspective as aligned with the kind of
culturalism that he in fact strongly repudiates. For instance, in her
reading of *When Memory Dies* alongside his political works, Sonali
Perera is anxious to position Sivanandan against Marxist critics like
John Berger and Timothy Brennan, and to align him instead with the
kind of poststructuralism that privileges "zigzagging prospects and
unverifiable outcomes."[34] Sivanandan's frequent focus on concrete issues
connected to cultural identity make critics like Perera oblivious to his
fundamental commitment to a universalist politics.[35]

Perera is unable to find the points of continuity between Sivanandan's
prose and his fiction, and she reads *When Memory Dies* as the author's
turn toward literature and "away from the language of manifestos . . . a
move towards an understanding of the dialectic as quotidian—to be
apprehended not in the context of revolutionary moments, but in the
struggle of the everyday." Thus, she alleges, the novel turns away from
the possibility of revolutionary struggles and toward the necessity of
serving the "*cultural politics* of the struggle":[36] "At the heart of the
novel . . . eschewing revolutionary violence, Vijayan discovers (as Sivanandan does) the Marxism *of* literature . . . this turn occurs when
Vijayan finally and firmly abjures the propagandist revolutionary
rhetoric of the Marxist university student groups to instead derive a
politics from reading Marx, Cabral and Avayyar."[37] It is unclear what
"Marxism *of* literature" as opposed to that of "revolutionary rhetoric"

33 A. Sivanandan, "The Liberation of the Black Intellectual," *Race and Class* 8:4
(1977), pp. 329–43.

34 Sonali Perera, *No Country: Working-Class Writing in the Age of Globalization*,
New York: Columbia University Press, 2014, p. 56.

35 Other critics have similarly interpreted the novel without accounting for the
author's politics; see, for instance, Gayathri Hewagama, "Anxious Nationals and Others,"
Sri Lanka Journal of the Humanities 37:1–2 (2011), pp. 135–48.

36 Perera, *No Country*, p. 54, emphasis mine.

37 Ibid., p. 68.

might mean, but what Perera offers is a fundamental misreading both of the novel and of Sivanandan's politics. What she characterizes as contradictions are, in fact, inseparable *complementarities* in his work: between literature and manifestos, and between everyday struggles and revolutionary moments. Vijay does not "abjure" revolutionary politics; the passage to which Perera refers signals a moment of growth in the young character, when he realizes that conflict and evolution do not merely mark a societal trajectory but also apply to the individual: "He understood contradiction out there in society, but he did not grasp it in people. He had not till now seen conflict as necessary to one's personal growth, as an essential part of life, its motor as natural as breathing. He had not seen that the dialectic is also a felt sensibility."[38] This is not to "eschew" revolutionary politics, as Perera would have it, but to extend the logic of dialectics to individual growth as well.

Perera's assertion that the novel signals the writer's own turn away from revolutionary struggles in favor of serving the "*cultural politics* of the struggle"[39] is strangely ignorant not only of Sivanandan's lifelong commitment to revolutionary politics, but also of his scathing critique of cultural politics. His piece "The Hokum of New Times," a critique of the cultural turn in the British Left, encapsulates his position on identitarian and culturalist politics:

> And the self that new timers make so much play about is become a small, selfish inward-looking self that finds pride in life-style, exuberance in consumption and commitment in pleasure—and then elevates them all into a politics of this and that, positioning itself this way and that way (with every position a politics and every politics a position) into a "miscellany of movements and organisations" stretching from hobbies and pleasure to services.[40]

Refusing to join the ranks of erstwhile comrades such as Stuart Hall in celebrating "new social movements" oriented around family, health, food, sexuality and the body, Sivanandan instead points to the debilitating limitations of these movements. They may contain subversive

---

38 Sivanandan, *When Memory Dies*, p. 291.
39 Perera, p. 54, emphasis mine.
40 Sivanandan, "The Hokum of New Times," p. 23.

possibilities, he argues, but their survival is based on their choice to not challenge fundamental economic and political structures. And, when accosted by the power of the state, the politics of the new social forces invariably turns into a "politics of accommodation."[41] It is not surprising, then, that much of culturalist politics remains narrow, inward looking, and restricted to choices of lifestyle and consumption; Sivanandan characterizes them as a

> sort of bazaar socialism, bizarre socialism, a hedonist socialism: an eat, drink and be merry socialism because tomorrow we can eat drink and be merry again . . . a socialism for disillusioned Marxist intellectuals who had waited around too long for the revolution—a socialism that holds up everything that is ephemeral and evanescent and passing as vital and worthwhile, everything that melts into air as solid, and proclaims that every shard of the self is a social movement.[42]

This rejection of a narrow politics of identity comes out of Sivanandan's own experience in his native Sri Lanka. As a member of the minority Tamil community, he underwent the persecution and devastation wreaked by a politics governed by ethnicity and religion. As a socialist, he also learned that when resistance confines itself to the domains of ethnicity or religion, it loses both its moral power and its political efficacy. As a consequence, he rejects a politics of identity in favor of a "politics of identification";[43] that is, he urges us to connect to struggles that do not directly touch our own social identities. This commitment reaches its apotheosis in his call to build a solidarity against capital's global assault on our social selves, as he reminds the reader that unity has to be "forged and re-forged . . . [and requires] a capacity for making other people's fight one's own."[44]

Sivanandan refuses to acknowledge the "novelty" of the Thatcherite moment. If the new movements are justified as reflection of the fragmentation of sociality caused by capital, Sivanandan asserts that capital has *always* fragmented the self as well as the social. It has always divided

---

41 Ibid., p. 17.
42 Ibid., p. 23.
43 Ibid., p. 15.
44 Ibid., p. 24.

labor, encouraged specialization and compartmentalization. Resistance to such fragmentation cannot itself embrace this condition; it cannot uphold its own fragmentation as a virtue. Of course, Sivanandan fully appreciates the social oppressions that generate what we know as "new" social movements. However, as he observes in an interview, if these battles are fought as particularistic reactions disconnected from other battles, other solidarities, then they lose their force:

> Any struggles of the oppressed, be it blacks or women, which are only for themselves and then not for the least of them, the most deprived, the most exploited of them, are inevitably self-serving and narrow and unable to enlarge the human condition . . . The black middle class, Black Sections, blacks in academia, do not interest me. The question for me is: what is it in the black and Third World experience, in the experience of the oppressed and the exploited, that gives one the imagination to see other oppressions and the will to fight for a better society for all, a more equal, just, free society, a socialist society?[45]

Conclusion

If Goonesinha's character in *When Memory Dies* embodies the limitations and the eventual corruption of an anticolonial position divorced from class struggle, Sivanandan's political writings identify a similar dynamic in the political and intellectual trends centered around identity—their particularism engenders a self-serving ethic rendering them ineffectual in the fight against capitalist oppression, and at times complicit with power structures. Just as the literary narrative exposes and rejects the bourgeois anti-colonialism of Goonesinha, Sivanandan refuses to be enamored of the New Left and its putative resistance battles.

Both, Sivanadan's novel and his political discourse emanate from a deep empathy for the devastated lives of ordinary people and his rage against oppressive regimes. His portrayal of the Tamil militancy,

---

45 A. Sivanandan, "The Heart Is where the Battle Is: An Interview with A. Sivanandan," *Race and Class* 59:4 (2018), pp. 3–14.

movingly depicted as a struggle against injustice, is informed by that
empathy. But the movement is also subjected to stringent critique and
ultimately rejected for its dogmatism and brutality. It is the anticolonial
labor leader, SW, who comes closest to embodying Sivanandan's view
of humane and principled resistance. In fact, Sivanandan's work, both
literary and political, is ultimately an attempt to grapple with the question of what constitutes meaningful resistance and how to forge
solidarities and lines of battle. He staunchly maintains that because
oppressive systems generate a fragmented social order, resistance must
challenge—and not simply reflect—that fragmentation; he thus rejects a
politics of particularism and parts ways with some of the core assumption of the postcolonial discipline in affirming what Neil Lazarus has
called an "extraordinary commitment to universalism,"[46] Yet, in rejecting culturalist positions, his works represent a postcolonial alternative
that meaningfully challenges colonial and elite discourses with its
commitment to historical specificity and subaltern agency—to the
portrayal of postcolonial subjects as actively engaged in the construction of their history rather than as colonized objects. Sivanandan
achieves precisely what the discipline has considered well-nigh impossible: honoring the particular while articulating the possibility of a radical
universalism.

---

46 Neil Lazarus, "The Prose of Insurgency: Sivanandan and Marxist Theory," *Race
and Class* 41:1–2 (1999), pp. 35–47.

Index

Orientalism/Orientalist, 7, 9, 10, 11, 14, 15, 86–90, 96, 103, 105, 107, 170, 191, 193, 203, 209. *See also* neo-Orientalism

Oxford Handbook of Postcolnial Studies (Huggan), 3–4

P

Padma (fictional character in *When Memory Dies*), 200

Palestinian experience, 17, 133, 171, 172–80, 181, 192

Palipana (fictional character in *Anil's Ghost*), 92–3, 94–5, 96, 97–9, 102, 103

Palli Samaj (Chattopadhyay), 77

Panchu (fictional character in *The Home and the World*), 75

Para (fictional character in *When Memory Dies*), 206, 208

Parry, Benita, 6, 7, 164

the particular. *See also* universal/ particular binary
  embrace of in postcolonial literature, 5
  and Jameson's view of the nation, 171
  as needing to be defended and privileged, 170
  as not in contradiction to the universal, 192
  Ondaatje's attentiveness and concern of, 87
  politics of particularism, 214
  recognition of, 18
  risks of focusing on, 177

as subject to repression, 163

as under threat from logic of the universal, 191

the universal as residing in, 17

Pather Dabi (Chattopadhyay), 77

patriarchy, 13, 14, 28, 29, 30, 32, 33, 59, 60, 61, 63, 65, 68, 69, 71–2, 75, 83, 85, 185, 186, 187

People's Liberation Front (Sri Lanka), 90, 200, 201

Perera, Sonali, 210, 211

Pirtha (fictional location in *Pterodactyl, Puran Sahay and Pirtha*), 142, 143–4, 145, 146, 147, 149, 151, 152

political agency, and postcolonial studies, 21–49

politics
  of accommodation, 212
  of class, 40
  of coercion, 54
  of colonialism, 199
  of difference, 150
  of force and fear, 62
  of gender, 43, 48
  of identification, 212
  of identity, 212
  of international charity, 150
  of the local, 16
  of myth making, 150
  of the oppressed, 126
  of particularism, 214
  of race and immigration, 210
  of racial identity, 206
  of resistance, 109, 110

postcolonial ecocriticism, 153–4